Plant Cell Physiology

A Series of Books in Biology

Editors: Donald Kennedy
Roderic B. Park

Plant Cell Physiology

A PHYSICOCHEMICAL APPROACH

Park S. Nobel

University of California,
Los Angeles

W. H. FREEMAN AND COMPANY
San Francisco

Printed in the United States of America

International Standard Book Number: 0-7167-0682-2
Library of Congress Catalog Card Number: 73-116896

9 8 7 6 5 4 3 2 1

Contents

Preface   vii

1 Cells   *1*

Introduction   *1*
Diffusion   7
Membrane Structure   *13*
Permeability of Membranes   *19*
Cell Walls   *25*

2 Water   *33*

Physical Properties of Water   *34*
Chemical Potential of Water   *42*
Central Vacuole and Chloroplasts   *52*
Water Potential and Plant Cells   *57*
Water Movement in Plants   *64*

3 Solutes   *75*

Chemical Potential of Ions   *76*
Fluxes and Diffusion Potentials   *84*
Active Transport   *99*
Principles of Irreversible Thermodynamics   *111*
Solute Movement Across Membranes and in the Phloem   *118*

4 Light   *129*

Wavelength and Energy   *130*
Absorption of Light by Molecules   *137*
De-excitation   *144*
Absorption Spectra and Action Spectra   *149*

5 Photosynthesis   *165*

Chlorophyll—Chemistry and Spectra   *167*
Other Photosynthetic Pigments   *174*
Excitation Transfers Among Chlorophylls and
    Other Photosynthetic Pigments   *180*
Photosynthetic Units and Enhancement Effects   *188*
Electron Flow and Photophosphorylation   *194*

6 Bioenergetics   *207*

Free Energy   *208*
Biological Energy Currencies   *215*
Chloroplast Bioenergetics   *221*
Mitochondrial Bioenergetics   *227*
Energy Flow   *229*

Appendices   *233*

I Frequently Used Variables and Their Units   *235*
II Frequently Used Constants and Their Numerical Values   *238*
III Conversion Factors   *240*
IV Abbreviations and Symbols   *243*
V Natural and Common Logarithms   *246*

Answers to Problems   *250*
Index   *255*

Preface

As both teaching and research become more interdisciplinary, many traditional boundaries between fields are tending to vanish. Thus, the student finds that his introductory textbooks in plant physiology, cell physiology, and biochemistry overlap to a great extent. The problem with such introductory texts is, however, that they often do not adequately treat some of the more abstract or mathematical aspects of their subject or related subjects. While adequate treatises covering such aspects in specific fields are available, they are of little help to the student not yet at an advanced level and often impose a sizable financial burden on him. The present text attempts to fill in this existing gap by covering certain biophysical and physicochemical areas of plant and cell physiology that the student at an advanced undergraduate or beginning graduate level can understand.

This book may also prove useful to researchers who want to broaden their background by peripheral reading. Both they and students will be helped, hopefully, by the effort to present in a practical manner certain physical ways of considering plant cell physiology in particular and biology in general. The problems at the end of each chapter will provide practice in quantitatively applying the appropriate equations.

Our main emphasis is on concepts that are important for a broad biological understanding of processes, particularly *in vivo*. We point out physiological consequences of physical principles, often by means of calculations. Although some knowledge of elementary calculus is important, it is our intention to encourage a student's rigorous development without placing undue demands on his background or memory. Thus, we will not include extensive experimental observations or attempt a complete coverage of the many possible applications of the concepts that are considered. Rather, stress will be on the underlying theoretical bases. We will develop in some detail the two physicochemical areas of thermodynamics and photochemistry. Specifically included are the principles governing ion and water movement in the various compartments of plant cells as well as the mechanism whereby light is absorbed and its radiant energy converted to chemical and electrical energy in photosynthesis.

The selection of material is based to some extent on what can be adequately treated in a one-quarter, semester, or term course on the specific topics that are discussed or on what can be incorporated as ancillary material into a full year's course on plant physiology. Consequently, no attempt is made to include all topics which might fit under the rather wide purview of the physicochemical principles important to an understanding of plants, but rather attention is directed toward the cellular and subcellular aspects.

The encouragement to undertake this project came from Professor George Laties, who also furnished valuable ideas on its content. Innumerable discussions with Dr. John Cram markedly contributed to the topics and the approach. Professor Chris Foote provided important suggestions, particularly concerning photochemistry. Dr. Peter Barry offered many useful criticisms on the sections covering ion and water relations. A critique by Professor Peter Ray substantially improved Chapters 1 and 2. A final version was carefully examined by Professor Jack Dainty. Miss Marjorie Macdonald did an excellent job on the typing. The author gratefully acknowledges the outstanding cooperation of these people, the permissions kindly granted by various authors and publishers to reproduce certain figures, and the patience of his wife during the preparation of this text.

January 30, 1970   P.S.N.

Ye rigid Ploughmen! Bear in mind
Your labour is for future hours.
Advance! Spare not! Nor look behind!
Plough deep and straight with all your powers!

From "*The Plough*," R. H. Horne, 1848.

Plant Cell Physiology

Chapter 1

Cells

Introduction

Classically, plant physiology is divided into such areas as water relations, mineral nutrition, metabolism, photosynthesis, and the enormous area of growth and development. A goal of the plant physiologist is to understand these areas in formal physical and chemical terms. Accurate models can then be constructed and a plant's response to its environment predicted. Such physicochemical explanations of plant processes are available so far for only some of the classical areas of plant physiology. For instance, ion and water movements across cellular membranes and the photosynthetic conversion of radiant energy from the sun into other forms of energy can be so described. It is to these topics that this book is addressed.

Chapters 1 to 3 present the physical description of water relations and ion transport involving plant cells. After a discussion of the concept of diffusion, we will consider the physical barriers to free diffusion caused by cellular and organelle membranes. The other physical barrier associated with plant cells is the massive cell wall, which limits the size and, consequently, the contents of the cells. In the treatment in Chapter 2 of the movement of water through cells in response to physical forces, we make use of the thermodynamic argument of chemical potential gradients. With the cell walls, membranes, and the solvent water already described, we consider in Chapter 3 the topic of solute movement through plant cells, which leads to an explanation of how electrical potential differences arise across membranes. The formal criteria for distinguishing diffusion from active transport are also developed, and the important parameter called the reflection coefficient is derived, using concepts from irreversible thermodynamics. Use of reflection coefficients allows an evaluation of osmotic pressure effects across membranes under real, not idealized, biological conditions. The thermodynamic arguments used to describe ion and water movements are equally applicable at the cellular level to animal cells.

The second half of the book deals with the interconversion of various forms of energy. In Chapter 4 we will consider the properties of light and its absorption. Upon the absorption of light by nonliving material, the radiant energy is usually converted rapidly to heat. The arrangement of photosynthetic pigments and their special molecular structures allow some of the sun's radiant energy to be converted by plants into other forms of energy before the eventual degradation of such light energy to thermal energy. In Chapter 5 we discuss the particular features of chlorophyll and the accessory pigments for photosynthesis which allow this energy conversion. Light energy absorbed by chloroplasts leads to the formation of ATP and NADPH$_2$. These compounds represent currencies for carrying chemical and electrical (redox potential) energy, respectively. How much energy they actually carry is discussed in the last chapter.

Generalized Plant Cell. Before embarking on a formal consideration of diffusion, we will outline the architecture or structure of certain plant cells and tissues. Figure 1-1, an arrangement within a representative leaf cell from a higher plant, illustrates only the larger subcellular structures. Surrounding the cell is a wall composed of cellulose and other polysaccharides. Since the cell wall contains numerous large interstices, it does not serve as the main permeability barrier to solute movement. Inside the cell wall and surrounding the cytoplasm is the plasma membrane or plasmalemma. This membrane exhibits differential permeability, and thus it regulates what enters and leaves the plant cell. The cytoplasm contains organelles like chloroplasts and mitochondria, in which energy is converted from one form to another. Also the nucleus and many other inclusions which function in the organization of information transfer and in cellular metabolism occur in the cytoplasm. In mature cells of higher plants as well as in a number of lower (evolutionarily less advanced) plant cells, there is a large central

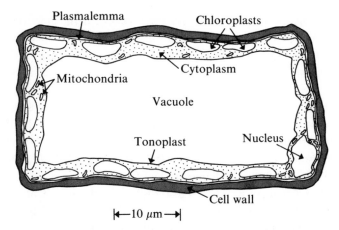

Figure 1–1. Schematic representation of a mature cell from the leaf of a higher plant, suggesting some of the complexity resulting from the presence of many membrane-surrounded subcellular bodies.

vacuole surrounded by a membrane known as the tonoplast. The tonoplast is usually quite large in area since the central vacuole can occupy up to 90% of a mature cell. Small cytoplasmic vesicles are often found associated with the tonoplast, and these may be involved in transport. Inside the central vacuole is a relatively simple aqueous solution, the solutes of which are mainly inorganic ions or organic acids, although considerable amounts of sugars and amino acids may also be present in some species. Water uptake into this vacuole accounts for a major part of the increase in plant cell size during growth.

Membranes separate the various compartments within the plant cell from each other. Diffusion of substances across these membranes is much slower than diffusion within the compartments. Thus organelle and vacuolar membranes can effectively control the contents and consequently the reactions occurring in the particular compartments which they surround. Diffusion can also impose limitations on the overall size of a cell since the time to diffuse a certain distance in free solution increases with the square of that distance—as will be quantitatively considered in the next section. As a consequence of the time-distance relation for diffusion, the amount of oxygen diffusing to a part of the cell remote from the plasmalemma may be insufficient to support normal rates of respiration there.

Although various plant cells share most of the features indicated in Figure 1–1, they are remarkably diverse in size. The nearly spherical cells of the green alga *Chlorella* are approximately 4 μm in diameter. [μ is the prefix meaning micro, which specifically indicates 10^{-6} (Appendix IV); m is the abbreviation for meter; thus μm is a distance unit equaling 10^{-6} meters and commonly referred to as a micron (it should be stressed that the symbols μm will be used in this text to refer to 10^{-6} m, instead of the frequently employed but less consistent convention of using simply μ).] Internal diffusion limitations are minimal in such small cells as *Chlorella* because molecules can readily diffuse the short distances involved in crossing the cell. On the other hand, some species of the intertidal green alga *Valonia* have cells up to a few centimeters (cm) in diameter. The genera *Chara* and *Nitella* include fresh water green algae having large internodal cells which may be 10 cm in length and 1 millimeter (mm) in diameter. Such giant algal cells have proved extremely useful for studying both passive and active ion fluxes. Special salt-bridges (commonly referred to as microelectrodes—see p. 89) can be inserted into *Chara* or *Nitella* internodal cells, and the electrical potential differences across the tonoplast and across the plasmalemma can each be measured. After cutting open these large internodal cells at one end, we can remove the vacuolar and cytoplasmic contents separately and determine the concentrations of ions in each phase. Evidence on whether or not a particular ion is in equilibrium across the membranes is provided by the measured electrical potential differences and the ionic concentrations.

Leaf Cells.   The diagram of a transverse section of a leaf as given in Figure 1–2 further illustrates some of the heterogeneity of cell types encountered in plants and serves to introduce certain anatomical features important for photosynthesis and transpiration. Leaves of plants like pea and spinach are generally a few hundred microns thick and have 4 to 10 cells in a cross-section (Fig. 1–2). The epidermis occurs on both the upper and the lower sides of the leaf and is usually one layer of cells thick. The cytoplasm of epidermal cells generally appears colorless since very few chloroplasts are present in it. Epidermal cells have a cutin-containing cuticle on the externally facing wall, which greatly reduces the outward diffusion of water from the leaf interior and at the same time hinders the diffusion of CO_2 in an inward direction. (Cutin refers to a diverse group of complex polymers composed principally of esters of monocarboxylic acids which contain two or three hydroxyl groups.) Between the epidermal layers is the leaf mesophyll, which is composed of both "palisade" and "spongy" cells. The palisade cells are usually elongated at right angles to and immediately beneath the upper epidermis (Fig. 1–2). The spongy mesophyll cells, which occur between the

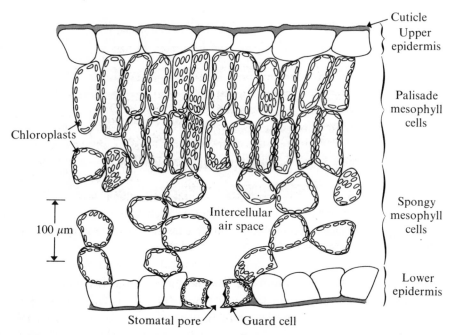

Cuticle
Upper
epidermis

Palisade
mesophyll
cells

Chloroplasts

Spongy
mesophyll
cells

Intercellular
air space

100 μm

Lower
epidermis

Stomatal pore   Guard cell

Figure 1-2. Schematic transverse section of a leaf indicating the arrangement of various cell types.

lower epidermis and the palisade mesophyll cells, are loosely packed with conspicuous intercellular air spaces between them. A spongy mesophyll cell from a pea leaf is about $40 \times 40 \times 60$ μm and contains approximately 50 chloroplasts. A neighboring palisade cell is generally more oblong and can be $30 \times 30 \times 120$ μm, containing up to 100 chloroplasts.

The pathways of least resistance for gases to cross the epidermis and thus to enter or exit from the leaf are through the spaces between pairs of guard cells, these pores being referred to as stomata or stomates (singular, stoma or stomate, respectively). The stomatal pores allow for the entry into the leaf of CO_2, which will be chemically "fixed" or incorporated into organic compounds in photosynthesis, and for the release of the photosynthetic product, oxygen, into the air surrounding the leaf. The inevitable loss of water vapor by transpiration also occurs through the stomatal pores. (See pp. 69-70.) Thus, the stomata act as a control which strikes a balance between freely admitting the CO_2 that is needed for photosynthesis and at the same time preventing excess water loss from the plant because of water vapor evaporating from the cell walls of cells within the leaf and then diffusing out into the surrounding atmosphere.

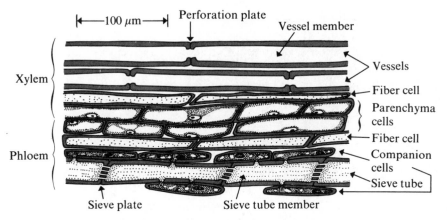

Figure 1–3. Longitudinal section through part of a vascular bundle in an angiosperm leaf, showing elements of both the xylem and the phloem.

Vascular Cells. The xylem and the phloem make up the vascular systems found in the roots, stems, and leaves of plants (Fig. 1–3). The xylem serves primarily in the upward movement of both water and nutrients from the soil to the upper portions of the plant. It is a tissue of various cell types which will be considered in more detail in Chapter 2 when water movement in plants is briefly discussed in terms of the water potential. The conducting cells in the xylem are the tracheids and the vessel members, both of which occur in long files of linearly arranged cells. These conducting cells have lost their protoplasts and often their end walls too, and thus the remaining cell walls border a low resistance channel for the passage of solutions (Fig. 1–3). Water moves up from the soil to the leaves in these hollow xylem cells in the direction of decreasing hydrostatic pressure. (See pp. 65–67.) Ions and other solutes accompany such movement of water to the leaf, where they can diffuse or be actively transported across the plasmalemmas of various leaf cells.

The distribution of most organic compounds throughout the plant takes place in the other vascular system—the phloem. A portion of the photosynthetic products made in the mesophyll cells of the leaf diffuses or is actively transported across cellular membranes until it reaches the conducting cells of the leaf phloem. By means of the phloem, the photosynthetic products, which are then mainly in the form of sucrose, are distributed throughout the plant. The carbohydrates produced by photosynthesis and certain other substances generally move in the phloem toward regions of lower concentration, although diffusion is not the mechanism. (See pp. 123–26.) The phloem is a tissue consisting of several types of cells, but in contrast with the xylem, the conducting cells of the phloem contain cytoplasm. (See Fig. 1–3 and the discussion in Chapter 3.) The conducting cells in the phloem are referred to as sieve cells and sieve tube members. They are joined end-to-end and thus form a transport system throughout the plant. Although these phloem cells often contain no nuclei at maturity, they remain metabolically active.

Thus plant cells differ greatly in size, shape, and predominant activity. It is these many cell types which provide not only the characteristic architecture of plant tissues but also the framework for describing the physical processes of diffusion (Chapter 1), water relations (Chapter 2), and solute transport (Chapter 3). The energy conversion processes take place in the organelles within these various cells. Specifically, light energy is absorbed (Chapter 4) by photosynthetic pigments located in the internal membranes of chloroplasts (Chapter 5) and then converted or transduced into other forms of energy useful to a plant (Chapter 6).

Diffusion

Diffusion is a spontaneous process leading to the movement of a substance from some region to adjacent regions where that species has a lower concentration. Diffusion results from the independent and directionally random thermal motion of the individual molecules of the solute and the solvent, requiring no energy input for it to occur. The net movement caused by diffusion is basically a statistical phenomenon since there is a greater probability for molecules to move from the concentrated to the dilute region than vice versa.

The steps involved in going from CO_2 in the air to the incorporation of carbon into a carbohydrate in the chloroplasts by photosynthesis is a good example of a phenomenon entailing many different diffusion processes. For instance, carbon dioxide diffuses from the atmosphere up to the leaf surface and then through the stomatal pores. After entering the leaf, diffusion of CO_2 occurs in the intercellular air spaces indicated in Figure 1–2. Next, CO_2 diffuses across the wet cell wall and the plasmalemma of a mesophyll cell in the leaf. Carbon dioxide, perhaps as HCO_3^-, could diffuse through the cytoplasm to reach the chloroplasts. Finally, CO_2 diffuses into a chloroplast and up to the enzymes that are involved in carbohydrate formation. Thus many diffusion steps are involved in just this one facet of photosynthesis. If the enzymes fixed all the CO_2 in their vicinity and no other carbon dioxide were to *diffuse* in from the atmosphere surrounding the plant, photosynthetic processes would stop. Diffusion is likewise involved in many other aspects of plant physiology, especially in moving substances across membranes. The mathematical formulation necessary for understanding both diffusion across a membrane and diffusion in free solution will be developed later in this chapter.

Fick's First Law.   Fick was one of the first to consider diffusion on a quantitative basis. For such an analysis, emphasis is placed on the concentration, *c*, of a certain species in a solution. It is assumed that the concentration of this species in some region is less than in a neighboring region. A net migration of molecules then occurs by diffusion from the concentrated to the dilute region. Such a molecular flow down a concentration gradient is analogous to the flow of heat down a temperature gradient from a warmer region to a cooler one. The analogy is actually rather good (especially for gases) since both processes depend on the random thermal motion of the molecules. In fact, the differential equations and their solutions which are used to describe diffusion are those which had previously been developed to describe heat flow.

To express diffusion quantitatively, consider a diffusive flux or flow, *J*. Specifically, let *J* be the number of particles of some species diffusing in a given direction and crossing a certain area per unit time, e.g., moles of particles per cm^2 in a second. From reasoning based on an analogy with heat flow, Fick deduced that the "force" or causative agent leading to the net molecular movement is the concentration gradient. A gradient is simply a measure of how a certain parameter changes with distance. The use of gradients of various quantities as driving forces is extremely important for discussing ion and water relations of plants. In the present instance, the driving force is the concentration gradient, which can be expressed as $\partial c / \partial x$ for diffusion in one dimension. The partial derivative is used here to indicate the change in concentration in the *x*-direction of Cartesian coordinates at some moment in time (constant *t*) and for given values of *y* and *z*. (For the one-dimensional case we are presently considering, the flux in the *x*-direction actually has the same magnitude at any value of *y* and *z*.) The following relation giving the dependence of the flux on the driving force is commonly referred to as Fick's first law of diffusion:

$$J = -D\frac{\partial c}{\partial x} \tag{1-1}$$

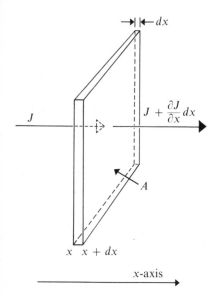

Figure 1–4. Diagram showing the dimensions and the fluxes which form the geometrical basis for the continuity equation.

where D is the diffusion coefficient, generally expressed in cm²/sec. Since D need not be a constant, it is properly called a coefficient in the general case. By convention, a flux from left to right in the direction of increasing x is considered to be positive. Since a net flow occurs toward regions of lower concentration, the minus sign is therefore needed in Equation 1–1. Fick's first law, which has been amply demonstrated experimentally, is the starting point for the present discussion of diffusion.

Continuity Equation and Fick's Second Law.　As indicated above, free diffusion in solution is an important process in the movement of solutes across plant cells and tissues. To discuss such phenomena adequately, we must find the dependence of the concentration on both space and time. We can readily derive such a space-time relationship after considering the concept of continuity, which is needed in order to transform Equation 1–1 into an expression that is convenient for describing the actual solute distributions caused by diffusion.

The flux J of some species is the amount per unit time crossing a given area, here considered to be an area perpendicular to the x-axis (Fig. 1–4). In general, J can change with position along the x-axis. Imagine a volume element of thickness dx in the direction of flow and of cross-sectional area A (Fig. 1–4). At x, let the flux across the surface of area A be J. At $x + dx$, the flux has changed to $J + (\partial J/\partial x)\, dx$ where $\partial J/\partial x$ is the gradient of the flux in the x-direction. The amount accumulating in the volume element Adx in unit time for this one-dimensional problem is simply the amount flowing in per unit time, which is JA, minus that flowing out, $[J + (\partial J/\partial x)dx]A$. The amount accumulating in the volume element can also be expressed in another way, namely as the product of the change in the concentration with time, $\partial c/\partial t$, times the volume element in which the change in concentration occurs, Adx. Equating these two different expressions that describe the accumulation in Adx, we obtain the following relation:

$$JA - \left(J + \frac{\partial J}{\partial x}dx\right)A = \frac{\partial c}{\partial t}Adx \tag{1-2}$$

The two JA terms appearing on the left-hand side of Equation 1–2 cancel each other. After dividing through by Adx, Equation 1–2 leads to the very useful expression known as the continuity equation:

$$-\frac{\partial J}{\partial x} = \frac{\partial c}{\partial t} \tag{1-3}$$

The continuity equation is simply a mathematical way of stating that matter cannot be created or destroyed under ordinary conditions. Thus if the flux of some species changes with position, Equation 1–3 indicates that the local concentration must consequently be increasing or decreasing with time. When we substitute Fick's first law (Eq. 1–1) into the continuity equation (Eq. 1–3), we obtain Fick's second law. For the important special case of constant D, this general equation for diffusion becomes

$$\frac{\partial c}{\partial t} = D\frac{\partial^2 c}{\partial x^2} \tag{1-4}$$

The solution of Equation 1–4 describes how the concentration of the solute changes with position and time as a result of diffusion. A determination of the particular function which satisfies this important partial differential equation requires knowledge of the special conditions for the specific problem under consideration. For the present purpose of describing the characteristics of solute diffusion in general terms, a representative solution useful for the consideration of diffusion under simple initial and boundary conditions is sufficient. For example, the following expression for the concentration can be shown by substitution into Equation 1–4 to satisfy the differential form of Fick's second law when D is constant:

$$c = \frac{M}{2(\pi Dt)^{\frac{1}{2}}} e^{-x^2/4Dt} \tag{1-5}$$

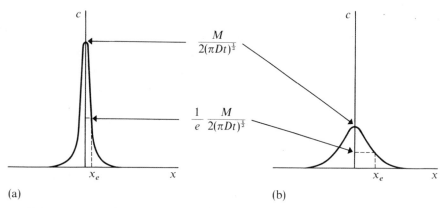

Figure 1–5.   Concentration c as a function of position x for molecules diffusing away from the origin ($x = 0$) according to Fick's second law: (a) statistical distribution for molecules at a time near $t = 0$, and (b) distribution occurring at a subsequent time t. x_e is the location where the concentration has dropped to $1/e$ of its value at the origin.

In Equation 1–5, M is the total amount of solute per unit area initially ($t = 0$) placed at the origin ($x = 0$), and c is the concentration at position x at any later time t.

Space-Time Relation for Diffusion.   Although the functional form of c given by Equation 1–5 is only one particular solution to Fick's second law (Eq. 1–4) and, furthermore, is restricted to the case of constant D, it nevertheless proves to be an extremely useful expression for understanding diffusion. It relates the distance a substance diffuses to the time necessary to reach that distance. The expression involves the diffusion coefficient, D, which can be determined experimentally. At the origin ($x = 0$), Equation 1–5 indicates that the concentration is $M/[2(\pi Dt)^{\frac{1}{2}}]$, which becomes infinitely large as t is turned back to 0—the starting time. This infinite value for c at $x = 0$ corresponds to having all the solute initially placed at the origin. For t greater than 0, the material begins to diffuse away from the origin, the distribution of molecules along the x-axis at two successive times being indicated in Figure 1–5. Since the total number of molecules does not change (it remains at M per unit area across any volume element perpendicular to the x-axis and extending from x values of $-\infty$ to $+\infty$), the area under each of the concentration profiles is the same.

By comparing the left-hand side of Figure 1–5 with the right-hand side, one can see that the average distance of the diffusing molecules from the origin increases with time. To estimate how far molecules diffuse in time t, a useful parameter is the distance at which the concentration has dropped to $1/e$ or 37% of its value at the origin. From Equation 1–5, the concentration at the origin is $M/[2(\pi Dt)^{\frac{1}{2}}]$. (See also Fig. 1–5.) Although somewhat arbitrary, this parameter describes the shift of the statistical distribution of the molecules with time. Specifically, the concentration drops to 37% of the value at the origin when the exponent of e in Equation 1–5 is -1. From Equation 1–5, this distance, x_e, is given by

$$x_e{}^2 = 4Dt \qquad\qquad (1\text{–}6)$$

The distance x_e along the x-axis is also indicated in Figure 1–5. Equation 1–6 is an extremely important relationship that indicates a fundamental characteristic of diffusion processes. The distance a population of molecules diffuses is proportional to the square root of both the diffusion constant and the time for diffusion. In other words, the time for diffusion increases with the square of the distance which needs to be traversed. We should stress that an individual molecule may diffuse a greater or lesser distance in time t than is indicated by Equation 1–6, which actually refers to the time required for the concentration at position x_e to become $1/e$ of the value at the origin.

To illustrate the space-time consequences of Equation 1–6, we will quantitatively consider the diffusion of small molecules in an aqueous solution. Diffusion coefficients determined for 10 mM solutions at 25° (we will use ° in this text as the abbreviation for degrees on the Celsius or centigrade temperature scale) are as follows: sucrose, 0.52×10^{-5} cm^2/sec; glucose, 0.67×10^{-5} cm^2/sec; glycine, 1.05×10^{-5} cm^2/sec; calcium (as the chloride), 1.19×10^{-5} cm^2/sec; and potassium (as the chloride), 1.92×10^{-5} cm^2/sec. Hence, the diffusion coefficients of small ions and other molecules in aqueous solutions are approximately 10^{-5} cm^2/sec. How long would it take to diffuse 50 μm, the distance across a typical leaf cell? From Equation 1–6, the time required for the population of molecules to shift this distance is $(50 \times 10^{-4})^2/[(4)(10^{-5})]$ or 0.6 second. Thus, diffusion is a fairly rapid process over subcellular distances. Next, consider the diffusion of the same substances over a distance of 1 meter. The time needed is $(100)^2/[(4)(10^{-5})]$ or 2.5×10^8 seconds, which is eight years! Diffusion is indeed not a rapid process over long distances. Thus inorganic nutrients in xylary sap would not ascend a tree by diffusion at a rate necessary to sustain life. On the other hand, diffusion is often sufficient for the movement of solutes within leaf cells and especially inside organelles like chloroplasts and mitochondria. In summary, diffusion in a solution is fairly fast over short distances (less than about 100 μm) but extremely slow for very long distances.

Diffusion of gases in the air surrounding and within leaves is necessary for both photosynthesis and transpiration. For instance, water vapor evaporating from the cell walls of leaf cells diffuses across the intercellular air spaces (Fig. 1–2) to reach the stomata and from there diffuses into the atmosphere. Carbon dioxide diffuses from the atmosphere through the open stomata to the surfaces of leaf cells while the photosynthetically evolved oxygen traverses the same pathway in the reverse direction, also primarily by diffusion. The diffusion coefficients for such movements are roughly 10^4 times greater than the D's describing the diffusion of a solute in a liquid. Specifically, the experimentally determined coefficients of the three gases mentioned above in air at 20° are approximately as follows: for water vapor, 0.25 cm^2/sec; for carbon dioxide, 0.16 cm^2/sec; and for oxygen, 0.20 cm^2/sec. The relative diffusion rates of gases in air are generally inversely proportional to the square root of the molecular weights. For H_2O, the molecular weight is 18 while for CO_2 it is 44. Thus water vapor should diffuse $\sqrt{(44)/(18)}$ or 1.56 times faster than carbon dioxide, as the above diffusion coefficients do indicate.

Because of the complicated anatomy of a leaf, the actual pathway for the movement of gas molecules in the intercellular air spaces (cf. Fig. 1–2) is not describable by the simple one-dimensional process used to derive Equation 1–6. Nevertheless, calculations using this equation do give useful estimates of the diffusion times for the many processes involving gaseous movements in a leaf. A typical distance for diffusion in such intercellular air spaces of a leaf might be 1000 μm. Using Equation 1–6 and the diffusion coefficients given in the previous paragraph, we can calculate that the times to diffuse 1000 μm for water vapor, carbon dioxide, and oxygen in air are from 10 to 16 milliseconds. This illustrates that diffusion of molecules in a gas is a fairly rapid process. However, the rate of photosynthesis in plants is often limited by the amount of CO_2 diffusing up to the chloroplasts while the rate of transpiration can be controlled by the time necessary for the diffusion of water vapor away from the leaf surface. In this latter case, the diffusion limitation prevents excessive water loss from the plant and hence, physiologically speaking, is quite useful.

Membrane Structure

A major barrier to diffusion into and out of plant cells is presented by the plasmalemma while the organelle membranes play an analogous role for

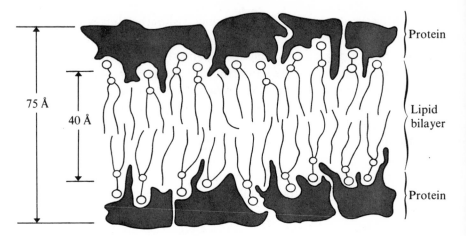

Figure 1–6. Bimolecular lipid leaflet model of a membrane having protein layers on both sides.

the various subcellular compartments and the tonoplast for the vacuole. For instance, water and carbon dioxide readily penetrate the plasmalemma, but ATP and metabolic intermediates usually do not diffuse across it at an appreciable rate. Before a mathematical description of the penetration of membranes by solutes, we need to consider briefly certain features of the structure of membranes.

Davson-Danielli Membrane Model. A widely accepted general model for membrane structure is the bimolecular lipid leaflet flanked on either side by protein layers (Fig. 1–6). Gorter and Grendel in 1925 estimated that the area covered by the lipids extracted from erythrocytes (red blood cells) was about twice the surface area of the cells. Thus the amount of lipid that was present was sufficient to form a double layer in the membrane. Moreover, the penetration of molecules across membranes often appeared to depend primarily on their relative lipid solubility. This circumstantial evidence eventually led to the concept of a lipid bilayer that was envisaged to be located in the center of biological membranes.

To help understand the resulting membrane model, which is generally attributed to Davson and Danielli, we must consider the charge distribution within lipid molecules. The arrangement of atoms in the hydrocarbon (containing only C and H) region of lipid molecules leads to bonding in which no charge imbalance develops. This hydrocarbon part of the molecule is thus nonpolar and tends to avoid water and is therefore called hydrophobic. Most lipid molecules in membranes also have a phosphate and/or an amine group. This region of the molecule becomes charged in aqueous solutions. Such charged regions interact electrostatically with the polar parts of other molecules. Since they interact attractively with water, the polar regions are termed hydrophilic. Many of the phospholipids in membranes are glycerol diesters, which have two different fatty acid side chains. A typical example found to be a major component of most membranes is phosphatidyl choline, also known as lecithin:

$$
\begin{array}{l}
\quad\quad\quad\quad\ \ \overset{\displaystyle O}{\overset{\displaystyle \|}{}} \\
CH_2\!-\!O\!-\!C\!-\!R \\[4pt]
\quad\quad\quad\quad\ \ \overset{\displaystyle O}{\overset{\displaystyle \|}{}} \\
CH\ \!-\!O\!-\!C\!-\!R' \\[4pt]
\quad\quad\quad\quad\ \ \overset{\displaystyle O}{\overset{\displaystyle \|}{}} \quad\quad\quad\ \ \overset{+}{} \\
CH_2\!-\!O\!-\!P\!-\!O\!-\!CH_2CH_2N(CH_3)_3 \\
\quad\quad\quad\quad\ \ \underset{\displaystyle O^-}{|}
\end{array}
$$

where R and R' are the hydrocarbon parts of the fatty acids. Various fatty acids which are commonly esterified to this phospholipid include palmitic (16C and no double bonds, which can be represented as 16:0), palmitoleic (16:1), stearic (18:0), oleic (18:1), linoleic (18:2), and linolenic (18:3)—the major fatty acid combined in various forms in the membranes of higher plant chloroplasts being linolenic. The hydrocarbon side chains from the esterified fatty acids affect the packing of the lipid molecules in the membrane. For instance, as the number of double bonds in the fatty acid side chain increases, the area per lipid molecule in a monolayer becomes greater. This change in intermolecular distances affects the permeability of such lipid layers and presumably also of biological membranes.

To form a bilayer, the lipid molecules could have their nonpolar portions adjacent to each other (Fig. 1–6), which facilitates hydrophobic interactions. The polar or hydrophilic regions are then on the outside. These outer charged regions of the lipids can attract water molecules and the charged parts of proteins, both of which are present in membranes. For instance, myelin is 30% protein by weight while up to 70% of mitochondrial membranes may be protein. Based on the low surface tensions experimentally observed for membranes, Davson and Danielli proposed that the membrane protein was adsorbed as monolayers on either side of the central lipid bilayer. Proteins are fairly heavily charged in aqueous solutions and can interact both with the polar end of the lipids and with the surrounding water molecules in an aqueous solution. This protein-water interaction would decrease the surface tension of membranes from that expected for a nonpolar region interacting with water. Thus the model was consistent with the low surface tension, the apparent presence of a lipid phase, and the substantial protein content of membranes.

A lipid bilayer with protein adsorbed on both sides as suggested by Davson and Danielli would be approximately 70 to 80 Ångstroms thick. [An Ångstrom, abbreviated Å, is 10^{-8} cm (Appendix III).] In particular, lipid bilayers are about 40 Å thick. Such a thickness is too small to be resolved by the light microscope, which has a limit of size resolution of about 2000 Å. Since about 1940, the electron microscope has been used to study membranes. Electrons are scattered by heavy metals in fixatives like OsO_4 and $KMnO_4$, which interact strongly with the membranes. A resolution of 10 Å is possible, and thus membranes can be resolved in electron micrographs of thin sections through cells. For nearly all membranes, two regions of heavy metal deposition about 20 Å wide are found on either side of a relatively clear space about 35 Å wide. These electron-dense bands were suggested to be protein layers, and the unstained central region of the membrane was proposed to be a lipid region, although the actual interactions of the fixatives leading to the local deposition of the heavy metals have not been unambiguously identified.

A very similar electron-scattering pattern has been found in the electron micrographs for various membranes like the plasmalemma and tonoplast as well as for the outer or limiting membranes of the organelles. Based on this consistently observed pattern of two electron opaque layers flanking a lighter area as seen in numerous electron micrographs, J. D. Robertson enunciated the unit membrane concept. Robertson speculated that the various cellular membranes may be similar in structure and may all have been derived from the plasma membrane. More than likely, this is an oversimplification, as we will consider below. For instance, the two allegedly protein layers on either side of the membrane vary in thickness and fixative interactions within the same cell as well as from cell to cell.

Mitochondrial and Chloroplast Membranes.   Both mitochondria and chloroplasts have extensive internal membrane systems, and both are highly involved with cellular metabolism. When membranes of such organelles are carefully investigated using electron microscopy, a globular substructure is found. For instance, particles with diameters near 100 Å and near 170 Å have been found in the lamellar membranes of chloroplasts using the freeze-etch technique (the frozen specimens are fractured, water is removed by sublimation, and then electron microscopy is performed using suitable replicas). These subunits appear to be embedded in the membrane, not adsorbed as monolayers on the surface. Thus, where high enzymatic activity is expected, divergences from the unit membrane become apparent. Enzymes implementing electron transport in respiration or in photosynthesis might be an integral part of the interior membranes of mitochondria or chloroplasts, respectively. Such membrane subunits could thermally rotate due to their own kinetic motion while remaining in the membrane. This allows successive interactions with various enzymes located in the membrane. Thus the location of various components involved with electron transport in a solid membrane system could ensure an orderly, rapid, directed passage of electrons from enzyme to enzyme. The proteins involved with electron transport vary in size and shape, and thus the internal membranes of chloroplasts and mitochondria would not be expected to be uniform and regular. Enzymes involved with ion transport and possibly with cell wall synthesis may be embedded at different sites in the plasmalemma. Furthermore, it has also been suggested that proteins involved with transport occur in the tonoplast. In short, a membrane may be a mosaic consisting of a lipid bilayer with adsorbed protein in some regions while in others it may have globular subunits.

The outer of the two mitochondrial membranes appears to be rather permeable to sucrose, various small anions and cations, adenine nucleotides, coenzyme A, and many other compounds, in contrast with the much less permeable inner mitochondrial membrane. The inner membrane apparently invaginates to form the mitochondrial cristae, in which are embedded the enzymes responsible for electron transport and the accompanying ATP formation. For instance, the inner membrane system contains various dehydrogenases, an ATPase, and cytochromes a, a_3, b, and c. (Cytochromes will be considered in Chapters 5 and 6.) These proteins are not in a simple flat monolayer adsorbed onto a lipid bimolecular leaflet but rather occur in organelle membranes which are at least partially globular in substructure. Electron microscopy has revealed small particles attached by stalks to the cristae, indicating another divergence from the simple Davson-Danielli model of a membrane. These structures embedded in or released from the mitochondrial membranes are believed to be involved in the phosphorylation accompanying respiration.

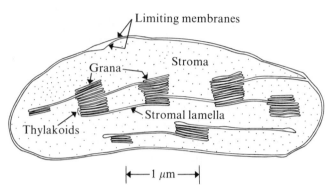

Figure 1–7.   Generalized chloroplast from a leaf mesophyll cell.

Inside the inner membrane of a mitochondrion is a viscous region known as the matrix. The citric acid cycle (Krebs cycle) enzymes as well as others are located there. For substrates to be catabolized via the citric acid cycle, they must cross two membranes to pass from the cytoplasm to the inside of the mitochondrion. Often the slowest or rate-limiting step in the oxidation of such substrates is their entry into the mitochondrial matrix. Since the inner mitochondrial membrane is highly impermeable to most molecules, transport across the membrane using a "carrier" (see pp. 107–8) is generally invoked to explain how various substances get into the matrix. These carriers situated in the inner membrane might shuttle important substrates from the lumen between the outer and inner mitochondrial membranes to the matrix. Because of the inner membrane, important ions and substrates in the mito-chondrial matrix do not leak out, and consequently such permeability barriers between various subcellular compartments improve the overall efficiency of the cell.

Chloroplasts (Fig. 1–7) are also surrounded by two membranes, the inner one of which may invaginate to form the complex internal lamellar system. Although of obvious importance for a full understanding of photosynthesis *in vivo*, very little is presently known about the permeability properties or the composition of the two limiting membranes. Chloroplast lamellar mem-branes are 52% lipid and 48% protein. Much of the chlorophyll and other photosynthetic pigments appears to be bound to the membrane proteins and lipids by hydrophobic forces. Also, the enzymes and other components involved with photosynthetic electron transport (see Chapters 5 and 6) are located in the chloroplast lamellar membranes. These membranes are about 100 Å thick, which is somewhat thicker than the plasmalemma or tonoplast. Usually the lamellae form flattened sacs, which are known as thylakoids or discs. When seen in an electron micrograph, a transverse section of a thylakoid looks like a pair of opposed membranes joined at the ends (cf. Fig. 1–7).

The actual organization of lamellar membranes within the chloroplast varies greatly with the species. The chloroplasts of red algae appear to have the simplest internal structure as the lamellae are in the form of single thylakoids separated by appreciable distances from each other. For most higher plant chloroplasts (Fig. 1–7), the characteristic feature is stacks of about 10 or more thylakoids known as grana, which are typically 0.4 to 0.5 μm in diameter, 10 to 50 of these grana occurring in a single chloroplast. The lamellar extensions between grana are called intergranal or stromal lamellae. The remainder of the chloroplast volume is known as the stroma, which contains the enzymes involved with the fixation of carbon dioxide into the various products of photosynthesis. For completeness, it should be pointed out that the blue-green algae and the photosynthetic bacteria do not contain chloroplasts, but their photosynthetic pigments still are generally located in membranes, often in lamellae immediately underlying the cell membrane. In some photosynthetic bacteria, the lamellae appear to have pinched off and formed discrete subcellular bodies known as chromatophores.

Permeability of Membranes

With this knowledge of the general structure of membranes, let us now turn to a quantitative analysis of the interactions between membranes and diffusing solutes. The rate-limiting step for movement of many molecules into and out of plant cells is diffusion through the plasmalemma. Because of the close packing and interactions between the component molecules of the membrane, such diffusion is greatly restricted compared with the relative ease of movement in an aqueous phase like the cytoplasm. It has proved quite useful to apply Fick's first law for describing such diffusion of molecules across a membrane (and this will be the mathematical approach adopted in this section). Once past the barrier presented by the membrane, the molecules may be distributed throughout the cell relatively rapidly by diffusion and by protoplasmic streaming.

Concentration Difference Across a Membrane. The driving force for diffusion of uncharged molecules into or out of plant cells is the concentration gradient across the plasmalemma, this movement being a special case suitable for the application of Fick's first law (Eq. 1–1). Since the actual

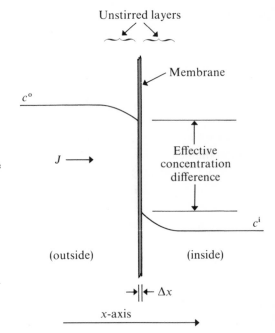

Figure 1–8. The effect of unstirred layers on the solute concentration near a membrane across which the molecules are diffusing.

concentration gradient is not known in the plasmalemma or any other membrane, the driving force is generally approximated by the average gradient across the membrane:

$$\frac{\partial c}{\partial x} \simeq \frac{\Delta c}{\Delta x} = \frac{c^i - c^o}{\Delta x} \tag{1–7}$$

where c^o is the concentration of the species outside the cell, c^i is the concentration in the cytoplasm, and Δx is the thickness of the plasmalemma which acts as the barrier restricting the penetration of the molecules into the cell. (See Fig. 1–8.) The concentrations c^o and c^i appearing in Equation 1–7 can equally well represent values in any two compartments separated by a membrane, such as the aqueous phases outside and inside the central vacuole of a plant cell.

The magnitude of the effective concentration difference across a membrane is made somewhat uncertain by the existence of unstirred layers (Fig. 1–8), as has been pointed out by J. Dainty. The solute moves across these layers next to the membrane not by mechanical mixing but by diffusion, indicating that a concentration gradient must also exist in the unstirred layers, as is illustrated in Figure 1–8. When the mixing in the solutions adjacent to the membrane is increased as by turbulence resulting from protoplasmic streaming on the inside of the cell or rapid stirring on the outside, the thickness of the unstirred layer is reduced. However, the unstirred layers are not eliminated. Under actual experimental conditions with good stirring, the external unstirred layer may be from 10 to 300 μm thick, which is much thicker than the membrane itself. Although diffusion is rapid in aqueous solutions compared with that in membranes, the unstirred layers represent an appreciable distance for molecules to diffuse across. Thus diffusion through the unstirred layer can become the rate-limiting factor for the entry into cells or organelles of molecules which rapidly penetrate the membrane itself. For convenience, the difference in concentration across the membrane will be taken as $c^i - c^o$, but this is an overestimate of the effective concentration difference, as indicated in Figure 1–8.

The difference in concentration, Δc, actually determining the diffusion of molecules across a membrane is the concentration just inside one side of the membrane minus that just within the other side. In Equation 1–7, the concentrations are those in the aqueous phases outside the membrane. Since membranes are quite different as solvents compared with aqueous solutions, the concentrations just inside the membrane can differ appreciably from those just outside in the aqueous solution; thus a correction factor must be applied to Equation 1–7 to give the actual concentration gradient existing in the membrane. This factor is known as the partition coefficient, K. It is essentially the ratio of the concentration of a solute in the membrane to that outside it (c^o or c^i), and consequently K for a particular molecule is often defined as the solubility of a solute in the membrane divided by the solubility in the aqueous bathing solutions. Practically, the partition coefficient is determined by measuring the ratio of the equilibrium concentration of some solute in a lipid phase (such as olive oil) to the concentration in an adjacent and immiscible aqueous phase. This rather simple convention for obtaining partition coefficients is based on the high lipid content of membranes and the numerous experimental results which show that the penetration of a membrane depends on the lipid solubility of the molecules. Partition coefficients have a wide range of values, most being between 10^{-4} and 10. Usually K is considered to be the same on the two sides of the membrane. Thus the corrected concentration difference leading to diffusion across the membrane is $K(c^i - c^o)$, where K characterizes a particular substance.

Permeability Coefficient.   To utilize Fick's first law for describing the entry of solutes into a cell [$J = -D\, \partial c/\partial x$ (Eq. 1–1)], we need some convenient way of expressing the flux, J. By convention, J is positive when the net flow is into the cell (left to right in Fig. 1–8). Let s be the amount of some substance that enters the cell; then ds/dt is the rate of entry. The flux J is the rate of entry of the substance per unit area or $(1/A)\,(ds/dt)$, where A is the area of the cellular membrane across which the substance is diffusing. Using the partition coefficient and this expression for the flux, we can write Fick's first law (Eq. 1–1) as follows:

$$\frac{1}{A}\frac{ds}{dt} = DK\frac{(c^o - c^i)}{\Delta x} \tag{1–8}$$

where ds/dt is positive when material enters the cell, i.e., when the external concentration, c^o, of the substance being considered is greater than the internal one, c^i, as Equation 1–8 indicates.

To describe quantitatively the amount of some substance penetrating a particular membrane, we must know the magnitude of the factor $DK/\Delta x$ appearing in Equation 1–8. This quantity is called the permeability coefficient, P. The permeability coefficient conveniently replaces three quantities, which in general would all need to be determined. Because of the tortuous pathway a molecule may take in diffusing across a membrane, Δx is not necessarily equal to the membrane thickness and cannot readily be measured. The partition coefficient is generally determined by using a lipid phase like olive oil, not the actual lipids occurring in the membrane, and thus K has some uncertainty. The diffusion coefficient of a molecule can vary with distance across the membrane although the actual dependence of D on x is not known in any membrane. However, P is a single, measurable quantity characterizing the membrane and the solute of interest and thus has proved to be a very useful parameter for describing diffusion. The units of P are length per time which is a velocity, e.g., cm/sec. Using the definition of the permeability coefficient, we can rewrite Equation 1–8 as

$$ds/dt = PA(c^o - c^i) \tag{1–9}$$

This equation is in a form useful for considering many experimental investigations of the diffusion of solutes into and out of plant cells.

Diffusion and Cellular Concentration. To describe how the solute concentration inside a cell changes with time due to diffusion across the surrounding membrane, we must first express s in Equation 1–9 in a suitable fashion and then integrate the equation. It is useful to introduce the approximation, particularly appropriate to plant cells, that the cell volume does not change during the time interval of interest. In other words, because of the rigid cell wall, the plant cell can be assumed to have a nearly constant volume, V, during the entry or exit of the solute being considered. The average internal concentration of this species, c^i, is equal to the amount of the particular solute divided by the cellular volume or s/V. Therefore, s can be conveniently replaced by Vc^i, meaning that ds/dt in Equation 1–9 equals Vdc^i/dt. For simplicity, we will assume that P is independent of concentration. Upon rearrangement and the insertion of integral signs, Equation 1–9 then becomes

$$\int_{c^i(0)}^{c^i(t)} \frac{dc^i}{c^o - c^i} = \frac{PA}{V} \int_0^t dt \qquad (1\text{–}10)$$

where $c^i(0)$ is the initial internal concentration (i.e., when $t = 0$) and $c^i(t)$ is that at a later time t.

The volume outside the cell is usually quite large compared with V, and consequently the external concentration, c^o, does not change appreciably. Such an approximation is also appropriate for experiments of short duration or where special arrangements are made to maintain c^o at some fixed value. For such cases where c^o is constant, Equation 1–10 can be integrated to give the following expression for P:

$$P = \frac{V}{At} \ln \frac{c^o - c^i(0)}{c^o - c^i(t)} \qquad (1\text{–}11)$$

Starting with a known c^o outside the cell and determining the internal concentration initially (i.e., for $t = 0$) and at some subsequent time t, we can calculate P from Equation 1–11 if V/A is known. Even when V/A is not known, the relative permeability coefficients for two substances can be determined. The above derivation of an expression for P can easily be extended to the case where the external concentration, c^o, is zero. The permeability coefficient then equals $(V/At)\ln [c^i(0)/c^i(t)]$, which is an expression appropriate for describing the diffusion of a photosynthetic product out of a chloroplast or of some substance from the cell into a large external solution initially devoid of that species. In general, permeability coefficients are useful for quantitatively describing the diffusion of substances such as metabolic substrates or products across cellular and subcellular membranes.

The time it takes a population of molecules to diffuse a given distance in a free solution is proportional to the square of the length moved, as discussed above [$x_e^2 = 4Dt$ (Eq. 1-6)]. On the other hand, when the rate-limiting step is diffusion through the membrane, the time to reach a given concentration inside a cell can be linearly proportional to the dimensions of the cell. This statement presupposes either mechanical mixing or rapid diffusion inside the cell to distribute quickly the solute molecules throughout the cell, once they diffuse across the membrane. For convenience of calculation in illustrating this point, consider a spherical cell of radius r. Then the volume V equals $(4/3)\pi r^3$ and the surface area A is $4\pi r^2$. Hence V/A is simply equal to $r/3$. For two spherical cells having the same permeability coefficient, Equation 1-11 indicates that the time to reach a given concentration inside is *linearly* proportional to the radius, i.e., t in this case equals $(r/3P)\ln [c^o - c^i(0)]/[c^o - c^i(t)]$. For the same P, a given level inside a small cell would still be reached sooner than it would be reached inside a large cell. However, when diffusion across the membrane is the slow step, the ratio of the times to reach a given internal concentration for these two cells equals the ratio of the radii while when diffusion in the internal solution is the rate-limiting factor, the time ratio would be closer to the square of the ratio of the radii.

A typical permeability coefficient for a small nonelectrolyte or uncharged molecule (e.g., *tert*-butyl alcohol) is 10^{-4} cm/sec while P for a small ion (e.g., K^+ or Na^+) is often about 10^{-7} cm/sec. Such a difference in permeability coefficients is mainly because of the much lower partition coefficients for charged particles. In other words, due to its charge, the electrolyte tends to be much less soluble in the membrane than is a neutral molecule with the result that the effective concentration gradient driving the charged species across the membrane is generally smaller for given concentrations in the aqueous phases on either side of the barrier.

Using these permeability coefficients and Equation 1-11, we can calculate the time required for a substance initially absent from a cell [$c^i(0) = 0$] to achieve an internal concentration equal to half the external concentration [$c^i(t) = \frac{1}{2}c^o$]. For spherical cells, V/A is $r/3$, and the conditions on the concentrations mean that [$c^o - c^i(0)]/[c^o - c^i(t)]$ equals $(c^o - 0)/(c^o - \frac{1}{2}c^o)$, which is 2. Substituting these relations into Equation 1-11 gives the result that the time needed is $(r/3P)\ln 2$, where r is the radius of the spherical cell, P is the permeability coefficient of the solute being considered, and $\ln 2$ equals 0.693 (Appendix III). For a cell 50 μm in diameter, which is reasonable for spongy mesophyll cells in certain leaves (cf. Fig. 1-2), the time for an initially absent species to reach half of the external concentration is

$\{(25 \times 10^{-4})/[(3)(10^{-4})]\}(0.693)$ or 6 seconds for the nonelectrolyte ($P = 10^{-4}$ cm/sec) and 2 hours for small electrolytes ($P = 10^{-7}$ cm/sec). Hence, the external membrane is an extremely good barrier for electrolytes, markedly hindering their entry into or egress from the cell. On the other hand, small nonelectrolytes can diffuse in and out of plant cells fairly readily, depending to a large extent on their relative lipid solubility.

Cell Walls

The rigidity of the cell wall helps determine the size and shape of the cell and ultimately the overall structure of the plant. This supportive role is performed in conjunction with the internal hydrostatic pressure, which causes an elastic distension of the cell walls, to be discussed below. The cell wall is also intrinsically involved in many aspects of the ion and water relations of a plant. Since it surrounds each cell, all fluxes of water and solutes into and out of a plant cell must cross the cell wall, usually by diffusion. Water which evaporates from a plant during transpiration comes directly from cell walls. (Some aspects of this process will be considered quantitatively in Chapter 2.) The cell wall in certain specialized cells can act as a channel. For instance, the conducting cells in the xylem have lost their protoplasts with the result that the pathway for the conduction of solutions in the xylem consists essentially of pipes or conduits made exclusively out of cell walls.

Cell walls vary from tenths to tens of microns in thickness and generally are divided into three regions. The primary cell wall surrounds dividing meristematic cells as well as the elongating cells during the period of cell enlargement. The cell wall often becomes thickened by the elaboration of a secondary cell wall inside the primary one, which makes the cell much less flexible. The cell wall also includes an amorphous third region between contiguous cells called the middle lamella, whose width is not universally agreed upon. Although cellulose also occurs there, the middle lamella may be composed mainly of the calcium salts of pectic acids, the presence of which causes adjacent cells to adhere together.

Chemistry and Morphology.   Cellulose is the most abundant organic component in the entire plant and animal kingdoms. It is the characteristic substance of the plant cell wall, constituting from 25% to 50% of the cell wall organic material. Cellulose is a linear (unbranched) polysaccharide consisting of 1,4-linked β-D-glucopyranose units the polymer being about 8 Å in its maximum width and 33 Å^2 in cross-sectional area. Since the glucose residues have their rings in the same plane, the cellulose polymer is ribbon-like. These polymers are organized into various entities in the cell wall. Approximately 100 parallel chains of cellulose form a structural unit known as an elementary microfibril. Elementary microfibrils are generally about 40 Å by 85 Å in cross-section. Approximately 20 such parallel units are organized into 1 microfibril. The microfibrils are about 250 Å in diameter and can be 10 μm long. They are the basic unit of the cell wall and are readily observed in electron micrographs. Although great variation exists, the microfibrils tend to be interwoven in the primary cell wall and parallel to each other in the secondary wall.

Interstices between the cellulose microfibrils are usually a few hundred Ångstroms across. In these interstices surrounding the cellulose microfibrils is a matrix of amorphous components which can occupy a larger volume of the cell wall than do the cellulose microfibrils themselves. In fact, the main constituent of the cell wall on a weight basis is actually water, the consequences of which will be considered in Chapter 2.

The cell wall matrix contains lignins, noncellulosic polysaccharides such as pectin, a small amount of protein, bound and free water, appreciable calcium, other cations, and sometimes silicates. Lignins are complex phenylpropanoid (C_6, C_3) polymers with varied subunit residues and constitute the second most abundant class of organic molecules in living organisms, being about 50% as prevalent as cellulose. Lignins tend to be hydrophobic and thus act as waterproofing agents for the cell walls. Pectin consists primarily of 1,4-linked α-D-galacturonic acid residues, the uronide carboxyl groups of which are normally dissociated and have a negative charge. This negative charge leads to the tremendous cation-binding capacity of cell walls. In particular, much of the divalent cation calcium (Ca^{++}) is bound, which may help link the various polymers together. Polymers based on 1,4-linked β-D-xylopyranose units (xylans) as well as on many other residues can also be extracted from cell walls. They are loosely referred to as hemicelluloses, e.g., xylans, mannans, galactans, and glucans. In general, hemicelluloses tend to have a low molecular weight (in the ten thousands) compared with pectin (about five to ten times larger) or cellulose (up to 1000 times larger). The presence of the negatively charged pectins hinders the entry of anions into plant cells. However, ions and other solutes generally pass through the cell wall much more easily than through the plasmalemma, as will be considered next.

Diffusion Across Cell Walls. The effective diffusion coefficients of certain small molecules are only ten to one hundred times less in the cell wall than in an aqueous solution, some D's being as high as about 10^{-6} cm^2/sec. Such relatively high values are due to the rather large interstices in the cell wall, which can be at least partially filled with unbound water. Thus the movement from the external solution up to the plasmalemma can be in aqueous channels through the cell wall.

The permeability coefficient in the cell wall can be calculated from its definition, $DK/\Delta x$, which was introduced above. The partition coefficient, K, would be close to 1 for the water-filled interstices of the cell wall. The thickness of the cell wall is often near 2 μm. (A discussion of the complications resulting from the tortuous nature of the aqueous channels from one side of the wall to the other will be omitted here.) Using a diffusion coefficient of 10^{-6} cm^2/sec, we can thus estimate P for the cell wall as $[(10^{-6})(1)]/(2 \times 10^{-4})$ or 5×10^{-3} cm/sec. Most of the permeability coefficients for small solutes crossing the plasmalemma range from 10^{-8} to 10^{-4} cm/sec. Hence, a cell wall generally has a higher permeability coefficient than does a membrane, which means that the wall is usually more permeable for small solutes than is the plasmalemma. Another point can be made by considering the quantity DK for the two cases. With the above numerical values, DK is 10^{-6} cm^2/sec in the cell wall while for a plasmalemma 100 Å thick, it is only 10^{-14} to 10^{-10} cm^2/sec. This indicates that molecules have much greater difficulty diffusing a given distance in the plasmalemma compared with the same distance in the cell wall.

Secondary cell walls are often interrupted by localized pits. In such regions, the primary cell walls also have local depressions where they are markedly decreased in thickness. A pit in the wall of a given cell usually occurs opposite a complementary pit in an adjacent cell, the cytoplasm of two adjacent cells being brought into close proximity at such a pit pair. The local absence of extensive cell wall substance facilitates the diffusion of molecules from one cell into the other. Another important way molecules move between plant cells is by means of the plasmodesmata (singular, plasmodesma). These are fine, membrane-flanked, cytoplasmic threads that pass from a protoplast, through a pit, directly into the protoplast of a second cell. A tobacco leaf cell can have 10 to 30 plasmodesmata per 100 μm^2 of cell surface, each plasmodesma having a diameter near 0.2 μm. Electron microscopy has revealed over ten times as many 300 Å diameter "microplasmodesmata" per unit area although great variation in size and frequency does exist. The meshwork of communicating cytoplasm created by such connections between cells is commonly referred to as the symplasm. The presence of the plasmodesmata provides a particularly effective pathway for solute movement between adjacent cells since no permeability barrier in the form of either a cell wall or a membrane then needs to be surmounted for diffusion of molecules from cell to cell.

Stress-Strain Relations of Cell Wall. Cell walls of mature plant cells are generally quite resistant to deformation. However, such structures do stretch when a stress is applied. Reversible elastic properties are generally described in terms of a measure of elasticity known as Young's modulus, which is the ratio of the applied stress (force per unit area) to the resulting strain (change in length per unit length):

$$\text{Young's modulus} = \frac{\text{stress}}{\text{strain}} = \frac{\text{force/area}}{\Delta L/L} \qquad (1\text{--}12)$$

Since $\Delta L/L$ is dimensionless, Young's modulus has the dimensions of force per unit area or pressure. A high value of this modulus of elasticity means that a large stress must be applied to produce a given strain.

Young's modulus for pure cellulose is quite large [about 10^5 kilograms (kg)/cm^2 or 5% of that for steel], which is consistent with the great strength of cell walls. Because of both the complicated three-dimensional array of microfibrils in the cell wall and the presence of many other components, Young's modulus for a cell wall is considerably less than for pure cellulose. For instance, the modulus of elasticity of the cell wall of *Nitella* cells has been experimentally found to be about 7000 kg/cm^2. [The footnote to Appendix III explains the common convention of expressing forces, such as those in Young's modulus (Eq. 1–12), in units of mass, e.g., kilograms in the present case.]

There is a pressure, P, acting uniformly in all directions inside plant cells. This P is essentially the internal hydrostatic pressure, also referred to as

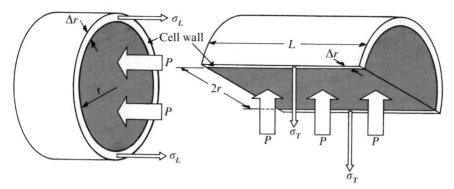

Figure 1–9. Schematic sections of a hypothetical cylindrical cell resembling the internodal cells of *Nitella* or *Chara*, which illustrates various dimensions and the stresses (σ_L and σ_T) existing in the cell wall.

the turgor pressure. (These terms will be discussed in Chapter 2.) Because of such an internal pressure, tensions or stresses generally exist in the cell wall. The magnitudes of these stresses vary with the physiological state of the plant as well as with direction in the cell wall, which we will now consider.

A cylinder, which closely approximates the large internodal cells of *Nitella* or *Chara* (Fig. 1–9), is a useful geometrical model for evaluating the various cell wall stresses. Let the radius of the cylinder be r. The force on an end wall is the pressure, P, times the area of the end wall, πr^2; thus the force is $P\pi r^2$. This force is balanced by a tension known as the longitudinal stress, σ_L, which occurs in the cell wall. The area over which σ_L acts is shown by the cut portion of the cell wall in the left-hand part of Figure 1–9, which indicates that the longitudinal stress occurs in an annulus of circumference $2\pi r$ (approximately) and a width equal to the thickness of the cell wall, Δr; the force in the cell wall is thus $(\sigma_L)(2\pi r)(\Delta r)$. This force is an equal and opposite reaction to $P\pi r^2$, and so

$$\sigma_L = \frac{rP}{2\Delta r} \qquad (1\text{–}13)$$

The longitudinal stress acts parallel to the major axis of the cylinder and resists the lengthwise deformation of the cell, such strain ultimately resulting from the internal hydrostatic pressure.

A tangential stress σ_T, which limits the radial expansion of the cell, also exists in the cell wall in response to the internal pressure. To help determine the magnitude of this stress, consider a cell split into half along a length, L (right-hand side of Fig. 1–9). The split part of the cell has an area of

2rL which is acted on by the pressure P, leading to a force of P2rL. This force is resisted by the tangential stress in the cell wall. As indicated in Figure 1–9, σ_T acts along two cell wall surfaces each of width Δr and length L. Thus the total force in the cut part of the cell wall is the area $(2\Delta rL)$ times the tangential stress. Equating this force $(\sigma_T 2\Delta rL)$ with that due to the internal pressure in the cell $(P2rL)$, we obtain the following relationship for the tangential stress:

$$\sigma_T = \frac{rP}{\Delta r} \qquad (1\text{–}14)$$

The tangential stress in the cell wall given by Equation 1–14 is twice as large as the longitudinal stress (Eq. 1–13). Thus, this simple cylindrical model illustrates the important point that the stresses in a cell wall can vary with direction.

To estimate the magnitudes of the stresses and strains in the cell wall, consider a *Nitella* or *Chara* cell 1 mm in diameter with a cell wall 5 μm thick. In this case, $r/\Delta r$ is 500 μm/5 μm or 100. A reasonable estimate of P is 6 bars. [A bar, which is a convenient unit for expressing pressures occurring in plants, equals 10^6 dynes/cm^2 or 0.987 atmosphere (Appendix III).] Using Equation 1–13, the longitudinal stress in the cell wall of such a cell is $[(100)(6)]/(2)$ or 300 bars; using Equation 1–14, the tangential stress is calculated to be 600 bars. One bar corresponds to 1.020 kg/cm^2 at sea level (Appendix III). Thus the longitudinal stress in the cell wall is $(300)(1.020)$ or 306 kg/cm^2, which is an appreciable tension. The strain produced by this stress can be calculated using the definition of Young's modulus (Eq. 1–12) and its particular value for the cell wall of 7000 kg/cm^2 cited above. From Equation 1–12, the fractional change in length is calculated to be $(306)/(7000)$ or 0.044, i.e., only about 4% in this case. Hence, even with an internal pressure of 6 bars, which leads to a longitudinal stress of 300 bars, the cell wall is not extended very much. The cell wall is indeed strong and therefore well suited for limiting the size of individual cells as well as for providing the structural support of a plant.

Problems

1–1. Consider a cylindrical *Nitella* cell 10 cm long and 1 mm in diameter, a spherical *Valonia* cell 1 cm in diameter, and a spherical *Chlorella* cell 4 μm in diameter.

(a) What is the area/volume in each case? (b) Which cell has the largest amount of surface area per unit volume? (c) Assume that the cell walls are equal in thickness. For a given internal pressure, which cell would have the highest cell wall stress?

1–2. A thin layer of some solution is inserted into a long column of water. One hour later, the concentration of the solute is 0.1 molal at the plane of insertion and 0.037 molal at a distance 3 mm away. (a) What is its diffusion coefficient? (b) When the concentration 9 cm away is 37% of the value at the plane of insertion, how much time has elapsed? (c) Suppose that a trace amount of a substance having a diffusion coefficient 100 times smaller than that of the main solute was also initially introduced. For the time in (b), where would its concentration drop to $1/e$ of the value at the plane of insertion?

1–3. Suppose that an unstirred air layer 1 mm wide is adjacent to a guard cell with a cell wall $2\mu m$ thick. (a) If D is 10^6 times larger for CO_2 diffusing in air compared with diffusion in the cell wall, what are the relative times involved in crossing the two barriers? (b) If it takes CO_2 just as long to cross an 80 Å plasmalemma as it does to cross the cell wall, what are the relative sizes of the two diffusion coefficients? (c) Assuming that the partition coefficient for CO_2 is 100 times greater in the cell wall than in the plasmalemma, in which barrier is the permeability coefficient larger and by how much?

1–4. Consider a solute having a permeability coefficient of 10^{-4} cm/sec for the plasmalemma of a cylindrical cell that is 10 cm long and 1 mm in diameter. Assume that its concentration remains essentially uniform within the cell. (a) How much time would it take for 90% of the solute to diffuse out into a large external solution initially devoid of that substance? (b) How much time would it take if diffusion occurred only at the two ends of the cell? (c) How would the times calculated in (a) and (b) change in order that 99% of the solute would diffuse out? (d) How would the times change if P were 10^{-6} cm/sec?

References

Bonner, J., and J. E. Varner, eds. 1965. *Plant Biochemistry*, Academic Press, New York.

Clowes, F. A. L., and B. E. Juniper. 1968. *Plant Cells*, Blackwell Scientific Publications, Oxford.

Crank, J. 1956. *The Mathematics of Diffusion*, Oxford University Press, Oxford.

Davson, H., and J. F. Danielli. 1952. *The Permeability of Natural Membranes*, 2nd ed., Cambridge University Press, Cambridge.

Esau, K. 1965. *Plant Anatomy*, 2nd ed., Wiley, New York.

Jacobs, M. H. 1967. *Diffusion Processes*, Springer-Verlag, New York.

Kamiya, N., M. Tazawa, and T. Takata. 1963. The relation of turgor pressure to cell volume in *Nitella* with special reference to mechanical properties of the cell wall. *Protoplasma* **57**: 501–21.

Siegel, S. M. 1962. *The Plant Cell Wall*, Pergamon Press, New York.

Stein, W. D. 1967. *The Movement of Molecules Across Cell Membranes*, Academic Press, New York.

Weast, R. C. 1968. *Handbook of Chemistry and Physics*, 49th ed., Chemical Rubber, Cleveland.

Chapter 2

Water

Water is the main constituent of most plant cells, as the discussion of both vacuoles and cell walls in the previous chapter has already suggested. The actual cellular water content varies with cell type and physiological condition. For example, the carrot root is about 85% water while the young inner leaves of lettuce contain up to 95% water. Water comprises only 10% of certain dry seeds and spores; when these entities become metabolically active, however, an increase in water content is essential for the transformation.

Water is the medium in which diffusion of solutes through plant cells takes place; it is an extremely suitable substance for temperature regulation; it is the solvent for many biochemical reactions; and it is rather incompressible for the pressures occurring under physiological conditions, the latter property underlying its role in plant support. Specifically, water has a high heat capacity and a high thermal conductivity for a liquid, both properties making it ideal for maintaining temperature equilibration. Water is also an extremely good solvent for polar substances and particularly for ions, which has far-reaching consequences for life since many biologically important substances are charged. The mineral nutrients needed for growth and the organic products of photosynthesis are all transported in aqueous solutions throughout the plant. In actively growing land plants, water continuity exists from the soil, through the plant, to the evaporation sites in the leaves. Another important aspect is that water is quite transparent to visible radiation, enabling sunlight to reach chloroplasts within the cells in leaves and in submerged plants in the ocean. Water is also intrinsically involved with metabolism. It is the source of oxygen evolved in photosynthesis and the hydrogen used for carbon dioxide reduction. The generation of the important energy currency, ATP, involves the extraction of the components of water from ADP plus phosphate, i.e., such a phosphorylation is a dehydration process which takes place in an aqueous solution under biological conditions. Thus a recognition of the many unique properties of water is crucial for an overall understanding of plant physiology.

A number of isotopically different forms of water can be prepared, which greatly facilitates experimental studies with this biologically important molecule. If deuterium (^{2}H) replaces both of the usual hydrogens, what is obtained is "heavy water" or deuterium oxide with a molecular weight of 20. The entry of water into chemical reactions in the plant can then be studied by analyzing the deuterium content of the various substances involved as reactants or products. Also, tritium (^{3}H), which is radioactive and has a half-life of 12.4 years, can be incorporated into water. Such tritiated water has been invaluable in measuring the rate of diffusion of water in plant tissue. As another alternative for tracing the pathway of water, the usual ^{16}O isotope can be replaced by ^{18}O. This "labeling" of water with ^{18}O was used to determine that the oxygen evolved in photosynthesis actually comes from water and not from carbon dioxide. (See Chapter 5.)

Physical Properties of Water

Water differs markedly from substances having closely related electronic structures, a point which can be illustrated by considering the series CH_4, NH_3, H_2O, HF, and Ne. Each molecule contains 10 protons and 10 electrons, the series from methane to neon representing a decrease in the number of hydrogen atoms per molecule. For this sequence, the melting points are $-184°$, $-78°$, $0°$, $-92°$, and $-249°$, respectively. A similar striking variation in boiling points occurs, viz., $-161°$, $-33°$, $100°$, $19°$, and $-246°$. The relatively high melting and boiling points for water are indicative of its strong intermolecular forces. In other words, thermal agitation does not easily disrupt the water-water bonding. This attraction between molecules

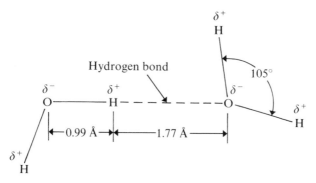

Figure 2–1. Schematic structure of the water molecule indicating the hydrogen bonding resulting from the electrostatic attraction between the net positive charge on a hydrogen ($\delta+$) in one molecule and the net negative charge on an oxygen ($\delta-$) in a neighboring water molecule.

is responsible for many of the characteristic features of water that we will consider next.

Hydrogen Bonding.   The strong intermolecular forces in water result from the structure of the H_2O molecule (Fig. 2–1). The internuclear distances between the oxygen and each of the two hydrogens are approximately 0.99 Å, and the H—O—H angle is about 105°. The oxygen atom is strongly electronegative and tends to draw electrons away from the hydrogen atoms. This leaves the oxygen with a partial negative charge ($\delta-$ in Fig. 2–1) while the two hydrogens become positive ($\delta+$). The positively charged hydrogens of water are electrostatically attracted to the negatively charged oxygens in neighboring water molecules. This leads to "hydrogen bonding" between water molecules, which has an energy of about 4.8 kilocalories per gram molecular weight (kcal/mole) of hydrogen bonds. Such bonding of water molecules to each other leads to increased order in aqueous solutions. In fact, liquid water becomes nearly crystalline in local regions, which is extremely important for determining the molecular interactions and orientations that occur in aqueous solutions.

Ice is a coordinated crystalline structure in which essentially all the water molecules are joined by hydrogen bonds. (See Fig. 2–1.) When heat is added so that the ice melts, some of these intermolecular hydrogen bonds are broken. The heat of fusion of ice at 0° is 80 cal/g or 1.44 kcal/mole. The total rupture of the intermolecular hydrogen bonds involving each of the hydrogens would require 9.6 kcal per mole of water. (The actual magnitude of the hydrogen bond energy assigned to ice depends somewhat on the particular operational definition used in its measurement.) The heat of fusion thus indicates that $(1.44/9.6)(100)$ or about 15% of the hydrogen bonds are broken when ice melts. Conversely, 85% of the hydrogen bonds remain intact for liquid water at $0°$. To heat water from $0°$ to $25°$ takes about 0.45 kcal/mole. If all of this energy were used to break hydrogen bonds, still over 80% of the bonds would remain intact at $25°$, such bonding leading to the semicrystalline order found in aqueous solutions. This extensive amount of intermolecular hydrogen bonds present in the liquid state contributes to the unique and biologically important properties of water that we will discuss throughout this chapter.

The energy necessary to separate molecules from a liquid and move them into an adjacent vapor phase without changing the temperature is given by the heat of vaporization. For water, the heat of vaporization at $100°$ is 540 cal/g or 9.75 kcal/mole. Per gram, this is the highest heat of vaporization of any liquid known and reflects the extensive hydrogen bonding in aqueous solutions. More pertinent to plant physiology is the heat of vaporization of water at temperatures encountered by plants. For instance, at $25°$ each mole of water evaporated takes 10.5 kcal, which means a substantial heat loss by the plant accompanies the evaporation of water in transpiration. Most of this vaporization energy is needed to break hydrogen bonds so that the water molecules can become separated in the gaseous phase. For instance, if 80% of the hydrogen bonds remained at $25°$, then $(0.80)(9.6)$ or 7.7 kcal/mole would be needed just to rupture them. The heat loss upon evaporation of water is one of the primary means of temperature regulation in land plants. It dissipates much of the heat absorbed as radiation as well as that from metabolic activity, other important heat losses occurring by convection, conduction, and the reradiation of energy (see p. 36).

Water is further characterized by having an extremely high surface tension, which is a force arising from interactions at the interface between two fluids. At $20°$, the surface tension at an air-water interface is 72.8 dynes/cm. Since a dyne is an erg/cm, surface tension also has the units of ergs/cm^2 or energy per unit area. It is actually the amount of energy required to expand the surface by unit area. To see why energy is required, consider water molecules which are brought from the interior of an aqueous solution to an air-water interface. A loss in the water-water attraction of intermolecular hydrogen bonds occurs with no compensating air-water attraction. Energy (72.8 ergs/cm^2) is thus needed to move water molecules from the interior of the

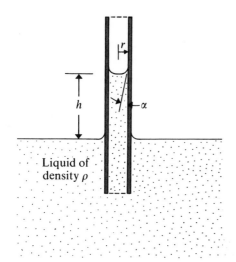

Figure 2–2. Quantities involved in the capillary rise of a liquid.

solution to the air-water interface and thereby to expand the surface area of the liquid.

The intermolecular water-water attraction occurring in the liquid state is generally referred to as cohesion while the attractive interaction between liquid water and a solid phase, such as the walls of a small tube or capillary, is called adhesion. When the water-wall attraction is appreciable, the walls are said to be wettable. At the opposite extreme where the intermolecular cohesive forces within the liquid are substantially greater than the adhesion between the liquid and the wall material, the upper level of the liquid in a capillary is lower than the surface of the free solution. Such a capillary depression occurs for liquid mercury in glass capillaries. For water in glass capillaries or in xylem vessels, the attraction between the water molecules and the walls is great (as will be discussed below), and therefore the liquid rises. Since capillary rise has such important implications for plant physiology, we will discuss its characteristics in a quantitative manner.

Capillary Rise. As an example appropriate to an evaluation of water rise in a plant, consider a wettable capillary of inner radius r dipping into some aqueous solution (Fig. 2–2). The strong adhesion of water molecules to the wettable wall leads to a rise of the fluid in the capillary. Since there is also a strong water-water cohesion in the bulk solution, water is concomitantly pulled up into the lumen of the capillary as water rises along the walls. Viewed another way, the air-water surface greatly resists being stretched, a property reflected in the high surface tension of water at gas-liquid interfaces. This resistance tends to minimize the area of the air-water interface, a condition achieved if water also moves up in the lumen as well as along the sides of the capillary. The tendency for water to rise along the walls of the capillary is thus transmitted to a volume of fluid. Let the height that the liquid rises in the capillary be h and the contact angle that the liquid makes with the capillary wall be α (Fig. 2–2). The extent of the rise depends on α, and so the properties of the contact angle will now be examined a little more closely.

The size of the contact angle depends on the magnitude of the liquid-solid adhesive force compared with that of the liquid-liquid cohesion. Specifically, when the adhesive force equals (or exceeds) the cohesive force in the liquid, α equals zero. This is the case for water in capillaries made of clear smooth glass or having walls with polar groups on the exposed surface. When the adhesive force equals half of the value of the cohesive force, then the contact angle is 90° and the level of the fluid in the capillary is the same as that in the bulk of the solution. This latter condition is closely approached for water-polyethylene adhesion, where α equals 94°. As the liquid-solid adhesive force becomes relatively less and less compared with the intermolecular cohesion in the liquid phase, the contact angle indicated in Figure 2–2 increases toward 180° and capillary depression occurs, e.g., for mercury interacting with most solid surfaces such as a glass one, α is near 150°.

We can calculate the extent of the capillary rise by considering the balance of two forces: (1) gravity acting downward and (2) surface tension which leads to a force in the upward direction in the case of wettable walls. The force pulling upward acts along the inside perimeter of the capillary, a distance of $2\pi r$, with a force per unit length of σ, the surface tension (sometimes represented by the symbol γ or T). Considering the contact angle α, the projected component acting vertically upward is $2\pi r\sigma \cos \alpha$. This upward force is balanced by the gravitational force acting on the liquid of density ρ and volume essentially $\pi r^2 h$. (Some fluid is also held in the meniscus as indicated in Fig. 2–2; for narrow capillaries, the fluid in the meniscus increases the effective height of the column by about $r/3$.) Thus gravity acts on a mass of fluid of approximately $\pi r^2 h\rho$ with a gravitational acceleration, g, and so the gravitational force is $\pi r^2 h\rho g$ acting downward. Since this equals $2\pi r\sigma \cos \alpha$ pulling in the opposite direction, the extent of rise, h, is given by

$$h = \frac{2\sigma \cos \alpha}{r\rho g} \tag{2–1}$$

Equation 2–1 indicates the readily demonstrated property that the extent of liquid rise in a capillary is inversely proportional to the radius of the tube. For water in glass capillaries as well as in many of the fine channels encountered in plants where the walls have a large number of exposed polar groups, the contact angle is near zero, in which case cos α appearing in Equation 2–1 can be set equal to 1. The density of water is 0.998 g/cm^3 at 20°, and g, the acceleration due to gravity, is about 980 cm/sec^2 (see Appendix II). Using a surface tension for water at 20° of 72.8 dynes/cm (Appendix II), we obtain the following relation between the height of the rise and the capillary radius:

$$h_{(cm)} = \frac{0.149}{r_{(cm)}} \qquad (2–2)$$

where (cm) in Equation 2–2 means that the two dimensions involved are each expressed in centimeters.

Although Equations 2–1 and 2–2 refer only to the height of capillary rise in a static sense, they still have important implications concerning the movement of water in plants. To be specific, consider a xylem vessel having a radius of 20 μm. From Equation 2–2, water will rise in it to a height of $(0.149)/(2 \times 10^{-3})$ or 75 cm. This capillary rise would be sufficient to account for the extent of the upward movement of water in small plants although it says nothing about whether the rate of such water movement is sufficient (to be considered below). For water to reach the top of a 30 meter $(3 \times 10^3$ cm) tree by capillary action, however, the vessel would have to be $(0.149)/(3 \times 10^3)$ or 0.50×10^{-4} cm (0.50 μm) in radius. This is much smaller than is observed for xylem vessels, indicating that capillary rise in channels of the size of the xylem cells cannot even account for the extent of the water rise in tall trees, let alone the rate of water movement. Furthermore, the vascular system is not open to the air at the upper end, and thus xylem vessels are not really analogous to the capillary indicated in Figure 2–2. Nevertheless, there is another aspect of water-wall adhesion that makes it capable of supporting water at great heights in a tree.

The numerous interstices in the cell wall of xylem vessels form a meshwork of many small tortuous capillaries, which not only can lead to an extensive capillary rise of water but could also cooperatively act to hold water in the lumen of the xylem vessel. A representative "radius" for these channels in the cell wall might be 50 Å. Based on Equation 2–2, a capillary of 50 Å radius could support a height of water of 2.98×10^5 cm or approximately 3.0 kilometers (km), far in excess of the needs of any plant. In other words, the cell wall could act as a very effective wick for water rise in its numerous small interstices although the actual rate of such movement up a tree is generally far from being sufficient to replace the water lost by transpiration. (We will return to this point later in the chapter.) As an alternative to leading to a capillary rise of 3.0 km, the pull due to the water-wall adhesion in the 50 Å capillaries could also be transmitted by cohesive forces to the bulk solution occurring in another tube. This could lead to the support of a certain mass of fluid in the other tube whose dimensions are not necessarily the same as the capillary having the air-water interface.

In the derivation of Equation 2–1, the upward force due to surface tension was balanced against the gravitational force acting on the fluid in that capillary. For the present case we will consider that the surface tension holds up the same *mass* of water against gravity, but in some other tube to which the small capillary is directly connected. For instance, the mass of the water in a cylinder of 50 Å radius and 3.0 km length equals that in a column 20 μm in radius and 0.019 cm long (the mass, $\pi r^2 L \rho$, is the same in each case, where r is the radius, L the length, and ρ the density). The upward directed force ($2\pi r \sigma \cos \alpha$) in each 50 Å capillary in the cell wall could thus support a short length (0.019 cm) of the water in a much larger xylem vessel. If the capillary forces in many 50 Å radius pores were all pulling upward on the water in a 20 μm radius xylem vessel, water could conceivably be held at a great height in the larger vessel. For instance, to hold water at 30 m (3×10^3 cm) in a 20 μm radius vessel, $(3 \times 10^3)/(0.019)$ or 1.6×10^5 such small capillaries of 50 Å radius cooperatively acting in parallel would be necessary (one 50 Å capillary could support a length of 0.019 cm in the 20 μm radius vessel). Thus water that is already present in the lumen of a xylem vessel can be sustained or supported at great heights by the appreciable water-wall attraction which develops in the interstices of the cell walls.

Implicit in the discussion of the pulling on water columns that occurs in capillary rise is that water can be put under tension. In other words, water must have a nonzero tensile strength, where the latter term refers to the maximum tension (force per unit area) that a substance can withstand before breaking. Theoretical calculations based on the strength of hydrogen bonds indicate that pure water should be able to withstand tensions in excess of 10,000 bars. [A bar is 10^6 dynes/cm^2 or 0.987 atmosphere (Appendix III).] Experimentally, water withstands negative pressures (tensions) of up to only approximately 300 bars at 20° without breaking. Any local imperfections in the semicrystalline structure of water, such as are caused by H$^+$ and OH$^-$ (which are always present even in pure water), markedly reduce the observed tensile strength from the theoretical value predicted based on hydrogen bond strengths. Moreover, the actual tensile strength is difficult to decide since the maximum tensions measured depend on the wall material, diameter of the vessel in which the determinations are made, and any solutes present in the water. Nevertheless, such a substantial, measurable tensile strength of 300 bars, which is provided by the intermolecular hydrogen bonds in the water, is nearly 10% of that for copper or aluminum and is sufficiently high to meet the demands encountered for water movement in plants. However, in contrast with the stable situation for metals, water under tension is actually in a metastable state. If minute gas bubbles combine in the water under tension, the column of liquid can be ruptured. Thus the introduction of another phase where the water adhesion is slight can disrupt the metastable state describing water under tension. For instance, the introduction of air can break the long columns of water under tension in the xylem vessels of a tall tree. It is because of the great cohesive forces between water molecules that an appreciable tension can exist in an uninterrupted water column in a wettable capillary or tube such as a xylem vessel. This property is important for the continuous movement of water from the root through the plant to the surrounding atmosphere during transpiration (to be discussed below).

Electrical Properties. Another important physical characteristic of water is its extremely high dielectric constant, which again is a consequence of its molecular structure. A high dielectric constant causes electrical forces between charged solutes dissolved in that solvent to be relatively low. To quantify the magnitude of electrical effects occurring in a fluid, consider two particles having charges Q_1 and Q_2 and separated from each other by a distance r. The electrical force exerted by one charge on the other is given by Coulomb's law,

$$\text{Electrical force} = \frac{Q_1 Q_2}{4 \pi \epsilon_o D r^2} \tag{2-3}$$

where ϵ_o is a proportionality constant known as the permittivity of a vacuum (electrical units are briefly discussed in Appendix II). In Equation 2–3, D is a dimensionless quantity called the dielectric constant. It equals unity in a vacuum and is 1.00058 in air at 0° and at a pressure of 760 mm Hg.

A substance composed of highly polar molecules such as water generally has a high dielectric constant. Specifically, D for water is 80.2 at 20° and 78.4 at 25°, which are extremely high values for dielectric constants of liquids. By contrast, the dielectric constant of the nonpolar liquid hexane is only 1.87, and such a low value is typical of many organic solvents. Based on these two vastly different dielectric constants and Equation 2–3, the attractive electrical force between ions such as Na$^+$ and Cl$^-$ is 80.2/1.87 or 43 times greater in hexane than in water. The much stronger attraction between Na$^+$ and Cl$^-$ in hexane reduces the amount of NaCl that will dissociate compared with the dissociation of this salt in aqueous solutions. Stated another way, the much weaker electrical forces in water compared with in organic solvents permit a larger number of ions to remain in solution. Water is thus a good solvent for charged particles.

The electrostatic interaction between ions and water partially cancels or screens out the local electrical fields produced by the ions; thus the strength of the electrical ion-ion interactions in aqueous solutions is less than they would be in a nonpolar solvent. Specifically, cations attract the negatively charged oxygens of the water molecule, and vice versa, while anions reciprocally attract the hydrogen atoms of water. The oriented water molecules around the charged particles produce local electrical fields opposing the fields of the ions. The resultant screening diminishes the electrical interaction between the ions and allows more of them to remain in solution. This is the molecular basis for the high dielectric constant of water.

The energy for the interaction between water and nonpolar molecules is usually less than the energy required to break water-water hydrogen bonds; therefore, nonpolar compounds are generally not very soluble in water. Certain substances such as detergents, phospholipids, and proteins have both a nonpolar and also a polar region in the same molecule. In aqueous solutions, these compounds can form aggregates, termed micelles, in which the nonpolar groups of the molecules are in the center while the charged or polar groups are external and interact with water, as was alluded to when we discussed membrane structure in Chapter 1. The lack of appreciable electrostatic interaction between water and the nonpolar regions of a molecule underlies the ability of biological membranes to limit the passage of water into and out of cells and organelles.

Chemical Potential of Water

Chemical potential is a thermodynamic way of quantitatively describing the free energy that is available for performing work. (See pp. 208–9.) A knowledge of the free energy or chemical potential of a substance under one condition compared with another is necessary in order to help predict the direction of spontaneous change or movement. For instance, a spontaneous change proceeds in the direction of decreasing free energy for the system. Such considerations of chemical potential have many applications in plant physiology, in particular: (1) in determining whether a certain substance is in equilibrium across some barrier and thus would not be expected to move spontaneously from one side to the other, or (2) in predicting the direction of net movement and the driving force acting on some species which has different chemical potentials on the two sides of a membrane or other surface separating the compartments under consideration.

The passive process of diffusion discussed in Chapter 1 describes molecules moving from some region to another one where their concentration is lower. In more formal terms, diffusion of a species proceeds in the direction of decreasing chemical potential for that substance. Thus, the concept of chemical potential was implicitly used in the development of Fick's equations in Chapter 1. Moreover, the importance of concentration gradients or differences in leading to movement of a substance has been established by the discussion of diffusion. In this section, we will present the effect of concentration on the chemical potential in a somewhat more sophisticated manner, using the concentration which is thermodynamically active.

The electrical potential affects the total energy of charged particles and hence must be considered when predicting the direction of their change or movement. (See Chapter 3.) It is well known that if an electrical potential gradient is placed across some solution containing a uniform concentration of ions throughout, then cations will spontaneously tend to move to regions of lower electrical potential, e.g., toward the negative electrode or cathode, while anions in such a conducting solution will drift toward the positively charged anode. Thus, to describe the total energy of charged species, an electrical term must also be included in the expression for the free energy or chemical potential of a particular substance.

The chemical potential also depends on the pressure, which usually means the hydrostatic pressure for situations of interest in plant physiology. When pressure is applied to an aqueous solution, the water and the solute molecules are pushed slightly closer together, which leads to an increase in energy for the system, meaning that water under pressure is at a higher energy or chemical potential than in the absence of applied pressure. Furthermore, the existence of pressure gradients can cause movements of fluids, such as the flow of crude oil in long-distance pipelines, blood in arteries, and sap in xylem vessels, emphasizing that pressure differences can affect the direction for spontaneous changes.

Under some conditions of interest in plant physiology, it may be convenient or necessary to include still other terms in the chemical potential besides those dealing with concentration, electrical potential, and pressure. Specifically, if a solution contains solid-liquid or liquid-gas interfaces, the chemical potential of water and of solutes depends on the interactions at these surfaces. For example, a considerable amount of water may be bound at the interface and thus be unavailable to partake in chemical reactions in the bulk of the solution, in which case it may be desirable to explicitly recognize such interactions by a special term in the chemical potential. Another possible contributor to the chemical potential under certain circumstances is gravity. Although the gravitational force can be neglected for ion and water movements across plant cell walls and membranes, it becomes important for the water movement in a tall tree.

Definition of Chemical Potential. The various types of driving forces introduced above can all contribute to the relative free energy or chemical potential, μ_j, of a particular species, j. The units of μ_j are energy per unit amount of the substance, generally expressed as joules/mole or cal/mole. Both for convenience and also since it has proved experimentally valid, the chemical potential of any species j, μ_j, is taken to be the following linear combination of the various component energies:

$$\mu_j = \mu_j{}^* + RT \ln a_j + \bar{V}_j P + z_j FE \tag{2-4}$$

The difference in chemical potential of species j at various locations can be used to predict the direction for spontaneous movement of that chemical substance (viz., toward lower μ_j, as will be discussed below), just as comparison of temperatures can be used to predict the direction for heat flow (to lower T). After defining and describing the various contributions to μ_j indicated in Equation 2–4, we will consider in greater detail the various terms for the important special case where species j is water.

The chemical potential, like other potential energies, is a relative quantity, meaning that it is expressed relative to some arbitrary energy level. Thus an additive constant or reference term, $\mu_j{}^*$, is included in Equation 2–4. For most applications of the chemical potential in plant physiology, one is interested in the difference in chemical potential between two particular locations, in which case only relative values of the chemical potential are important. In other words, the arbitrariness of $\mu_j{}^*$ is of little consequence because it is added to each of the chemical potentials under comparison. Thus $\mu_j{}^*$ cancels out when the chemical potential in one location is subtracted from that in another in order to obtain the chemical potential difference between the two locations.

For thermodynamic considerations, the influence of the amount of a particular species j on its chemical potential is handled by the activity of that species, a_j. The activity of species j is related to its concentration, c_j, by means of an activity coefficient, γ_j:

$$a_j = \gamma_j c_j \tag{2-5}$$

The activity coefficient can be viewed as a correction factor which quantifies deviations from ideal behavior since the thermodynamic activity of a species is generally less than its concentration. For ideal solutions, γ_j is 1 and the activity of species j equals its concentration. This condition can be approached for situations dealing with certain dilute aqueous solutions that are important in biology, especially for the neutral species involved. Activity coefficients of charged species can deviate markedly from unity. (See pp. 79–81.) In the expression for the chemical potential, Equation 2–4, the term involving the activity appears as $+ RT \ln a_j$. Therefore, the greater the activity of species j (loosely speaking, the higher its concentration), the larger will be the chemical potential or free energy of that compound. The appearance of the logarithmic form can be "justified" in a number of different ways, all of which are in the final analysis based on agreement with empirical observations. (See pp. 86–87 for the particular justification to be used in this text.) The factor RT multiplying $\ln a_j$ is necessary to convert the activity term to units of energy per mole.

The term $\bar{V}_j P$ in Equation 2–4 represents the effect of pressure on chemical potential. Since essentially all measurements in plant physiology are made at ambient atmospheric pressure, it is convenient to define P as the pressure in excess of this, and such a convention will be adopted here. $\bar{V}_j$ is the differential increase in volume of a system per mole increase of species j, other species, as well as pressure, temperature, and electrical potential remaining constant:

$$\bar{V}_j = \left(\frac{\partial V}{\partial n_j}\right)_{n_i, P, T, E} \tag{2-6}$$

$\bar{V}_j$ is called the partial molal volume of species j. (μ_j is actually the partial molal free energy, as will be discussed in Chapter 6.) We will estimate its value for water when the chemical potential of water is specifically considered below.

The possible electrical effects on the free energy of a substance are handled by the term $z_j FE$ in Equation 2–4, where z_j is the charge carried by species j, F is a constant known as the Faraday (see p. 77), and E is the electrical potential. Because water is uncharged ($z_w = 0$), the electrical term does not contribute to its chemical potential. However, the electrical potential is of central importance when discussing ions and also the origin of membrane potentials, both of which will be examined in detail in Chapter 3, where we will explicitly consider the $z_j FE$ term. The full expression for the chemical potential, μ_j, given by Equation 2–4 and including $z_j FE$, is often referred to as the electrochemical potential when discussing the properties of charged particles.

The constant term μ_j^*, appearing in Equation 2–4, is the chemical potential of a specific reference state. From the preceding definitions of the various pertinent quantities, this reference state is attained when the activity is 1, the hydrostatic pressure equals atmospheric pressure, the species is uncharged or the electrical potential is zero, and the temperature equals that for the system under consideration. It has proved convenient to define unit activity in slightly different ways for the solute and the solvent. When γ_j equals 1, a 1 molal solution of solute j has an activity of unity. For water, the standard reference state is taken to be pure water at atmospheric pressure and at the temperature of the system under consideration. Hence, water has an activity of unity when its concentration is 55.6 molal. (The thermodynamic terms and concepts involved in the chemical potential will be the basis for most of the mathematical development in Chapters 2, 3, and 6.)

Water Activity and Osmotic Pressure.   The presence of solutes in an aqueous solution tends to decrease the activity of water, a_w. As a first approximation, the decrease in a_w as more and more solutes are added can be viewed as simply a dilution effect. In other words, the concentration or the mole fraction (to be defined below) of water becomes less when the water molecules are displaced by those of the solute. As its concentration decreases, we would expect a lowering of the chemical potential of water, as does indeed occur. The presence of solutes also leads to an osmotic pressure, π, in the solution. An increase in the concentration of solutes raises the osmotic pressure, indicating that π and a_w change in opposite directions. In fact, the osmotic pressure and water activity are related, the formal definition of π being

$$\pi = -\frac{RT}{\bar{V}_w} \ln a_w \tag{2–7}$$

where the subscript w refers to water. As solutes are added, a_w decreases from its value of unity for pure water, $\ln a_w$ is therefore negative, and thus π is positive, which is consistent with the arguments presented above. Equation 2–7 indicates that $RT \ln a_w$, a term appearing in the chemical potential of water (cf. Eq. 2–4), is equal to $-\bar{V}_w\pi$.

For many purposes in plant physiology, it is convenient to relate the concentration of solutes directly to the osmotic pressure instead of expressing π in terms of the water activity, a_w, as is done in Equation 2–7. In general, the greater the concentration of solutes, the more negative $\ln a_w$ becomes and the larger the osmotic pressure. Thus some way of expressing a_w in terms of the properties of the solutes would seem to be an appropriate approach for expressing π as a function of the various solute concentrations. The ensuing derivation will not only show how a_w can be so expressed but will also serve to indicate the many approximations necessary in order to achieve a rather simple expression for π.

The activity of pure water is unity while in general a_w equals $\gamma_w N_w$, γ_w being the activity coefficient of water and N_w its mole fraction. The mole fraction of a species is simply the fraction of the total moles in some system comprised by that species. Thus N_w is given as follows:

$$N_w = \frac{n_w}{n_w + \sum_j n_j} = 1 - \frac{\sum_j n_j}{n_w + \sum_j n_j} \qquad (2\text{--}8)$$

where n_w is the number of moles of water, n_j is the number of moles of solute j, and the summation, $\sum_j$, is over all solutes present in the system being considered. Equation 2–8 also expresses the familiar relation that N_w equals 1 minus the mole fraction of solutes. For an ideal solution, γ_w equals 1. This condition of unit activity coefficient is approached for dilute solutions in which case n_w is much greater than $\sum_j n_j$. ($n_w >> \sum_j n_j$ can be taken as one way of defining a dilute solution, where the symbol $>>$ means "is much greater than.") Using Equation 2–8 and assuming a dilute solution, we obtain the following relations for $\ln a_w$:

$$\ln a_w \cong \ln N_w = \ln \left(1 - \frac{\sum_j n_j}{n_w + \sum_j n_j}\right) \cong - \frac{\sum_j n_j}{n_w + \sum_j n_j} \cong - \frac{\sum_j n_j}{n_w} \qquad (2\text{--}9)$$

The penultimate step in Equation 2–9 is based on the series expansion of a logarithm [$\ln (1 - x) = -x - x^2/2 - x^3/3 - \ldots$], and the last two steps both employ the approximation $(n_w >> \sum_j n_j)$ relevant to a dilute solution. Equation 2–9 is thus restricted to dilute ideal solutions. Nevertheless, it is a useful expression which clearly indicates that in the absence of solutes $(\sum_j n_j = 0)$, ln a_w is zero and a_w is unity while the presence of solutes decreases the activity of water from the value of 1 for pure water.

To obtain a rather familiar form for expressing the osmotic pressure, we can incorporate the approximation for ln a_w given by Equation 2–9 into the definition of osmotic pressure, Equation 2–7, which yields

$$\pi_s = -\frac{RT}{\bar{V}_w}\left(-\frac{\sum_j n_j}{n_w}\right) = RT \sum_j \frac{n_j}{\bar{V}_w n_w} = RT \sum_j c_j \qquad (2\text{--}10)$$

where $\bar{V}_w n_w$ is the total amount of water in the system, $n_j/\bar{V}_w n_w$ is the concentration of species j (c_j), and the summations in Equation 2–10 are over all solutes. Osmotic pressure is often defined by Equation 2–10, but this is justified only in the limit of dilute ideal solutions. In order to stress that many approximations are involved in equating the osmotic pressure to $RT \sum_j c_j$, π_s instead of π has been used in Equation 2–10, and this convention will be followed throughout the text. The effect of solute concentration on osmotic pressure as described by Equation 2–10 was first clearly shown by the botanist W. Pfeffer in 1877. The measurement of osmotic pressures and the recognition of their effects have been crucial for an understanding of the water relations of plants.

Relatively dilute solutions are capable of having large osmotic pressures. The cellular fluid expressed from plants like pea or spinach often contains about 0.3 mole of osmotically active particles per liter of water. This fluid is referred to as being 0.3 osmolal by analogy with molality, which refers to the total concentration, e.g., 0.1 molal $CaCl_2$ is about 0.3 osmolal since most of the $CaCl_2$ is dissociated. At 20°, RT has the value of 24.37 liter-bars/mole. (See Appendix III for various values of RT.) Using Equation 2–10, the osmotic pressure is then (24.37) (0.3) or 7.3 bars (essentially 7 atmospheres). Thus an 0.3 osmolal solution has a substantial osmotic pressure.

Hydrostatic Pressure.   Because of the rigid cell walls, fairly large hydrostatic pressures can exist in plant cells while in animal cells such pressures generally are relatively small. In addition to being involved in the support of the plant, such high intracellular hydrostatic pressures are important for the movement of water and solutes in the xylem and probably also in the phloem. The term expressing the effect of pressure on the chemical potential of water (cf. Eq. 2–4) is $\bar{V}_wP$, where $\bar{V}_w$ is the partial molal volume of water and P is the hydrostatic pressure in the aqueous solution in excess of the ambient atmospheric pressure. The approximate value of $\bar{V}_w$ can be estimated using the following argument. When 1 mole (18.0 g) of water is added to water, the volume increases by 18.0 cm³ since the density of water at 20° is 0.998 g/cm³. In other words, $\bar{V}_w$ is 18.0 cm³/mole in the case of pure water. Although $\bar{V}_w$, defined according to the partial derivative given in Equation 2–6, can be influenced by the various solutes actually present, it generally is close to 18.0 cm³/mole for a dilute solution, a value that will be assumed for the calculations in this book.

Various units are used for expressing pressures, atmospheres and bars being commonly employed in plant physiology. One atmosphere of hydrostatic pressure can support a column of mercury that is 76.0 cm high or a column of water 10.3 m in height. Most current research concerning the water relations of plants uses pressures in bars, which is a unit in the centimeter-gram-second system, viz., a bar is 10^6 dynes/cm², which equals 0.987 atmosphere. (An extensive list of conversion factors for bars, atmospheres, and other pressure units is given in Appendix III, which also includes values for related quantities such as RT expressed in units employing both atmospheres and bars.) Pressure is force per unit area which is dimensionally the same as energy per unit volume, e.g., one bar is 0.100 joule/cm³ or 0.0239 cal/cm³ (Appendix III). Since $\bar{V}_w$ has the units of cm³/mole, the quantity $\bar{V}_wP$ appearing in Equation 2–4 and hence μ_j itself can be expressed in joules/mole or cal/mole.

Matric Potential. For certain applications in plant physiology, another term is frequently included in the chemical potential of water, viz., $\bar{V}_w\tau$, where τ is called the matric potential or matric pressure. The use of this term is sometimes convenient for dealing explicitly with interactions occurring at interfaces although in most circumstances these interfacial forces can also be adequately represented by their contributions to π or P. To make this statement a little more meaningful, we will briefly consider the influence of the liquid-solid interfaces at the surface of colloids on the chemical potential of water.

When water molecules are associated with interfaces such as are provided by colloidal particles suspended in an aqueous solution, they have less of a tendency either to react chemically in the bulk solution or to escape into a surrounding vapor phase. This occurs because water has a finite binding constant at the postulated solid-liquid interfaces, resulting in water molecules continually going on and coming off the interfacial surface. This ties up some of the water molecules and consequently lowers the thermodynamic activity of the water, a_w, especially near the surfaces of the colloids. As has been discussed above, the presence of solutes also lowers the water activity, an effect that can be expressed by Equation 2–10. As a useful first approximation, we can consider that these two different effects which lower the water activity are additive:

$$\pi = \pi_s + \tau \qquad (2\text{–}11)$$

where π_s is the osmotic pressure of solutes defined by Equation 2–10 and τ is the matric pressure resulting from the water-solid interactions at the surfaces of the colloids. The osmotic pressure, π, given in Equation 2–11 is determined by the actual activity of water regardless of the reason for its being different from unity, i.e., π still equals $-(RT/\bar{V}_w) \ln a_w$, as it must by Equation 2–7. Equation 2–11 should not be viewed as a relation defining τ but rather as one example where it may be useful to represent interfacial forces by a separate term.

Although π and a_w may be the same through some system, π_s and τ in Equation 2–11 could both vary. For instance, in the bulk of the solution the water activity may be lowered predominantly by the presence of the solutes while at or near the surface of colloids, the main factor decreasing a_w from 1 could be the interfacial attraction and binding of water.

Other areas of plant physiology where matric potentials have been invoked are descriptions of the chemical potential of water in the soil or in cell walls. The latter will be considered in detail at the end of this chapter, where we will show that interfacial interactions between water and the many surfaces lining the interstices of the cell wall lead to a tension in the cell wall water. In this case, a tension is a negative hydrostatic pressure, i.e., P is less than zero. Although not really necessary, P is sometimes used to refer only to positive pressures, in which case the tension in the cell wall could be defined as a positive matric potential arising out of the attractive interactions at the many interfaces which are present.

Water Potential.   From the definition of chemical potential given by Equation 2–4 and the formal expression for osmotic pressure (Eq. 2–7), we can write the chemical potential of water, μ_w, as

$$\mu_w = \mu_w{}^* - \bar{V}_w \pi + \bar{V}_w P \qquad (2\text{–}12)$$

where the electrical term (z_jFE) is not included since $z_w = 0$. The quantity $\mu_w - \mu_w^*$ has proved to be of considerable importance in studies of the water relations of plants. For a system at a constant pressure, it represents the particular work capacity of water at some point in the system compared with the work capacity of pure water at atmospheric pressure and at the same temperature as the system under consideration. More to the point, a difference in the value of $\mu_w - \mu_w^*$ at one location compared with another indicates that water is not in equilibrium between the two locations, and thus there will be a tendency for water to flow toward the region where $\mu_w - \mu_w^*$ is lower. A quantity proportional to $\mu_w - \mu_w^*$ and increasingly used in the studies of plant water relations is the so-called water potential, Ψ. This is conveniently defined as

$$\Psi = \frac{\mu_w - \mu_w^*}{\bar{V}_w} = P - \pi \qquad (2\text{–}13)$$

which follows directly from Equation 2–12. Equation 2–13 indicates that an increase in hydrostatic pressure raises the water potential while an increase in osmotic pressure lowers it. In the next two sections, the values of Ψ on both sides of cellular and subcellular membranes will be considered in detail.

Some of the older terminology describing plant water relations can be identified from Equation 2–13. For instance, $-\Psi$ is the quantity called "diffusion pressure deficit" or "suction pressure." Although these expressions are quite colorful, the use of the terms water potential (Ψ) and chemical potential of water (μ_w) are more universally adopted in biology, as well as in other disciplines, and will be used in this text. The hydrostatic pressure, P, is often referred to as the turgor pressure when discussing the protoplast or the wall pressure when we consider the pushing of the cell wall back against the protoplast.

Work must be performed to raise an object in the gravitational field of the earth. Thus vertical position also affects the energy and, consequently, the chemical potential of a substance. When water moves an appreciable distance vertically in the gravitational field, the term $\rho_w gh$ should be added to the water potential given by Equation 2–13, where ρ_w is the density of water, g is the acceleration due to gravity (close to 980 cm/sec², but see Appendix II for details), and h is the vertical distance in the gravitational field. In plant physiology, the magnitude of $\rho_w g$ is conveniently expressed as 0.098 bar/m. Thus when water moves 10 m vertically upward in a tree, the gravitational contribution to the water potential is increased by about 1 bar.

Central Vacuole and Chloroplasts

The water relations of both the large central vacuole and also the chloroplasts will be considered next, using the water potential defined above. We will focus attention on the situation when there is no net flow of water across the limiting membranes surrounding these subcellular compartments and for the special case of nonpenetrating solutes. (The more general case of penetrating solutes will be discussed in Chapter 3 after a consideration of the properties of solutes and the introduction of concepts from irreversible thermodynamics.) The central vacuole occupies up to 90% of the volume of a mature plant cell, which means that under such circumstances most of the cellular water is in the vacuole. The vacuolar volume is generally from 10^4 to 10^5 μm^3 for the mesophyll cells in a leaf but can be much larger in certain algal cells. Because its size is similar to that of the cell, the vacuole cannot be easily removed from the plant cell without rupturing its surrounding membrane, the tonoplast. In other words, procedures which remove the cell wall and open up the plasmalemma usually also break the tonoplast, especially for small cells. Chloroplasts are much smaller than the central vacuole, often having volumes near 30 μm^3 *in vivo* although the sizes vary considerably with the plant species. When chloroplasts are carefully isolated, suitable precautions will ensure that their limiting membranes remain intact. Such intact chloroplasts can be placed in solutions having various osmotic pressures. The resulting movement of water into or out of the isolated plastids can be precisely measured, which provides information on the chloroplast contents (as will be discussed below and in Chapter 3).

Water Relations of the Central Vacuole. A prerequisite for predicting whether and in what direction water will move is knowledge of the value of its chemical potential in the various compartments under consideration. At thermodynamic equilibrium, the water potential is the same in the various communicating phases, such as those separated by membranes. For instance, when water is in equilibrium across the tonoplast, the value of the water potential is the same in the vacuole as it is in the cytoplasm. No force then drives water across this membrane, and no net flow of water occurs into or out of the vacuole. The tonoplast most likely cannot withstand an appreciable difference in hydrostatic pressure across it, and thus P may well have the same value in the cytoplasm and the vacuole. With this simplifying assumption and for the equilibrium situation where Ψ is the same in the two phases, Equation 2–13 gives

$$\pi^{\text{cytoplasm}} = \pi^{\text{vacuole}} \qquad (2\text{–}14)$$

The vacuole appears to be a relatively homogeneous aqueous phase while the cytoplasm is a more complex phase containing many colloids and membrane-bounded organelles. Since the vacuole contains few colloidal or other interfaces, any matric potential in it is probably negligible compared with the osmotic pressure resulting from the vacuolar solutes. Expressing osmotic pressure by Equation 2–11 ($\pi = \pi_s + \tau$), and assuming τ^{vacuole} is negligible, we can replace π^{vacuole} in Equation 2–14 by π_s^{vacuole}, i.e., the decrease in vacuolar water activity is due essentially only to the presence of solutes. On the other hand, the water activity in the cytoplasm is presumably lowered considerably both by solutes and also by the presence of interfaces. In terms of Equation 2–11, this means that both $\pi_s^{\text{cytoplasm}}$ and $\tau^{\text{cytoplasm}}$ contribute to $\pi^{\text{cytoplasm}}$. Equation 2–14 hence indicates that $\pi_s^{\text{cytoplasm}} + \tau^{\text{cytoplasm}}$ equals π_s^{vacuole}. Since $\tau^{\text{cytoplasm}}$ is a positive quantity, we conclude that at equilibrium, the osmotic pressure in the vacuole due to solutes, π_s^{vacuole}, must be larger than $\pi_s^{\text{cytoplasm}}$. In other words, Equation 2–14 leads to the prediction that the vacuole has a higher concentration of osmotically active solutes than does the cytoplasm.

It is well known that the central vacuole greatly expands as the cell develops. For water to enter the vacuole during this expansion, Ψ^{vacuole} must be less than $\Psi^{\text{cytoplasm}}$, which by extension suggests that π^{vacuole} is larger than $\pi^{\text{cytoplasm}}$ when the vacuole is expanding. If $\tau^{\text{cytoplasm}}$ remains the same throughout development, a higher osmotic pressure in the vacuole means that $\pi_s^{\text{vacuole}} - \pi_s^{\text{cytoplasm}}$ in a young growing cell must be even larger than the values satisfying Equation 2–14, which were discussed above. Thus, at least in the developing plant cell, active transport of solutes from the cytoplasm into the vacuole would be expected in order to provide the higher solute osmotic pressure in the vacuole.

Various speculations exist concerning the role of the large central vacuole in plant cells. For instance, the vacuole might act as a storage site for metabolites, ions, or toxic products. As a consequence of the large central vacuole, the cytoplasm occupies a thin layer around the periphery of the cell (Fig. 1–1). This causes the cytoplasm to have a relatively large surface area (across which diffusion can occur) without at the same time requiring a large cytoplasmic volume. Because they can occupy most of the volume of plant cells, vacuoles are important for maintaining the plant structurally. Specifically, they provide large, relatively simple compartments in which hydrostatic pressures lead to the cellular turgidity necessary for support of the plant. The actual function of the central vacuole most likely entails a combination of the various possibilities indicated.

Boyle-Van't Hoff Relation.   The volume of a chloroplast or other membrane-bounded body changes in response to variations in the osmotic pressure of the external solution. This is a consequence of the properties of membranes, which generally allow water to move readily across them while certain solutes such as sucrose cannot. Such differential permeability leads to the "osmometric behavior" characteristic of many cells and organelles. The conventional expression quantifying this volume response to changes in the osmotic pressure is the Boyle-Van't Hoff relation:

$$\pi^o(V - b) = RT \sum_j \varphi_j n_j = RT\, n \qquad (2\text{–}15)$$

where π^o is the osmotic pressure of the external solution; V is the volume of the cell or organelle; b is the so-called nonosmotic volume or osmotically inactive volume and is frequently considered to be the volume of a solid phase within volume V which is not penetrated by water; n_j is the number of moles of species j within $V - b$; the osmotic coefficient, φ_j, is generally construed as a correction factor; and $n = \sum_j \varphi_j n_j$ is the apparent number of osmotically active moles in $V - b$. In this chapter, the Boyle-Van't Hoff relation will be derived from classical thermodynamics, using the concept of chemical potential, while in Chapter 3 an extension based on irreversible thermodynamics will be made. Although the derived Boyle-Van't Hoff expression will only be used to interpret the osmotic responses of chloroplasts, the equations that will be developed are actually quite general and can be applied equally well to data obtained with mitochondria or other membrane-bounded entities.

The Boyle-Van't Hoff relation applies to the situation where equality of the water potential has been achieved across the membrane surrounding a cell or organelle. When Ψ^i equals Ψ^o (the superscript i refers to the inside of the cell or organelle while the superscript o designates the outside), net water movement across the membrane ceases. This equilibrium condition means that the volume of the chloroplast or other entity has a specific value. When the chloroplast volume is measured, the external solution is generally at atmospheric pressure ($P^o = 0$); from Equation 2–13 ($\Psi = P - \pi$), the water potential in the external solution then is

$$\Psi^o = -\pi^o \qquad (2\text{–}16)$$

As is the case for Ψ^o (Eq. 2–16), the water potential inside the chloroplasts or other membrane-surrounded bodies also depends on the osmotic pressure. In addition, the internal hydrostatic pressure, P^i, may be different from atmospheric pressure and should be included in the expression for Ψ^i. Macromolecules and solid-liquid interfaces inside the chloroplasts can lead to a matric potential, τ^i. To emphasize this point, the internal osmotic pressure, π^i, will be considered as the sum of the solute and interface contributions, in the manner expressed by Equation 2–11. Using Equation 2–13, Ψ^i therefore is

$$\Psi^i = P^i - \pi^i = P^i - \pi_s{}^i - \tau^i \qquad (2\text{–}17)$$

For an ideal solution inside the chloroplasts, $\pi_s{}^i$ equals $RT \sum_j (n_j{}^i)/(\bar{V}_w n_w{}^i)$ by Equation 2–10. Solutions of real solutes necessitate the introduction of an activity coefficient for solute j, γ_j, which approaches 1 as the solution becomes more dilute. To handle deviations from ideal behavior for the solutes, $n_j{}^i$ can thus be replaced by $\gamma_j{}^i n_j{}^i$. Making these changes and equating the water potential outside the chloroplast (Eq. 2–16) to that inside (Eq. 2–17), the condition for water equilibrium across the limiting membranes of the chloroplast or other membrane-bounded entity is

$$\pi^o = RT \frac{\sum\limits_j \gamma_j{}^i n_j{}^i}{\bar{V}_w n_w{}^i} + \tau^i - P^i \qquad (2\text{–}18)$$

In order to appreciate the refinements that this thermodynamic approach introduces into the customary expression describing the osmotic responses of cells and organelles, Equation 2–18 should be compared with the conventional Boyle-Van't Hoff relation (Eq. 2–15). The amount of water inside the chloroplast or other membrane-bounded body is $\bar{V}_w n_w{}^i$ since $n_w{}^i$ is the number of moles of internal water and $\bar{V}_w$ is the volume of one mole of water. This factor in Equation 2–18 can be identified with $V - b$ in Equation 2–15. Instead of being designated the nonosmotic volume, b is more appropriately called the nonwater volume, for it includes the volume of the internal solutes. The osmotic coefficient, φ_j in Equation 2–15, is generally less than 1 as is the activity coefficient of an internal solute, $\gamma_j{}^i$, in Equation 2–18. But $\gamma_j{}^i$ cannot simply be equated to φ_j since other factors are also involved (to be considered in Chapter 3). Finally, the possible hydrostatic and matric contributions included in Equation 2–18 are neglected in the usual Boyle-Van't Hoff relation. In short, although certain approximations and assumptions have crept into Equation 2–18 (e.g., assuming solutes do not cross the limiting membranes and using dilute solution considerations), it is still a far more satisfactory expression for describing osmotic responses than is the conventional Boyle-Van't Hoff relation.

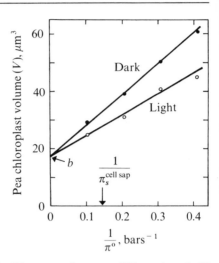

Figure 2–3. Osmotic volume responses for pea chloroplasts isolated from plants in the light or dark. [Data are taken from P. S. Nobel, *Biochimica et Biophysica Acta* **172**, 134–43 (1969); by permission.]

Osmotic Responses of Chloroplasts. To illustrate the use of Equation 2–18 for interpreting osmotic data, we will consider osmotic responses of pea chloroplasts suspended in external solutions of various osmotic pressures. Since it is customary to plot the volume V versus the reciprocal of the external osmotic pressure, $1/\pi^o$, certain algebraic manipulations are needed to put Equation 2–18 into a more convenient form for discussing such osmometric studies. By transferring $\tau^i - P^i$ to the left-hand side of Equation 2–18 and then multiplying both sides by $(\bar{V}_w n_w^i)/(\pi^o - \tau^i + P^i)$, $\bar{V}_w n_w^i$ can be shown to be equal to $(RT \sum_j \gamma_j^i n_j^i)/(\pi^o - \tau^i + P^i)$. The measured chloroplast volume, V, can be represented by $\bar{V}_w n_w^i + b$, i.e., as the sum of the aqueous and the nonaqueous contributions. Figure 2–3 indicates that the volume of pea chloroplasts varies linearly with $1/\pi^o$ over a considerable range of external osmotic pressures, and consequently $\tau^i - P^i$ occurring in Equation 2–18 and in the above expression must be negligibly small for pea chloroplasts compared with the various values of π^o employed. In other words, $V - b$ (or $\bar{V}_w n_w^i$) equals $(RT \sum_j \gamma_j^i n_j^i)/\pi^o$ for pea chloroplasts. We will return to such considerations in Chapter 3, where we will further refine the Boyle-Van't Hoff relation to include the case where solutes can cross the limiting membranes.

Cell sap expressed from pea leaves was found to have an osmotic pressure of 7.02 bars. At this external osmotic pressure (indicated by an arrow in Fig. 2–3), pea chloroplasts have a volume of 35 μm^3 when isolated from plants which are in the dark but only 29 μm^3 when isolated from illuminated plants. Since these are the volumes at the same osmotic pressure that occurs in the cell, they are presumably reliable estimates of pea chloroplast volumes *in vivo.* Another point raised by the data presented in Figure 2–3 refers to the effect of light on the chloroplast volume *in vivo.* Although the basis for the size changes is not fully understood, chloroplasts in many plants do have a larger volume in the dark than in the light, as indicated in Figure 2–3 for the specific case of pea chloroplasts. The decrease in volume upon illumination of the plants is observed by phase contrast and electron microscopy as a flattening or decrease in thickness of the chloroplasts. This flattening, which amounts to about 20% of the thickness, is in the vertical direction for the chloroplast depicted in Figure 1–7.

The intercept on the ordinate in Figure 2–3 is the chloroplast volume that would be obtained at an infinite external osmotic pressure since $1/\pi^{\circ}$ equaling zero is the same as a π° of infinity. For such an infinite π°, all the internal water would be removed ($n_w^i = 0$), and the volume, which is actually obtained by extrapolation, is that of the nonaqueous components of the chloroplasts. (Some uncertainty exists for water that is tightly bound to proteins and other substances, at least some of this water presumably not being removed even at the hypothetical infinite osmotic pressures considered here.) Thus, the intercept on the ordinate for a V versus $1/\pi^{\circ}$ plot corresponds to b in the conventional Boyle-Van't Hoff relation (Eq. 2–15). This intercept, which is also indicated by an arrow in Figure 2–3, corresponds to 17 μm^3 for chloroplasts both in the light and in the dark. Using the chloroplast volumes obtained for a π° of 7.02 bars and 17 μm^3 for the nonwater volume b, we find that the water content of chloroplasts is $[(35 - 17)/35](100)$ or 51% by volume in the dark and $[(29 - 17)/29](100)$ or 41% in the light. These relatively low water contents in the organelles are consistent with the extensive internal lamellar system and the prevalence of CO_2 fixation enzymes in chloroplasts, which were mentioned in Chapter 1. Thus osmometric responses of certain cells and organelles can be used to provide information on their fractional water content.

Water Potential and Plant Cells

In this section, we will shift our emphasis from a consideration of the water relations of subcellular bodies to those of whole cells, and we will extend the development to include the case of water fluxes. Whether and how much water enters or leaves a plant cell depends on the water potential outside compared with that inside. The external water potential Ψ° can often be varied experimentally, and the direction as well as the magnitude of the resulting water movement then gives information about Ψ^i. Moreover, under certain conditions to be discussed next, the equilibrium value of Ψ^o can be used to estimate the internal osmotic pressure, π^i.

Incipient Plasmolysis.   For usual physiological conditions, a positive hydrostatic pressure exists inside a plant cell, i.e., it is under turgor. By suitably adjusting an external solution that bathes such a turgid cell, it is possible to reduce P^i to zero and thereby obtain an estimate of π^i, as the following argument indicates. Consider placing the cell in a solution at atmospheric pressure ($P^o = 0$) which contains no solutes ($\pi^o = 0$). Thus Ψ^o is zero [$\Psi = P - \pi$ (Eq. 2–13)] while Ψ^i is $P^i - \pi^i$. If the cell can be assumed to be in equilibrium with this external solution ($\Psi^o = \Psi^i$), P^i must then equal π^i. Now suppose that π^o is gradually raised from its initial zero value. For example, the osmotic pressure outside the cell can be increased by adding solute to the external solution. If the cell remains in equilibrium, then π^o equals $\pi^i - P^i$ ($P^o = 0$ since the external solution is at atmospheric pressure). As π^o is increased, P^i will tend to decrease while π^i usually does not change very much. More precisely, because the cell wall is quite rigid, a plant cell will not change its volume appreciably in response to changes in P^i. [Since the cell wall has elastic properties (cf. Chapter 1), some water flows out as P^i decreases and the cell shrinks, a point that will be returned to shortly.] Therefore, if the cell volume can be assumed not to change in response to changes in π^o and no internal solutes leak out, π^i will remain constant. As the external osmotic pressure is raised, π^o will eventually become equal to π^i. In such a plant cell at equilibrium, P^i is zero, which means that no internal hydrostatic pressure is exerted against the cell wall when π^o equals π^i. The cell would thus lose its turgidity. If π^o were increased even further, water would appreciably flow out of the cell and plasmolysis would occur as the plasmalemma pulls away from the rigid cell wall. Ignoring for the moment any overall volume changes of the cell, we find that the condition for water to just begin to move out of the cell—a situation referred to as the point of incipient plasmolysis—is

$$\pi^o{}_{\text{plasmolysis}} = \pi^i \qquad\qquad (2\text{–}19)$$

Equation 2–19 suggests that only a relatively simple measurement, $\pi^o{}_{\text{plasmolysis}}$, is needed in order to estimate the osmotic pressure, π^i, occurring inside an individual plant cell.

The existence of an internal hydrostatic pressure within a plant cell leads to stresses in the cell wall and a resulting elastic deformation or strain, as the considerations in Chapter 1 indicated. The decrease of P^i to 0, which occurs in taking a turgid plant cell to the point of incipient plasmolysis, must therefore be accompanied by a contraction of the cell as the wall stresses are removed. This decrease in volume means that some water will actually flow out of the cell before the point of incipient plasmolysis is reached. If no internal solute leaves as the cell shrinks, then the osmotic pressure inside will increase (the same amount of solute in a smaller volume). As a useful first approximation, the increase in osmotic pressure can be assumed to follow reciprocally the change in volume, i.e., the product of π^i and the cellular volume can be taken to be approximately constant. With this assumption, the osmotic pressures in cells—described by Equation 2–19 and determined by using the technique of measuring the point of incipient plasmolysis—can be corrected to the original value by using the ratio of the initial volume to the final volume of the cell. For some plant cells, the change in volume is only a few percentage points, in which case fairly accurate estimates of π^i can be obtained from plasmolytic studies alone.

Measurements of $\pi^\circ_{plasmolysis}$ often give values near 7 bars for cells in storage tissues like onion bulbs or carrot roots and in leaves like those of pea and spinach. These values of the external osmotic pressure provide information on various contributors to the water potential inside the cell, as Equation 2–19 indicates. For the case where water is in equilibrium within the plant cell at the point of incipient plasmolysis, the term π^i in Equation 2–19 is the osmotic pressure both in the cytoplasm and in the vacuole. Under certain circumstances it is convenient to replace π^i by $\pi_s^i + \tau^i$ (Eq. 2–11), where π_s^i is the osmotic pressure contributed by the internal solutes and τ^i is the matric potential. For instance, this relation was invoked when the implications of Equation 2–14 ($\pi^{cytoplasm} = \pi^{vacuole}$) were discussed, and the various arguments presented at that time carry over to the present case. Specifically, since the possible matric potential in the vacuole is probably negligible, $\pi^\circ_{plasmolysis}$ should be a rather good estimate of $\pi_s^{vacuole}$. Moreover, $\tau^{cytoplasm}$ is most probably significant, as the water activity in the cytoplasm can be lowered by the many interfaces present; thus $\pi^\circ_{plasmolysis}$ is an upper limit for $\pi_s^{cytoplasm}$. We can see, therefore, that determination of the external osmotic pressure at the point of incipient plasmolysis provides information on the osmotic pressure existing in different compartments within the plant cell.

Plant-Air Interface.   A loss of water from plants, indeed sometimes also its uptake, occurs at cell-air interfaces. The chemical potential of water in the cells compared with that in the adjacent air determines the direction for water movement at such plant-air interfaces. It can readily be shown that water molecules in an aqueous solution continually escape into a surrounding gas phase. At the same time, water molecules also condense back into the liquid. The rates of escape and condensation depend *inter alia* on the chemical activities of water in the gas and the liquid phases, the two flows becoming equal at equilibrium. The gas phase adjacent to the given solution then contains as much water as it can hold at that temperature and still remain in equilibrium with the liquid; thus it is said to be saturated with water vapor for the particular solution under consideration. The partial pressure exerted by the water vapor under this condition is known as the saturation vapor pressure.

The saturation vapor pressure depends on the temperature and the solution but is independent of the relative or absolute amounts of liquid and vapor. When air surrounding pure water is saturated with water vapor (100% relative humidity), the gas phase then has the maximum vapor pressure possible at that temperature. The saturation vapor pressure of pure water increases markedly with temperature, being equivalent to 4.6 mm of Hg at 0°, 9.2 mm at 10°, 17.5 mm at 20°, 31.8 mm at 30°, and 55.3 mm at 40°. Thus air of 100% relative humidity at 0° would be only (4.6/55.3)(100) or 8% relative humidity when heated to 40°. As solutes are added to the liquid phase and the activity of its water is thereby lowered, the saturation vapor pressure in the gas phase becomes less.

The partial pressure of the water vapor determines the chemical activity of water in a gas phase, a_{wv}. If water vapor behaved as an ideal gas, then

$$a_{wv} = \frac{P_{wv}}{P_{wv}{}^*} = \frac{\% \text{ relative humidity}}{100} \qquad (2\text{–}20)$$

where P_{wv} is the partial pressure of water vapor in the air under consideration and $P_{wv}{}^*$ is the saturation vapor pressure in equilibrium with pure liquid water at the same temperature. The relative humidity defined by Equation 2–20 is a readily measured quantity reflecting the activity of water in a particular gas phase and has been extensively used in studying the water relations of plants. For water existing as water vapor in air at atmospheric pressure ($P = 0$), the chemical potential of the water as defined by Equation 2–4 is simply $\mu_w{}^* + RT \ln a_{wv}$. Using the expression for the activity of water vapor given by Equation 2–20, the water potential of water vapor in a gas phase such as air, Ψ_{wv}, is then

$$\Psi_{wv} = \frac{RT}{\bar{V}_w} \ln \left(\frac{\% \text{ relative humidity}}{100} \right) \qquad (2\text{–}21)$$

where the definition of water potential given in Equation 2–13 ($\Psi = (\mu_w - \mu_w{}^*)/\bar{V}_w$) has been used.

If the leaf and the air temperatures are the same, water equilibrium across the plant-air interface occurs when the water potential in the leaf cells equals that of the surrounding atmosphere. To measure Ψ^i, the leaf can be placed in a closed chamber and the relative humidity adjusted so that there is no net water gain or loss by the leaf. In practice, such a determination is rather difficult since small changes in relative humidity have large effects on $\Psi_{wv}{}^{air}$. To see why this is so, consider the factor $RT/\bar{V}_w$ appearing in Equation 2–21. The gas constant R is 8.3143 joules/mole-$^\circ K$ while $\bar{V}_w$ is 17.984 cm^3/mole at 20° (Appendix II). At 20°, $RT/\bar{V}_w$ therefore is (8.3143)(293.16)/(17.984) or 135.5 joules/cm^3, which is a rather large quantity. This can perhaps be appreciated better by converting it to bars. One bar is 10^6 dynes/cm^2 or 0.1 joule/cm^3 (Appendix III). Thus $RT/\bar{V}_w$ at 20° equals 1355 bars.

Next, let us calculate some values of water potentials in air to illustrate the effect of the large magnitude of the factor $RT/\bar{V}_w$. By Equation 2–21, a relative humidity of 100% corresponds to a water potential in the vapor phase of (1355)[ln (100/100)], which equals 0, since the natural logarithm of unity is zero. (Note that this would be in equilibrium with pure water at atmospheric pressure, which also has a water potential equaling zero.) For a relative humidity of 99%, $\Psi_{wv}{}^{air}$ given by Equation 2–21 equals (1355)[ln (99/100)], which is $- 13.6$ bars. [Recall that ln $(1 - x)$ is about $- x$ for $x << 1$, such as is the value 0.01 in the present case.] Hence, going from 100% to 99% relative humidity corresponds to a decrease of water potential of 13.6 bars. Small changes in relative humidity indeed reflect marked differences in the water potential in air!

An important consequence of the large magnitude of $RT/\bar{V}_w$ can be appreciated by considering values of the water potential that may occur within the plant. Although the actual value of Ψ^i depends on the ambient conditions as well as on the type and physiological status of the plant, a representative internal water potential for a green leaf of a garden vegetable might be about $- 5$ bars. From Equation 2–21, the relative humidity corresponding to a water potential of $- 5$ bars is 99.6%. (Incidentally, such an extremely high value for the relative humidity at equilibrium with a Ψ^{leaf} of $- 5$ bars indicates why it is rather difficult to determine Ψ^{leaf} by measuring the $\Psi_{wv}{}^{air}$ for which no water is gained or lost by the leaf.) Even during a rainstorm, the relative humidity of the air rarely exceeds 99%. Consequently, since the relative humidity is lower than 99.6% under most natural conditions, water is continually being lost from a leaf having an internal water potential of -5 bars (throughout this discussion, the leaf is assumed to be at the same temperature as the air). Ψ^i ranges from -4 to -30 bars in the leaves of most land plants. Quite a few desert plants, however, have internal water potentials as low as -50 bars. Even in this case of adaptation to arid climates, water still tends to leave the plant unless the relative humidity is above 96%.

Water Flux.   When the water potential inside a cell differs from that outside of it, the water is no longer in equilibrium, and we can expect a water movement toward the region of lower water potential. Attention will here be specifically focused on water flow into and out of plant cells. This volume flux of water, J_w, is assumed to be proportional to the difference in water potential ($\Delta\Psi$) across the membrane or membranes restricting the flow. The proportionality factor indicating the permeability to water flow at the cellular level is expressed by a water conductivity coefficient, L_w (L_w is usually experimentally the same as L_P, a coefficient also describing water conductivity, which will be referred to below and formally introduced in Chapter 3 in a rather different manner):

$$J_w = L_w\Delta\Psi = L_w(\Psi^o - \Psi^i) \tag{2-22}$$

In Equation 2–22, J_w is the volume flow of water per unit area of the barrier per unit time. It can have units of cm^3/cm^2-sec or cm/sec, which is a velocity. In fact, J_w is the average velocity of water moving across the barrier being considered, an important point that we will return to later. L_w can be given in cm/sec-bar, in which case the water potentials would be expressed in bars. When Equation 2–22 is applied to cells, Ψ^o is the water potential in the external solution while Ψ^i usually refers to the water potential in the vacuole; then L_w reflects the conductivity for water flow across the cell wall, the plasmalemma, and the tonoplast all in series.

When the value of the water conductivity is known, the water potential difference necessary to give an observed water flux can be calculated by using Equation 2–22. For the internodal cells of *Nitella* and *Chara*, L_w for water entry is about 10^{-5} cm/sec-bar. For convenience of calculation, we will consider cylindrical cells which are 10 cm long and 1 mm in diameter as an approximate model for such algal cells. The surface area across which the water flux occurs is $(2\pi r)(l)$, where r is the cell radius (0.05 cm) and l the length (10 cm). Thus the area equals $(2\pi)(0.05)(10)$ or π cm^2. (The area of each end of the cylinder, πr^2, is much less than $2\pi rl$, and in any case a water flux from the external solution across them would not be expected since they are in contact with other cells, not the bathing solution.) The volume of a cylinder is $\pi r^2 l$, which equals $(\pi)(0.05)^2(10)$ or $\pi/40$ cm^3 in the present case. Internodal cells of *Nitella* and *Chara* grow relatively slowly, a change in volume of about 1% per day being a possible growth rate for the fairly mature cells which were used in determining L_w. This growth rate means that the water content increases by about 1% of the volume per day, and therefore the total volume flux of water into the above cell is $(0.01)(\pi/40)$ cm^3/day. Since there are 24 hours/day and 3600 sec/hour, such an inflow of water per day is equivalent to $(0.01)(\pi/40)(1/24)(1/3600)$ or $3\pi \times 10^{-9}$ cm^3 of water moving into a cell/sec. This water influx occurs across a surface area of π cm^2 per cell, and so the rate of volume flow of water per cm^2 is $(3\pi \times 10^{-9})/(\pi)$ or simply 3×10^{-9} cm^3/cm^2-sec. But such a quantity is precisely what is meant by J_w in Equation 2–22. Using the appropriate value of L_w for these internodal cells, 10^{-5} cm/sec-bar, Equation 2–22 indicates that $\Delta\Psi$ is $(3 \times 10^{-9})/(10^{-5})$ or 3×10^{-4} bar. In other words, the internal water potential (Ψ^i) needed to sustain the water influx accompanying a growth of about 1% per day is 3×10^{-4} bar less than the outside water potential (Ψ^o). *Nitella* and *Chara* can grow in pond water, which is a dilute aqueous solution often having a water potential near -0.07 bar. Thus Ψ^i need be only slightly more negative than -0.07 bar to account for the influx of water estimated above.

Equation 2–22 is strictly true when water is the only substance moving across the permeability barrier. If solutes also move, their osmotic pressure effective in causing water flow is reduced. We will discuss this aspect in detail in Chapter 3 when we examine the properties of solutes; here we will present only one of the conclusions. It proves convenient to consider the total volume flow, J_v, which is the sum of the volume flux of water plus that of the solutes. J_v is not proportional to $\Delta\Psi$ as is J_w (Eq. 2–22), but rather to $\Delta P - \sigma\Delta\pi$:

$$J_v = L_P(\Delta P - \sigma\Delta\pi) \qquad (2\text{--}23)$$

where σ is a factor lying between 0 and 1 (to be derived and discussed in detail in Chapter 3). When σ equals 1, $\Delta P - \sigma\Delta\pi$ is $\Delta P - \Delta\pi$, which is the same as $\Delta\Psi$ ($\Psi = P - \pi$ by Eq. 2–13), and Equation 2–23 then reduces to Equation 2–22. However, when σ is zero, the driving force is simply represented by the difference in hydrostatic pressure, ΔP. Such a situation is relevant to the movement of fluid in the xylem, a topic which we will consider in the next section in terms of Poiseuille flow in response to gradients in the hydrostatic pressure.

Water Movement in Plants

Water flows as a continuous stream from the soil to the root to the stem to the leaves and then out through the stomata into the atmosphere. As a useful first approximation, the driving force for the flux across any segment of the overall pathway can be taken as the gradient of the water potential existing from one side to the other of that individual part. Therefore, for a given water flux (J_w in Eq. 2–22), the resistance of each segment determines the water potential difference across it that is necessary to sustain the water movement. The greater the resistance (or, alternatively, the lower the conductivity as expressed by L_w or L_P in Eqs. 2–22 and 2–23), the larger is the $\Delta\Psi$ required to maintain a given water flux. Complications in predicting the water flow occur when the solute also moves since gradients of the chemical potential of solutes can affect the movement of water (as will be discussed in the next chapter). In the following discussion we will cover certain components of the plant in the order that they are involved in water movement from the soil to the air and then summarize the possible water potentials in various parts of the soil-plant-air system.

The Root.   Nearly all water enters a land plant by way of the root, from which it is conducted to other parts through the xylem. To reach the xylem, water crosses the root epidermis, the cortex, and then the endodermis. Relatively little is quantitatively known about the water potential and the resistances involved in the various cell layers of the root.

Water may fairly easily traverse the single-cell layer of the epidermis to reach the cortex. The root cortex often consists of 5 to 10 cell layers, the cytoplasm of adjacent cells being continuous because of the plasmodesmata. The collective protoplasm of the interconnected cells is referred to as the symplasm, as we mentioned in Chapter 1. In the symplasm, permeability barriers in the form of plasmalemmas and cell walls do not have to be surmounted for diffusion from cell to cell, which facilitates the movement of water and solutes in this pathway across the cortex. Some of the water flow across the root cortex occurs in and along the cell walls.

Upon reaching the endodermis, most of the cell wall pathway for water movement is blocked by the Casparian strip. This is a continuous band around the radial walls of the endodermal cells, i.e., it blocks those walls in which water and solutes could have passed across the endodermal layer. The Casparian strip is impregnated with suberin (a polymer of fatty acids) and lignin. It is generally considered as part of the primary cell wall, but suberin and lignin are also deposited all the way across the middle lamella and in the secondary walls. Water and ions entering the xylem therefore cannot flow through or around the cell walls of the endodermal cells but rather must move through their cytoplasm. Thus the endodermis serves to retard the passage of solutes and water from the root to the xylem, and vice versa. Inside the endodermis are parenchyma cells, known as the pericycle, which surround the vascular tissue containing the conducting vessels of the xylem. During the water movement through the plant that accompanies transpiration, the hydrostatic pressure in the xylem is reduced and can become negative, as will be discussed below. This decreases the water potential $[\Psi = P - \pi$ (Eq. 2–13)] in the xylem and promotes water movement from the soil down a water potential gradient to the root xylem.

The Xylem—Poiseuille's Law.   Before discussing the characteristics of water flow in the xylem, we will review briefly some of the anatomical features of its cells. The conducting xylem elements usually have thick, lignified secondary walls and contain no protoplasts. Two types of conducting cells are distinguished in the xylem, the vessel members (primarily found in angiosperms) and the phylogenetically more primitive tracheids, the latter occurring in angiosperms, gymnosperms, and the lower vascular plants. Most tracheids are tapered at the ends while the generally shorter and broader vessel members abut each other with rather blunt ends. The cell walls of the vessel members are perforated in the area of union with other vessel members, especially the end walls for the vessel members that are arranged end-to-end to form a xylem vessel. The section of the cell wall of a vessel member bearing the holes is called the perforation plate, which in the case of a simple perforation plate (Fig. 1–3) can essentially eliminate the end wall between the individual members in a vessel. Although xylem elements actually vary considerably in their diameters (from 10 μm all the way up to 500 μm), for convenience in calculating they will be approximated as cylinders with radii of 20 μm. Conducting cells of the xylem range in length from a few hundred microns to over 2 meters, the latter reportedly occurring in some trees. Other types of cells such as fiber and parenchyma cells (Fig. 1–3) also occur in the xylem. Xylem fibers, which provide structural support for the plant, are long thin cells having heavily lignified cell walls and are devoid of protoplasts at maturity. The living parenchyma cells in the xylem are probably important for the lateral movement of water and solutes into and out of the conducting cells.

To describe water movement in the xylem quantitatively, an expression is needed to relate the volume flow rate of water per unit area, J_w, and the particular driving force which is causing this flux. For cylindrical tubes, an appropriate relationship is that given by Poiseuille's law. The water movement is assumed to be nonturbulent and to be driven by a gradient in hydrostatic pressure, $\partial P/\partial x$. According to Poiseuille's law, J_w depends on this force in the following way:

$$J_w = -\frac{r^2}{8\eta}\frac{\partial P}{\partial x} \qquad (2\text{--}24)$$

where r is the radius of the cylinder and η is the viscosity of the solution. (To obtain the volume flow rate per tube instead of per unit area, Equation 2–24 should be multiplied by πr^2, which gives a form of Poiseuille's law that is possibly more familiar.) The customary unit for viscosity is the poise, which is a dyne-sec/cm^2. For instance, the viscosity of water at 20° is 0.01002 poise (Appendix II). Since positive water flow ($J_w > 0$) occurs in the direction of decreasing hydrostatic pressure ($\partial P/\partial x < 0$), Equation 2–24 contains a minus sign.

Next, we will use Poiseuille's law (Eq. 2–24) to estimate the magnitude of the pressure gradient necessary to cause a specified water movement in the conducting cells of the xylem. The average water flow in the xylem of a transpiring tree, J_w, is often about 0.1 cm/sec. In other words, the macroscopic velocity of sap ascent in a tree can be near 0.1 cm/sec, which equals 3.6 m/hour. For a viscosity of 0.010 poise and a xylem element having a 20 μm radius, the pressure gradient required to satisfy Equation 2–24 is $-(8)(0.01)(0.1)/(2 \times 10^{-3})^2$ or -2×10^3 dynes/cm^3. As expected, the pressure decreases along the direction of water flow.

Since a bar is 10^6 dynes/cm^2 (Appendix III), the above $\partial P/\partial x$ satisfying Poiseuille's law equals -2×10^{-3} bar/cm. Such an estimate of the pressure gradient is consistent with experimental observations on the $\partial P/\partial x$ accompanying water flow in horizontal xylem vessels. For the vertical vessels in a tree, however, a static hydrostatic pressure gradient due to gravity exists even in the absence of flow. [This can be appreciated by considering a vertical column of pure water ($\pi = 0$) at equilibrium, where the water potential, Ψ, is $P + \rho_w g h$; $\rho_w g h$ increases vertically upward, and P must decrease by the same amount in order for Ψ to remain unchanged as it does at equilibrium.] Since $\rho_w g$ equals 0.098 bar/m (Appendix III), this additional pressure gradient amounts to a one bar decrease per 10.2 meters moved upward or -1.0×10^{-3} bar/cm. For transpiring plants, the total $\partial P/\partial x$ in the vertical sections of the xylem is often about -3×10^{-3} bar/cm. Based on the above calculations, this pressure gradient is sufficient to overcome gravity (-1×10^{-3} bar/cm) and to cause water movement in the xylem vessels by Poiseuille flow (-2×10^{-3} bar/cm needed in the above example).

The pressure gradient necessary for a given J_w across a cell wall can also be estimated by using Poiseuille's law. Since the interfibrillar spaces or interstices in a cell wall have diameters near 100 Å, we can assume r to be about 50 Å for purposes of calculation. (Complications due to the tortuosity of the aqueous channels through the interstices will be omitted here.) For J_w equal to 0.1 cm/sec, Equation 2–24 indicates that a pressure gradient of $-(8)(0.01)(0.1)/(50 \times 10^{-8})^2$ or -3.2×10^{10} dynes/cm^3, which equals -3×10^4 bars/cm, would be required for water flow through the cell walls, cf. the $\partial P/\partial x$ of -2×10^{-3} bar/cm needed in the xylem element having a 20 μm radius. Thus, a $\partial P/\partial x$ over 10^7 times greater is necessary for Poiseuille flow through the small interstices of a cell wall than for the same flux through the lumen of the above xylem element, indicating the sensitivity of Poiseuille flow to the radius of the channel. Because of the tremendous pressure gradients required to force water through the small interstices available for water conduction in the cell wall, water does not flow rapidly enough up a tree in the cell walls to account for the observed rates of water movement.

Tension in the Cell Wall Water.   After being conducted to and also across the leaves in the xylem vessels, water is distributed to the individual leaf cells probably by flowing mainly along and in the cell walls. Since such water is often in contact with air, interfacial phenomena at the air-wall surfaces play an important role in determining the forces acting on the water in the cell wall and consequently its water potential there, $\Psi^{\text{cell wall}}$.

Because water tightly adheres to the surfaces surrounding the many interstices in the wettable cell walls, the main contributor to the water potential in the cell wall can be considered to be the matric potential or pressure, τ. This matric pressure resulting from the water-wall attraction is really a negative hydrostatic pressure that develops from surface tension effects. These can be analyzed by considering the pressures that develop in a liquid contained in a cylindrical pore, the arguments being basically the same as those presented in discussing capillary rise in the first section of this chapter. As indicated there, one of the forces acting on the fluid in a narrow pore of radius r is due to surface tension σ. This force equals $2\pi r\sigma \cos \alpha$ (see Fig. 2–2), where α is the contact angle, a quantity which is essentially zero for the case of wettable walls. Since the adhesive forces at the wall are transmitted to the body of the fluid by means of the water-water cohesion, a tension or negative hydrostatic pressure develops in the fluid. The total force resisting the surface adhesion can be viewed as this tension times the area over which it acts, πr^2. Equating these two forces gives the following expression for the tension developed in the fluid contained within a cylindrical pore:

$$\text{Tension} = \frac{2\sigma \cos \alpha}{r} \qquad (2\text{--}25)$$

Adhesion of water at interfaces generally creates tensions, such as that described by Equation 2–25, in the bulk of the fluid. It has sometimes been considered to be convenient in plant physiology to treat such negative hydrostatic pressures arising from interfacial interactions as positive matric pressures, a convention mentioned above.

The strong water-wall adhesive forces, which are transmitted throughout the interfibrillar spaces by water-water hydrogen bonding, conceivably can greatly reduce the water potential in the cell wall, as the following calculation indicates. At 20°, the surface tension of water is 72.8 dynes/cm or 7.28×10^{-5} bar-cm (Appendix II). The voids between the fibers in the cell wall are often about 100 Å across, and for wettable walls, cos α equals 1. For water in such cylindrical pores, Equation 2–25 indicates that the tension would be $(2)(7.28 \times 10^{-5})(1)/(50 \times 10^{-8})$ or 291 bars. Thus 291 bars is an estimate of the negative hydrostatic pressure or tension that could develop in the aqueous solution within cell wall interstices of typical dimensions, supporting the contention that $\Psi^{\text{cell wall}}$ can be markedly less than zero. Moreover, the previous discussion of the tensile strength of water indicates that the hydrogen bonding in water could withstand such a tension.

Of considerable importance in transpiration is the relative value of the water potential in the cell wall compared with that in the adjacent vapor phase. From Equation 2–21, Ψ_{wv}^{air} corresponding to a relative humidity of 95% at 20° is (1355) ln (0.95) or -69 bars. According to Equation 2–25, a tension of 69 bars would occur in a water-containing cylindrical pore with wettable walls having a radius of $(2)(7.28 \times 10^{-5})(1)/(69)$ or 2.11×10^{-6} cm, which is 211 Å. In other words, water in 211 Å radius interstices in the cell walls of leaf mesophyll cells would be in equilibrium with air of 95% relative humidity in the intercellular spaces. If the relative humidity near the cell wall surface were decreased, water in such interstices could be lost, but it would still remain in the finer pores where a larger matric potential or tension can be created. The large tensions that potentially could be present in the cell wall generally do not occur in living cells since water is usually available and gets "pulled" into the interstices, thus filling them. However, when plant material dries out, such large tensions resulting from interfacial inter-actions can and do develop.

Stomata. Most of the water that evaporates from cell walls in the interior of the leaf diffuses along the intercellular air spaces to the stomata and then out into the surrounding atmosphere. The surface area of the intercellular air spaces is generally about ten times larger than the external leaf area. Thus a very large surface is available from which evaporation of water can take place. Although the epidermal cells occupy a much greater fraction of the exposed leaf surface than do the stomata, the waxy cuticle covering them greatly reduces the water loss from their cell walls. The water vapor that does diffuse through the waxy cuticle of the epidermal cells is known as cuticular transpiration. However, the usual pathway of least resistance for water vapor leaving the leaf during transpiration is through the open stomata.

The stomatal aperture is controlled by the conformation of the two guard cells surrounding the pore. (See Fig. 1–2.) These cells are kidney-shaped, may be 40 μm long, and contain chloroplasts (epidermal cells are generally devoid of chloroplasts). When the guard cells are relatively flaccid, the stomatal pore is nearly closed, as is the case for most plants at night. Upon illumination or decrease in the local carbon dioxide concentration, the guard cells somehow take up water and become more turgid relative to the sur-rounding epidermal cells, thereby opening the stomatal pore. The metabolic basis of such changes in stomatal aperture and the complicated interplay of the many external stimuli are not fully understood. The increase in guard cell turgidity relative to that in the epidermal cells causes the guard cells to expand, and their opposed cell walls (those on either side of the pore) become concave. As the kidney-shaped guard cells thus bow outward, an elliptical pore develops between the two cells. The formation of this pore is actually a consequence of the unequal thickening and elasticity of the cell wall sur-rounding each guard cell. The distance between the guard cells across the open pore is generally 6 to 10 μm, and the length of the pore may be about 20 μm. Stomata are usually more numerous on the under surface compared with the upper surface of leaves, a frequency of 10,000 per cm^2 being representative. For most plants, the pores of the open stomata correspond to 0.5% to 2% of the leaf surface area.

To indicate the amount of water vapor that may be diffusing across the unstirred air layer at the surface of leaves, we will make an estimate using Fick's first law [$J = -D\ \partial c/\partial x$ (Eq. 1–1)]. As mentioned in Chapter 1, the diffusion coefficient for water vapor in air at 20° is about 0.25 cm^2/sec. The concentration gradient, $\partial c/\partial x$ will here be approximated by the concentration difference of water vapor, Δc, divided by the distance across the unstirred layer, Δx. For a wind velocity of 5 kilometers/hour (3 miles/hour), the unstirred air layer at the surface of a representative leaf may be about 1 mm thick. Let us consider water vapor moving from just outside the stomata at 95% relative humidity to 50% relative humidity in the surrounding air by diffusing across such an unstirred layer that is 1 mm thick. It will be assumed that the water vapor diffuses from an open surface or plane at 95% relative humidity and that the air temperature is constant. At 20°, 100% relative humidity corresponds to 0.0173 mg of water/cm^3; 95% is then 0.0164 mg/cm^3 while 50% relative humidity is 0.0087. Thus, the concentration difference for water vapor across the unstirred air layer is 0.0077 mg/cm^3. Hence, the flux of water is $(0.25)(0.0077)/(0.1)$ or 0.019 mg/cm^2-sec using Fick's first law. For leaves under field conditions similar to this one (20°, 5 km/hour wind velocity), the rate of water loss by transpiration can be about 0.02 g/cm^2-hr, which is 0.006 mg/cm^2-sec. Thus, the value calculated assuming an open surface from which water vapor can diffuse in this case gives about a threefold overestimate of the actual rate of transpirational loss of water per unit area of plant leaf.

Water Potential Components in the Soil-Plant-Atmosphere Continuum.   Possible values of the water potential in various parts of the soil-plant-atmosphere system are estimated in Table 2–1. The plant is considered to act as a continuous pathway along which water moves from one region to another where the water potential is in general lower. The values listed in Table 2–1 do not apply to all plants, nor even to the same plant at all times. Rather, they serve to organize the various aspects discussed above. Moreover, the relative contributions of P, π, gravitational effects, and relative humidity are indicated in various parts of the soil-plant-atmosphere continuum.

First, let us consider the soil water potential, Ψ^{soil}. The pores in soil provide many air-liquid interfaces where surface tension effects lead to a negative hydrostatic pressure (cf. Eq. 2–25); thus P^{soil} is indicated as -2 bars in Table 2–1. This interfacial contribution often dominates Ψ^{soil} and is generally referred to as the soil matric pressure. It is found that the actual magnitude of Ψ^{soil} varies greatly with the environmental condition and the type of soil. In freshly irrigated soil, the water potential can be -0.1 bar while permanent wilting of plants often occurs when Ψ^{soil} decreases below about -15 bars.

The particular value of Ψ^{soil} for wilting depends on the specific plant

Table 2–1: Representative values for the various components of the water potential in the soil-plant-atmosphere system. Ψ equals $P - \pi + \rho_w gh$ in the liquid phases (Eq. 2–13 plus the gravitational term) and is $(RT/\overline{V}_w) \ln (\%$ relative humidity$/100)$ in the gas phases (Eq. 2–21), which are at $20°$.

Phase	P	$-\pi$	$\rho_w gh$	$\dfrac{RT}{\overline{V}_w} \ln \left(\dfrac{\%\ \text{relative humidity}}{100} \right)$ (in bars)	Ψ
Top of soil near root	-2	-1	0		-3
Xylem of root near ground surface	-5	-1	0		-6
Xylem in stem at 10 m above ground	-8	-1	1		-8
Vacuole of leaf cell at 10 m	2	-11	1		-8
Cell wall of leaf cell at 10 m	-7	-2	1		-8
Gas just outside stomata at 95% relative humidity				-69	-69
Atmosphere surrounding plant at 50% relative humidity				-941	-941

being considered, as the following argument indicates. Consider the case in Table 2–1 where the water potential in the vacuole of a leaf cell 10 m above the ground is initially -8 bars. As the soil dries out, Ψ^{soil} decreases and eventually becomes -10 bars. When the soil water potential becomes -10 bars, Ψ^{leaf} must be less than this for water movement from the soil to the leaf to continue. A Ψ^{leaf} of -10 bars could occur for P^{vacuole} equal to zero, $\rho_w gh^{\text{vacuole}}$ remaining 1 bar for this leaf 10 m above the ground and π^{vacuole} being unchanged at 11 bars—the value given in Table 2–1. (Actually, as the hydrostatic pressure in a leaf cell decreases, the elastic properties of the cell wall ensure that the cell would shrink somewhat, and thus π^{vacuole} would increase, as it does in the analogous situation describing incipient plasmolysis mentioned in the previous section.) Zero hydrostatic pressure in the vacuole means that the leaf has lost its turgor, and so it wilts in response to a decreasing Ψ^{soil}. If the soil dries out even further from the level that causes wilting and if water movement from the soil to the leaf still occurs (i.e., if Ψ^{leaf} is less than Ψ^{soil}), cellular water would be lost from the leaf. The vacuolar contents then become more concentrated, and $\pi^{vacuole}$ would be increased. For xerophytes in arid areas, the osmotic pressure in the leaves is usually close to 30 bars. The value of Ψ^{soil} where wilting occurs for such plants would be considerably lower (i.e., more negative, which means a drier soil) than for the plant indicated in Table 2–1. Thus a high osmotic pressure in the leaves can be viewed as an adaptation to a dry climate.

The primary driving force for water movement in the xylem is $\partial P^{xylem}/\partial x$ (Table 2–1), which can lead to a flow describable by Poiseuille's law (Eq. 2–24). The xylem sap, which contains mainly water plus some minerals absorbed from the soil, usually does not have an osmotic pressure in excess of 2 bars. The hydrostatic pressure, on the other hand, has much larger values and can change markedly during the day. During extremely rapid transpiration, great tensions (negative hydrostatic pressures) of up to 100 bars can develop in the xylem of some plants. These tensions are maintained by the cohesion of water molecules resulting from the intermolecular hydrogen bonding, as discussed above. When transpiration ceases, as can occur under conditions of very high relative humidity in the air surrounding the plant, the hydrostatic pressure in the xylem often becomes positive. This leads to guttation in which xylem fluid is exuded from the leaves.

The marked changes in hydrostatic pressure in the xylem during the day can cause trees to have observable diurnal fluctuations in their diameters! When transpiration is rapid, the tension in the xylem causes the tree to contract, as the water adhering to the walls of the xylem vessels is pulled inward. At night, the hydrostatic pressure in the xylem may become positive. The pressure on the cell walls is then outward, and the tree diameter actually increases.

The unstirred layer of air at the leaf surface often provides the largest resistance to water movement accompanying transpiration. As indicated in the introduction to this section, the resistance of any particular component is essentially the force across it divided by the resulting flux. The total flow of water in the steady state is approximately the same across each of the components in the soil-plant-atmosphere continuum. Thus, the effective resistance to water flow is closely indicated by the decrease in water potential across that component. (The actual force depends on the characteristics of the particular structure; for instance, changes in the osmotic term of the water potential would have relatively little effect on the flow along the xylem, which depends essentially on the hydrostatic pressure gradient alone.) The

drop in water potential from the surface of the leaf to the atmosphere surrounding the plant often represents the largest force involved in water
movement through the plant although factors like the wind speed, stomatal
opening, and internal resistance within the leaf must be considered in individual cases. For the specific example presented in Table 2–1, the drop in
water potential from the gas phase just outside the stomata at 95% relative
humidity to the surrounding air at 50% relative humidity is over 90% of
the entire drop in water potential from the soil to the atmosphere. Since the
total water flow is fairly uniform in magnitude across each component, the
greatest resistance for overall water movement from the soil through the
plant to the atmosphere is contributed by the unstirred air layers at the
surfaces of the leaves in this particular case.

Problems

2–1. Suppose that the capillary rise of water in a 2 mm diameter capillary with
wettable walls is 1.5 cm. (a) If the walls of the capillary are treated so that the
contact angle becomes 60°, what is the height of the rise? (b) If the original
capillary is tilted 45° from the horizontal, what is the vertical height of the
rise? (c) If sucrose is added to the solution in the original capillary so that the
density becomes 1.2 g/cm^3, what is the height of the rise? (d) What is the rise
of water in a capillary similar to the original one but with a 1 μm radius? (e)
In which of the 4 cases is the greatest weight supported by capillary (surface
tension) forces?

2–2. Consider a neutral solute that has a concentration of 0.1 molal on one side
of a barrier permeable only to water and 1 molal on the other side. Let its
partial molal volume be 40 cm^3/mole and the temperature be 20°. (a) If the
activity coefficient is unity on both sides, what is the hydrostatic pressure
difference (in bars) across the barrier at equilibrium? (b) If γ_{solute} is 0.5 on
the more concentrated side and if other conditions are unchanged, what is
ΔP across the barrier? (c) If P on the 0.1 molal side is the same as atmospheric
pressure, what is the chemical potential of the solute there?

2–3. (a) By what percent is the activity of water reduced for an osmotic pressure
of 10 bars at 20°? (b) Assuming activity coefficients are unity, what concentration of a solute corresponds to a π of 10 bars at 20°? (c) In the vacuole of
a certain cell, the mole fraction of water is 0.98, the hydrostatic pressure is
8.0 bars, and the temperature is 20°. Assuming activity coefficients are unity,
what is the water potential in the vacuole?

2–4. Suppose that chloroplasts are isolated from a plant cell whose cytoplasm has
an osmotic pressure of 4 bars at 20°. When the chloroplasts are placed in

solutions at 20° containing an impermeable solute, the volumes are 36 μm^3 at an external osmotic pressure of $3\frac{1}{3}$ bars, 28 μm^3 at 5 bars, and 20 μm^3 at 10 bars. Assume that activity coefficients are unity. (a) What is the volume of the chloroplasts in the plant cell? (b) What is the nonaqueous volume per chloroplast? (c) What volume fraction of the chloroplast is occupied by water *in vivo*? (d) What is the content of osmotically active particles per chloroplast?

2–5. Consider a cell that has a water conductivity coefficient, L_w, equal to 10^{-5} cm/sec-bar. Let the internal osmotic pressure be 10 bars and the internal hydrostatic pressure be 6 bars at 20°. (a) What is the net water flux into or out of the cell when it is placed in pure water at atmospheric pressure? (b) What is the water flux at the point of incipient plasmolysis? (c) What is the water flux when the external solution is in equilibirium with a gas phase at 97% relative humidity?

2–6. Assume that a horizontal xylem element has a cross-sectional area of 0.004 mm² and conducts water at 20° at a rate of 0.02 ml/hour. (a) What is the mean velocity of the fluid in the xylem element? (b) What pressure gradient is necessary to cause such a flow? (c) If the pressure gradient remained the same but cell walls with interstices 200 Å across filled the xylem element, what would be the mean velocity of fluid movement?

References

Briggs, G. E. 1967. *Movement of Water in Plants*, Blackwell Scientific Publications, Oxford.

Bull, H. B. 1964. *An Introduction to Physical Biochemistry*, Davis, Philadelphia.

Dainty, J. 1963. Water relations of plant cells. *Advances in Botanical Research* **1**, 279–326.

Davies, J. T., and E. K. Rideal. 1963. *Interfacial Phenomena*, 2nd ed., Academic Press, New York.

Dick, D. A. T. 1966. *Cell Water*, Butterworths, London.

Edsall, J. T., and J. Wyman. 1958. *Biophysical Chemistry*, Vol. I, Academic Press, New York.

Eisenberg, D., and W. Kauzmann. 1969. *The Structure and Properties of Water*, Oxford University Press, Oxford.

Meidner, H., and T. A. Mansfield. 1968. *Physiology of Stomata*, McGraw-Hill, New York.

Nobel, P. S. 1969. The Boyle-Van't Hoff Relation. *Journal of Theoretical Biology* **23**, 375–79.

Pauling, L. 1964. *College Chemistry*, 3rd ed., W. H. Freeman and Company, San Francisco.

Salisbury, F. B., and C. Ross. 1969. *Plant Physiology*, Wadsworth, Belmont, Calif.

Slatyer, R. O. 1967. *Plant-Water Relationships*, Academic Press, New York.

Chapter 3

Solutes

In this chapter we will turn our attention to a description of the properties of solutes, especially in regard to their crossing of membranes. The chemical potentials in the aqueous phases on the two sides of a membrane or other region across which movement is by diffusion will be compared in order to predict the direction of the passive solute fluxes as well as the driving forces leading to such motion. Moreover, the fluxes of charged species will be shown to set up the electrical potential differences observed across biological membranes.

Many of the solute properties important in plant physiology are intertwined with those of the ubiquitous solvent, water. For instance, the osmotic pressure term in the chemical potential describing the free energy of water is mainly due to the decrease of the water activity caused by the solutes. The movement of water through the soil to the root and then to the xylem influences the entry of dissolved nutrients and their subsequent distribution throughout the plant. However, in contrast with water, solute molecules can carry a net positive or negative electrical charge. For such charged particles, the electrical terms must be included in the chemical potentials, which leads to a consideration of electrical phenomena in general and an interpretation of the potentials present across biological membranes in particular. The thermodynamic criteria for judging whether an observed ionic flux into or out of a cell can be accounted for by passive diffusion depend on differences in both the concentration and the electrical potential between the inside and the outside. Ions can also be actively transported across a membrane, in which case metabolic energy is involved in some way in moving solutes in an energetically uphill direction.

When both solutes and water traverse the same barrier, the classical thermodynamic approach is replaced by a description based on irreversible thermodynamics. The various forces and fluxes are then viewed as being interdependent, which means that the movement of water across a membrane influences the movement of solutes, and vice versa. This more general approach helps explain why the effective osmotic pressure difference across a membrane that is permeable to solutes is often much less than the theoretical osmotic pressure difference, a phenomenon depending on the reflection coefficients of the solutes.

Chemical Potential of Ions

The free energy of a particular solute, j, can be represented by its chemical potential, μ_j, as discussed in Chapter 2. Since a substance would spontaneously tend to move to regions of lower free energy (see pp. 208–9), μ_j is a useful parameter for analyzing passive movements of solutes. Using a linear combination of the various component energies, the chemical potential of any species j was given by Equation 2–4 as follows: $\mu_j = \mu_j^* + RT \ln a_j + \bar{V}_j P + z_j F E$. Since water is uncharged ($z_w = 0$), the electrical term does not enter into its chemical potential. For ions, however, $z_j F E$ becomes important. In fact, for charged solutes under conditions of biological interest, the electrical term is usually far larger than that for the hydrostatic pressure. The chemical potential defined by Equation 2–4 is therefore commonly referred to as the electrochemical potential when dealing with ions, as the $\bar{V}_j P$ component is usually ignored. Although this emphasizes the role played by electrical potentials, "chemical potential" is only a shorthand expression for the sum of *all* the different component energies pertaining to a particular species, and it is not really necessary to use a special term like electrochemical potential.

Electrical Potential.   The electrical potential E at some location is used to describe the relative amount of electrical energy of some charged substance present there. It is relative since the location of the level of zero potential is arbitrary. It corresponds to energy since work must be done to move a positive charge from there to a region with a higher electrical potential. For instance, if the charge is expressed in coulombs and the potential in volts, then the amount of work in joules is simply the product of the charge that is moved and the electrical potential difference (final minus initial potential). The charge carried by an ion of species j, z_j, is a positive or negative integer indicating the electronic charge of a single ion. For instance, z_j is $+1$ for the potassium ion and -2 for sulfate (SO_4^{--}). One unit for charge is the coulomb, e.g., a proton has a charge of 1.6021×10^{-19} coulombs. Thus a mole or Avogadro's number of protons would have a charge equal to $(6.02252 \times 10^{23})(1.6021 \times 10^{-19})$ or 96,487 coulombs. Such a unit consisting of Avogadro's number of charge equivalents (i.e., one mole of single charges) is called the Faraday, F. This quantity appearing in the electrical term of the chemical potential (cf. Eq. 2–4) equals 96,487 coulombs/mole or 96,487 joules/mole-volt (a coulomb-volt is a joule), which can also be expressed as 23,060 cal/mole-volt (Appendix II).

To illustrate the rather large contribution that the electrical term can make to the chemical potential of a charged substance compared with the effect of hydrostatic pressure, consider a small monovalent cation ($z_j = +1$) having a partial molal volume $\bar{V}_j$ equaling 20 cm^3/mole. The question to be asked is what electrical potential difference (ΔE) in volts (v) corresponds to the same contribution to the chemical potential of such an ion as a hydrostatic pressure (ΔP) of one bar? In other words, what is ΔE so that $z_j F \Delta E$ equals $\bar{V}_j \Delta P$ under these conditions? One bar is 10^6 dynes/cm^2 or 0.1 joule/cm^3 (Appendix III). Thus, ΔE need be $(20)(0.1)/[(1)(96,487)]$ or only 2.1×10^{-5} v (0.021 mv). This is an extremely small electrical potential difference! For comparison, the difference in electrical potential across a biological membrane is often near 100 mv, which is $(100)/(0.021)$ or 4800 times larger than the potential difference calculated here. Stated another way, 100 mv across a membrane would make the same contribution to the chemical potential difference as a drop of 4800 bars of hydrostatic pressure from one side of the barrier to the other for the above case of a monovalent cation having a $\bar{V}_j$ of 20 cm^3/mole. Most hydrostatic pressures encountered in plant physiology are only a few bars. Thus, hydrostatic pressure drops across membranes are usually negligible in comparison with other contributions to the chemical potential differences of ions from one side of the membranes to the other.

Another consequence of the relatively large magnitude of electrical effects is the general occurrence of electroneutrality in plant cells and organelles. Thus, in regions that are large compared with atomic dimensions the total charge carried by the cations is closely compensated for by a nearly equal charge of opposite sign carried by the anions. If there were a net charge in some region such as near a membrane, then an electrical potential difference would exist from one part of the region to another. The magnitude of such an electrical potential difference, ΔE, is related to the capacitance of the region as follows:

$$Q = C\Delta E \tag{3–1}$$

where Q is the net charge and C is the capacitance. (In keeping with most of the plant physiology literature, the E's appearing in the electrical equations throughout this book refer to electrical potentials, not electric field intensities, as they do in many physics texts.) The unit for capacitance is the farad, which equals 1 coulomb/volt. The capacitances of most biological membranes are approximately the same per unit area, about 1 microfarad (μf)/cm^2.

For convenience in estimating the net charge inside a cell which would lead to a typical membrane potential, let us consider a spherical cell of radius r. Suppose that the uncanceled or net charges are uniformly distributed in space at a concentration, c. [For a conductor (a body in which electrical charges can freely move) such as an aqueous solution, the uncanceled or net charges would not remain uniformly distributed. Rather, they repel each other and collect at the inner surface of the sphere; thus, the quantity c is actually the hypothetical concentration of the net charge, if it were uniformly distributed throughout the interior of the sphere.] The charge Q within the sphere of radius r is $(4/3)\pi r^3 cF$. (c can be in moles/cm^3 and here refers to the net concentration of uncompensated singly charged particles; F, which is in coulombs/mole, is necessary to convert from concentration to electrical charge.) The capacitance of the sphere, C, is $4\pi r^2 C'$, where C' is the capacitance per unit area. After substituting these values of Q and C into Equation 3–1 and rearranging, one obtains the following expression for the electrical potential difference in the case of a spherical capacitor:

$$\Delta E = \frac{rcF}{3C'} \tag{3–2}$$

Equation 3–2 gives the electrical potential difference from the center of the sphere to just outside its surface. For a conductor, the internal uncompensated charges are found near the surface; thus ΔE in that case actually occurs across the bounding surface (such as a membrane) surrounding the spherical body under consideration. Equation 3–2 indicates that the electrical potential difference that is developed is directly proportional to the average concentration of net charge enclosed and inversely proportional to the capacitance per unit area of the sphere.

To apply Equation 3–2 to a specific example, consider a spherical cell with a radius of 30 μm and an electrical potential difference across the membrane (inside negative) of -100 mv, a value close to that occurring for many cells. Assuming a typical membrane capacitance per unit area of 1 μf/cm^2, to what net charge concentration in the cell does this potential correspond? Since a farad is a coulomb/volt, one μf/cm^2 is 10^{-6} coulomb/v-cm^2 while F equals 96,487 coulombs/mole (Appendices II and III). Using Equation 3–2, c equals $3C'\Delta E/rF$, and the average concentration of net charge would be $(3)(10^{-6})(-0.1)/[(30 \times 10^{-4})(96,487)]$ or -1.0×10^{-9} moles/cm^3, which is -1.0×10^{-6} moles/liter (-1 μM). The sign of the charge is negative, indicating more internal anions than cations. The average concentration of the net or uncanceled charge leading to a considerable electrical potential difference is rather small, an important point to be considered below. (It should be emphasized that the uncompensated charges would not be uniformly distributed in space but rather would repel each other and thus collect near the membrane; in fact, the electrical potential difference essentially occurs only across the membrane itself since the electrical potential is constant throughout a conductor, such as is approximately the case for an aqueous solution.)

It is useful to compare the net charge concentration averaged over the volume of the cell (c in Eq. 3–2) with the total concentration of anions and cations in a plant cell. Specifically, since the positive and negative ions in plant cells can each have a concentration near 0.1 M, the above calculated excess of -1 μM is only about one extra negative charge per 10^5 anions $[(0.1)/(10^{-6}) = 10^5]$. Put another way, the total charge of the cations inside such a cell equals or compensates that of the anions to about one part in 100,000. When cations are taken up by a cell to any appreciable extent, either anions must accompany them and/or cations must be released from inside the cell. Otherwise, if marked departures from electrical neutrality were allowed to occur in some region, sizable electrical potential differences would build up.

Activity Coefficients of Ions.   Next, we will turn our attention from the electrical term in the chemical potential to the activity one, more specifically to the chemical activity itself. As mentioned in Chapter 2, the activity of species j, a_j, is the thermodynamically effective concentration. For charged particles in an aqueous solution, this activity can differ appreciably from the actual concentration, c_j, a point that has not always been adequately recognized in dealing with ions. By Equation 2–5, a_j equals $\gamma_j c_j$, where γ_j is the activity coefficient of species j.

A quantitative description of the dependence of the activity coefficients of ions on the concentration of the various species in the solution was developed by Debye and Hückel. In a local region around a particular ion, the electrostatic forces describable by equations like 2–3 constrain the movement of other ions. As the concentration increases, the average distance between the ions becomes less, thereby facilitating ion-ion interactions. For instance, Equation 2–3 indicates that the electrostatic interaction between two charged particles varies inversely as the square of their separation, and thus the electrical forces increase greatly as the ions get closer and closer together. As ions of opposite sign attract each other, the various other interactions of both of the ions are restricted, which lowers their effective concentration or activity.

A simple and approximate form of the Debye-Hückel equation appropriate for estimating the value of activity coefficients of ions in relatively dilute aqueous solutions at 25° is

$$\log \gamma_{\pm} = \frac{0.509 \; z_+ z_- \sqrt{\frac{1}{2} \sum_j c_j z_j^2}}{1 + \sqrt{\frac{1}{2} \sum_j c_j z_j^2}} \tag{3-3}$$

where the plus and minus refer to cation and anion, respectively, concentrations are expressed in molarities, and the summations indicated in Equation 3–3 are over all the charged species. Thermodynamics per se cannot predict the activity coefficient of a single ion, and so $\gamma_{\pm}$ represents the mean activity coefficient of some cation-anion pair having charges z_+ and z_-. Since z_- is negative, Equation 3–3 indicates that $\log \gamma_{\pm}$ is less than zero, and so $\gamma_{\pm}$ is less than 1. Thus, the activities of ions in dilute aqueous solutions are less than their concentrations, as would indeed be expected.

To estimate $\gamma_{\pm}$ under conditions approximating those that might occur in a biological system, let us consider an aqueous solution containing 0.100 M of both monovalent cations and anions and 0.025 M of both divalent cations and anions. For this solution, $\frac{1}{2} \sum_j c_j z_j^2$, which is known as the ionic strength, is $\frac{1}{2}[(0.100)(1)^2 + (0.100)(-1)^2 + (0.025)(2)^2 + (0.025)(-2)^2]$ or 0.200 M. From Equation 3–3, $\log \gamma_{\pm}$ is then $(0.509)(1)(-1)(\sqrt{0.200})/(1 + \sqrt{0.200})$

or -0.157 for the monovalent ions. This corresponds to a mean activity coefficient of only 0.70, a value considerably less than one.

The activity coefficient depends on all the ions in the solution, as indicated by the ionic strength terms which appear in Equation 3–3. Therefore, even when a particular ionic species itself is dilute, its activity coefficient can still be appreciably less than one because of the many electrostatic interactions with other ions. The departure from 1.00 for activity coefficients is even greater for divalent and trivalent ions than for monovalent ions, as the z_+z_- factor in Equation 3–3 indicates. Thus, although activity coefficients of ions are often set equal to unity for convenience, this is obviously not always justified. A practical difficulty arising under most experimental situations is that c_j is much easier to determine than is a_j, especially for compartments like the cytoplasm or the interior of a chloroplast. In those circumstances where a_j has been replaced by c_j, caution must be exercised in the interpretations or conclusions. It should be pointed out that the activity coefficients for nonelectrolytes and water are generally much closer to unity than are those for ions, and so the assumption involved in replacing a_j by c_j for such neutral species is not as severe as for the charged substances (e.g., γ_{sucrose} is about 0.96 for 0.3 M sucrose). An all-inclusive theory for activity coefficients is rather complicated and is beyond the scope of this text. Equation 3–3 is presented only to illustrate in a quantitative manner that activity coefficients of ions can be appreciably less than 1.00 under conditions that may occur in a plant cell.

Nernst Potential.   Having considered the electrical and the activity terms in a little detail, let us now turn to the role of these quantities in the chemical potential of ions. Specifically, let us consider the deceptively simple and yet extremely important relationship between the electrical potential difference across a membrane and the accompanying distribution of ions across it at equilibrium.

When ions of some species j exist in equilibrium across a membrane, their chemical potential is the same outside (o) as it is inside (i), which means that $\mu_j{}^o$ equals $\mu_j{}^i$. The hydrostatic pressure term frequently makes only a negligible contribution to the chemical potential of ions, as discussed above, and therefore $\bar{V}_j P$ can be omitted from μ_j in the present case. With this approximation and the definition of chemical potential (Eq. 2–4), the condition for equilibrium of ionic species j across the membrane is given by:

$$\mu_j{}^* + RT \ln a_j{}^o + z_j F E^o = \mu_j{}^* + RT \ln a_j{}^i + z_j F E^i \qquad (3\text{–}4)$$

The term μ_j^* in Equation 3–4 is a constant referring to the same standard state of species j in the aqueous solutions on either side of the membrane, and so it can be canceled from the equation.

Upon solving Equation 3–4 for the electrical potential difference, $E^i - E^o$, across the membrane *at equilibrium*, one obtains the following important relationship:

$$E_{N_j} = E^i - E^o = \frac{RT}{z_j F} \ln \frac{a_j^o}{a_j^i}$$

$$= \frac{59.2}{z_j} \log \frac{a_j^o}{a_j^i} \text{ mv at } 25° \qquad (3\text{–}5)$$

The electrical potential difference E_{N_j} in Equation 3–5 is called the Nernst potential of species j. It has been derived by assuming equality of the chemical potential of some charged species on two sides of a membrane but can be considered in a broader context, as will be mentioned below. For convenience of calculation, the natural logarithm, ln, is often replaced by 2.303 log, where log is the common logarithm to the base 10 (see Appendices III, IV, and V). The quantity $2.303 \, RT/F$ equals 58.2 mv at 20°, 59.2 mv at 25° (cf. Eq. 3–5), and 60.2 mv at 30° (Appendix III). Using such numerical values, the Nernst potential can be expressed in the useful form presented in the second line of Equation 3–5.

Equation 3–5, which is known as the Nernst equation, is an equilibrium statement showing how the internal and external activities of ionic species j are related to the electrical potential difference across the membrane. At equilibrium, a tenfold difference in activity of a monovalent ion across some membrane is equivalent to a 59 mv difference in electrical potential (at 25°). Hence, a relatively small electrical potential difference can balance a large difference in activity across a membrane. For some calculations, the ratio of the external to the internal activity coefficient of species j, γ_j^o/γ_j^i, is set equal to one (a less stringent assumption than setting both γ_j^o and γ_j^i equal to one). Under this condition, the ratio a_j^o/a_j^i in Equation 3–5 becomes the ratio of the concentrations, c_j^o/c_j^i. Such a substitution may be justified when the ionic strengths on the two sides of the membrane are approximately the same but can lead to errors when the outside solution is much more dilute than the internal one.

Regardless of the actual electrical potential difference existing across a membrane (E_M), a Nernst potential for an individual ionic species j, E_{N_j}, can always be calculated from Equation 3–5 by using the ratio of the outside to the inside activity (a_j^o/a_j^i) or concentration (c_j^o/c_j^i). If that particular species of ion were in equilibrium across the membrane, E_{N_j} would equal the potential difference across the membrane, E_M. For many plant cells, the Nernst potential for potassium is close to the electrical potential difference measured across the membrane under consideration, e.g., the plasmalemma or the tonoplast. In such circumstances, potassium may actually be in equilibrium across that membrane, and no energy would be expended in moving it from one side to the other. If some ionic species cannot penetrate the membrane or is actively transported across it, E_{N_j} can markedly differ from E_M. In fact, the minimum amount of energy needed to transport ions across a membrane is proportional to the difference between E_{N_j} and E_M, as will be discussed below. It should also be pointed out that the aqueous phases designated as inside and outside can have more than one membrane intervening between them. For instance, the vacuolar sap and an external solution, which are often the compartments considered experimentally, have two membranes separating them, the plasmalemma and the tonoplast. The thermodynamic arguments remain the same in the case of multiple membranes with E_M and E_{N_j} referring to the electrical potential differences between the two phases actually under consideration, regardless of how many membranes occur between them.

Data obtained on potassium by L. N. Vorobiev for the large internodal cells of the green freshwater alga, *Chara australis*, are convenient for illustrating the use of the Nernst equation. The potassium ion activity in the medium bathing the cells (a_K^o, where the atomic symbol K when used as a subscript is the conventional shorthand notation for K^+) was 0.096 mM while a_K^i in the vacuole was measured as 48 mM. (See Appendix I for a comment on the units of activity.) Thus, a_K^o/a_K^i was $(0.096)/(48)$ or $1/500$. Using Equation 3–5 (with a factor of 58.2 since measurement was at 20°), the Nernst potential for potassium is 58.2 log $(1/500)$ or -157 mv. The actual measured electrical potential of the vacuole relative to the external solution, E_M, was -155 mv, very close to the calculated Nernst potential for potassium; thus potassium appears to be in equilibrium between the external solution and the vacuole. The potassium concentration in the vacuole of these *Chara* cells was 60 mM. The activity coefficient for potassium in the vacuole, γ_K^i, equals a_K^i/c_K^i, and therefore γ_K^i was $(48)/(60)$ or 0.80 while the potassium activity coefficient in the bathing solution, γ_K^o, was about 0.96. For this case of large differences in the internal and the external concentrations, the ratio γ_K^o/γ_K^i is $(0.80)/(0.96)$ or 0.83, which differs appreciably from 1.00. If concentrations instead of activities had been used in Equation 3–5 ($c_K{}^o/c_K{}^i = 0.1/60 = 1/600$), E_{N_K} would have been -162 mv, which is somewhat lower than the measured potential of -155 mv. Using the concentration ratio, the statement that potassium can be in equilibrium from the bathing solution to the vacuole could not have been made with such certainty.

Equilibrium does not require that the various forces acting on a substance be zero but rather that they cancel each other. In the above example for *Chara*, the factors that tend to cause potassium ions to move are the differences in both the activity and also the electrical potential across the membranes. The activity of potassium was much higher in the vacuole than in the external solution; therefore the activity term in the chemical potential represents a driving force on potassium directed from the inside of the cell to the bathing solution. The electrical potential is considerably lower inside the cell, and hence the electrical driving force on the positively charged potassium ions tends to cause potassium entry into the cell. At equilibrium, these two tendencies for movement in opposite directions are balanced, and no net flux of potassium occurs. However, the chemical potentials of most ions are generally not equal in all phases of interest, and passive movements toward lower μ_j's occur, a topic that we will turn to next.

Fluxes and Diffusion Potentials

Fluxes of many different solutes are continually occurring across biological membranes. Influxes take mineral nutrients into a growing cell while certain products of metabolism flow out of cells. The primary concern of this section will be the passive fluxes of charged solutes, which means the ionic movements in the direction of decreasing chemical potential. Although the mathematical expressions on the next pages are rather formidable, the underlying approach is really quite straightforward. First, the flux of some species is related to the driving force causing the movement. The driving force is then expanded in terms of the relevant components of the chemical potential. Next, the consequences of having simultaneous passive fluxes of more than one type of ion are examined. This leads directly to an expression describing the electrical potential difference across a membrane in terms of the properties of the ions penetrating it.

Flux and Mobility.   To start the analysis, let us consider some charged species j that can cross a particular membrane. At thermodynamic equilibrium, the chemical potential of j, μ_j, does not change with time or position, and there would be no net flux of this solute across the membrane. When μ_j changes with position but not with time, the situation is referred to as a steady state, a condition often used to approximate problems of biological interest. For the moment, μ_j will be allowed to change with both position and time, and later the development will be restricted to the steady state case.

When μ_j is not the same on the two sides of the membrane, a net passive movement or flux of species j, J_j, will occur toward the side with the lower chemical potential. It is the gradient in chemical potential of species j, $\partial\mu_j/\partial x$, which acts as the driving force for this J_j. (As in Chapter 1, the discussion will again be for the one-dimensional case.) The greater $\partial\mu_j/\partial x$, the larger is the flux of species j. As a very useful approximation, J_j is taken to be proportional to $-\partial\mu_j/\partial x$, the minus sign being required as a net positive flux occurs in the direction of decreasing chemical potential. The magnitude of a flux across some plane is also proportional to the local concentration of that solute, c_j, i.e., for a given driving force, the amount that moves across the membrane depends on how much of the substance is actually present. Thus, J_j can be expressed as follows for the one-dimensional case of crossing a plane perpendicular to the x-axis:

$$J_j = u_j c_j \left(-\frac{\partial\mu_j}{\partial x} \right) \tag{3-6}$$

where u_j appearing in Equation 3–6 is called the mobility of species j. A mobility is generally the ratio of some velocity to the force which causes the motion, and it will be considered next for the special case of the solute fluxes under discussion.

Equation 3–6 is a representative example from the large class of expressions relating various flows to their causative forces. In this particular case, J_j is the rate of flow of moles of species j across unit area of the membrane and can be expressed in moles/cm²-sec. Such a molar flux of species j divided by its local concentration gives the mean velocity with which this solute moves across the membrane. For instance, c_j can be in moles/cm³; J_j/c_j then has the units of cm/sec and actually represents the average velocity with which a molecule of j crosses the plane of interest. [Perhaps this important point can be better appreciated by considering it in a different way. Namely, the mean velocity of species j moving across the barrier times the number of those molecules per unit volume which can move (i.e., c_j) gives the flux of that species, J_j.] By Equation 3–6, this average velocity, J_j/c_j, equals the mobility of species j, u_j, times $-\partial\mu_j/\partial x$, the latter being the force on j that causes it to move. Thus the mobility turns out to be simply the proportionality factor between the mean velocity of motion and the causative force. The greater the mobility of some species, the larger is its velocity in response to a given force.

The particular form of the chemical potential of species j, μ_j, to be substituted into Equation 3–6 depends on the specific application in mind. For charged particles moving across biological membranes, the appropriate μ_j is $\mu_j{}^* + RT \ln a_j + z_j FE$. (As mentioned before, the $\bar{V}_j P$ term makes only a relatively small contribution to μ_j of ions and therefore is not included.) For treating the one-dimensional case described by Equation 3–6, μ_j must be differentiated with respect to x, which leads to $RT (\partial \ln a_j/\partial x) + z_j F (\partial E/\partial x)$ in the present case. The quantity $\partial \ln a_j/\partial x$ equals $(1/a_j)(\partial a_j/\partial x)$, which is $(1/\gamma_j c_j)(\partial \gamma_j c_j/\partial x)$ $[a_j = \gamma_j c_j$ (Eq. 2–5)]. Using the above form of μ_j appropriate for charged solutes and this expansion of the derivative, $\partial \ln a_j/\partial x$, the net flux of species j appearing in Equation 3–6 can be written

$$J_j = -\frac{u_j RT}{\gamma_j} \frac{\partial \gamma_j c_j}{\partial x} - u_j c_j z_j F \frac{\partial E}{\partial x} \qquad (3\text{–}7)$$

Equation 3–7 is a general expression for the one-dimensional flux of species j across a membrane or even just in a free solution in terms of the driving forces: the gradients in activity and electrical potential.

Before proceeding, let us examine a little more closely the first term on the right-hand side of Equation 3–7. When γ_j varies across the membrane, $\partial \gamma_j/\partial x$ can be considered to represent a driving force on species j. For constant γ_j, the first term on the right-hand side of Equation 3–7 becomes simply $-u_j RT(\partial c_j/\partial x)$, i.e., it is proportional to the concentration gradient. In the absence of electrical potential gradients ($\partial E/\partial x = 0$) or for neutral solutes ($z_j = 0$), equation 3–7 then indicates that J_j equals $-u_j RT(\partial c_j/\partial x)$. But this is just the type of flux described by Fick's first law $[J = -D \, \partial c/\partial x$ (Eq. 1–1)] with $u_j RT$ taking the place of the diffusion coefficient, D. (The only driving force considered in Chapter 1 was in fact the concentration gradient.) This agreement between the present thermodynamic approach and the *seemingly* more empirical Fick's first law is quite important. It serves to justify the logarithmic term for activity in the chemical potential $[\mu_j = \mu_j{}^* + RT \ln a_j + \bar{V}_j P + z_j FE$ (Eq. 2–4)]. In other words, if the activity of species j appeared in Equation 2–4 in a form other than $\ln a_j$, then Equation 3–7 would not reduce to Fick's first law under the appropriate conditions. Since Fick's first law has been amply demonstrated experimentally, such a disagreement between theory and practice would necessitate some modification in the expression that was used to define chemical potential. Stated another way, Equation 2–4 must be able to stand the test of being experimentally checked.

The various terms in the chemical potential can be justified or "derived" by different methods, such as the above comparison with Fick's first law which indicates that the ln a_j form is the appropriate way of handling the activity term. It should be pointed out, however, that all such derivations are based on conclusions from empirical observations. Rather than being all-inclusive theoretical formulations, thermodynamic expressions for the chemical potential like Equation 2–4 are really only approximations that have been found to agree with experiment. Nevertheless they are extremely valuable since they can be used to describe closely and elegantly rather complicated phenomena, as is indicated throughout this text.

In contrast to the case for a neutral solute, the flux of a charged particle also depends on an electrical driving force, which is represented in Equation 3–7 by $-\partial E/\partial x$. A charged solute spontaneously tends to move in an electrical potential gradient—a cation moving in the direction of lower or decreasing electrical potential. This is analogous to a neutral solute diffusing in the direction of decreasing concentration. Of course, the concentration gradient also affects charged particles. For instance, if a certain type of ion were present in some region but absent in an adjacent one, the ions would diffuse into the latter region. As such charged particles diffuse toward regions of lower concentration, an electrical potential difference is created. This electrical potential difference is referred to as a diffusion potential (to be discussed in detail below). It turns out that the interrelationship between concentration and electrical effects is extremely important in biology since most membrane potentials are in large part diffusion potentials which arise because of different rates of movement of the various ions across the membrane.

Diffusion Potential in a Solution. Let us now use Equation 3–7 to derive the electrical potential difference created by ions diffusing down a concentration gradient in a solution containing one type of cation and its accompanying anion. This derivation is relatively simple compared with the more biological one to follow, and thus it may more clearly illustrate the relationship between concentration gradients and the accompanying electrical potential differences. It is assumed that initially the cations and the anions are concentrated at one side of the solution. In time, they will *diffuse* across the solution to regions of lower concentration. In general, one of the ionic species will have a higher mobility, u_j, than the other. Ions of the former type will tend to diffuse faster than their oppositely charged partners, resulting in a microscopic charge separation. This slight charge separation sets up an electrical potential gradient leading to the diffusion potential. Under certain simplifying assumptions to be presented next, the magnitude of the electrical potential difference so created can be fairly readily calculated.

For convenience of analysis, consider the case where only two monovalent species are present in some solution, a cation $(+)$ and an anion $(-)$, and assume that their activity coefficients are constant. As the previous calculations on electrical effects have indicated, solutions are essentially neutral in regions that are large compared with atomic dimensions. Thus, c_+ equals c_-, and the concentration of either species can be designated as c. Furthermore, no charge imbalance will develop in time, which means that the flux of the cation across some plane in the solution equals that of the anion across the same plane. (A very small charge imbalance does develop which sets up the electrical potential gradient, but this unbalanced flux is transitory and in any case negligible compared with J_+ or J_-.) Both of the fluxes, J_+ and J_-, can be expressed by Equation 3–7 and then equated to each other, which gives

$$- u_+ RT \frac{\partial c}{\partial x} - u_+ cF \frac{\partial E}{\partial x} = - u_- RT \frac{\partial c}{\partial x} + u_- cF \frac{\partial E}{\partial x} \qquad (3\text{–}8)$$

where the plus sign on the right-hand side of Equation 3–8 occurs because the monovalent anion has a negative charge $(z_- = -1)$. Rearrangement of Equation 3–8 yields the following expression for the electrical potential gradient:

$$\frac{\partial E}{\partial x} = \frac{u_- - u_+}{u_+ + u_-} \frac{RT}{Fc} \frac{\partial c}{\partial x} \qquad (3\text{–}9)$$

Equation 3–9 indicates that a nonzero $\partial E/\partial x$ occurs when the mobilities of the anion and cation are different. If u_- is greater than u_+, the anions move or diffuse faster than the cations. As some individual anion moves ahead of its partner cation, an electric field is set up in such a direction as to speed up the cation and slow down the anion until they both move at the same speed, thus preserving electrical neutrality.

To obtain the difference in electrical potential produced by diffusion across the planes of differing concentration, Equation 3–9 must be integrated. In going from region I to region II, the change in electrical potential is $\int_{I}^{II}(\partial E/\partial x)dx$ or $E^{II} - E^{I}$ while the concentration term is $\int_{I}^{II}(1/c)(\partial c/\partial x)dx$, or $\ln(c^{II}/c^{I})$. Using these two relations, Equation 3–9 becomes

$$E^{II} - E^{I} = 59.2 \frac{u_- - u_+}{u_+ + u_-} \log\frac{c^{II}}{c^{I}} \text{ mv at } 25° \qquad (3\text{–}10)$$

where ln has been replaced by 2.303 log and the value 59.2 mv at 25° has been substituted for 2.303 RT/F (Appendix III). In the general case, the anions and the cations have different mobilities. As such ions diffuse to regions of lower chemical potential in the solution, an electrical potential difference—given by Equation 3–10 and called a diffusion potential—is set up across the concentration gradient.

A diffusion potential occurs at the open end of the special salt-bridges used for measuring electrical potentials across membranes, these salt-bridges commonly being referred to as microelectrodes. Such salt-bridges are hollow glass tubes drawn to a fine tip and filled with an electrolyte solution. The measuring electrode and its electrical lead are connected to the thick end of the glass tube while the fine end is open and provides an electrically con-ducting pathway into the cell or tissue. Ions diffuse from this fine tip and give a diffusion potential between the interior of the salt-bridge and the aqueous compartment into which the tip is inserted. This potential is in series with the biological potential being measured and, consequently, is added to it. To estimate the magnitude of this unwanted but ever-present potential, a concentration ratio of 100 across the salt-bridge tip will be assumed, and the diffusion potential for a typical electrolyte, NaCl, will be calculated using Equation 3–10. The mobility ratio, u_{Cl}/u_{Na}, is about 1.52 and so $(u_- - u_+)/(u_+ + u_-)$ is $(0.52)/(2.52)$ or 0.21. In going from a region where the concentration of NaCl is say 100 mM to one where it is 1 mM, the diffusion potential calculated from Equation 3–10 is $(59.2)(0.21)\log(1/100)$ or -25 mv. When measuring biological membrane potentials, this is an unacceptably large diffusion potential across the tip of the special salt-bridge. On the other hand, for KCl as the electrolyte, the mobility ratio of anion to cation, u_{Cl}/u_{K}, is 1.04, and thus $(u_- - u_+)/(u_+ + u_-)$ is $(0.04)/(2.04)$ or 0.02. This leads to a diffusion potential of $(59.2)(0.02)\log(1/100)$ or only -2 mv when the concentration ratio is 100. Thus KCl is a much more suitable electrolyte for the salt-bridges than is NaCl from the point of view of minimizing the diffusion potential across the fine tip.

Membrane Fluxes. As is the case for diffusion potentials in free solution, membrane potentials also depend on the different mobilities of the various ions. However, in this case the "solution" in which the diffusion takes place toward regions of lower chemical potential is actually the membrane itself. The discussion in Chapter 1 indicated that a membrane is often the main barrier or rate-limiting step for the diffusion of molecules into and out of cells or organelles, and, consequently, it is expected to be the phase across which the diffusion potential is expressed. Under biological conditions, a number of different types of ions are present, and so the situation is more complex than for the single cation-anion pair analyzed above. Furthermore, the quantities of interest such as $\partial E/\partial x$ and γ_j are those within the membrane, and hence they are not accessible to experimental measurement. The ways of dealing with these difficulties will now be considered.

To calculate membrane diffusion potentials, certain assumptions are necessary before an integration of fluxes or gradients can be made across the membrane. As a start, the electrical potential, E, will be assumed to vary linearly with distance across the membrane. This means that $\partial E/\partial x$ is a constant equal to $E_M/\Delta x$, where E_M is the electrical potential difference across the membrane and Δx is the membrane thickness. This assumption of a constant electric field across the membrane was originally suggested by D. E. Goldman. It appreciably simplifies the integration conditions leading to an expression describing the electrical potential difference across biological membranes. As another very useful approximation, the activity coefficient of species j, γ_j, will be assumed to be constant across the membrane (a less severe restriction than setting it equal to 1). As discussed in Chapter 1, a partition coefficient is needed to describe concentrations within a membrane since the solvent properties of a membrane are different from those of the aqueous solutions on either side of it where the concentrations are actually determined. Thus, c_j appearing in Equation 3–7 should be replaced by $K_j c_j$, where K_j is the partition coefficient for species j. Incorporating these various simplifications and conditions, one can rewrite Equation 3–7 as follows, after transferring the electrical term to the left-hand side:

$$u_j K_j c_j z_j F \frac{E_M}{\Delta x} + J_j = -u_j RT K_j \frac{\partial c_j}{\partial x} \qquad (3\text{–}11)$$

To cast Equation 3–11 into a form that can be integrated, it is advantageous to put all terms containing the concentration on the same side of the equation. Furthermore, since the two most convenient variables are c_j and x, their differentials should appear on opposite sides of the equation.

Being guided by these two objectives and after multiplying each term by $\Delta x/u_j z_j F E_M$, Equation 3–11 can be rearranged to give the following expression:

$$\frac{z_j F E_M}{RT \Delta x}\, dx = -\frac{K_j dc_j}{K_j c_j + \dfrac{J_j \Delta x}{u_j z_j F E_M}} \tag{3-12}$$

where $(\partial c_j/\partial x)\, dx$ has been replaced by dc_j in anticipation of the restriction to steady-state conditions.

When the term $J_j \Delta x/(u_j z_j F E_M)$ is constant, Equation 3–12 can be readily integrated from one side of the membrane to the other. The factors Δx, z_j, F, and E_M are all fixed, and so only J_j and u_j need be further considered. The flux J_j is generally assumed not to change with time or position, a situation known as a steady state. A steady-state value for J_j means that the fluxes of species j through any plane parallel to and within the membrane are all the same; therefore the concentration of species j in these regions is not changing with time, i.e., the ions are not accumulating or being depleted in any of the regions of interest. The mobility, u_j, of each species is also assumed to be constant within the membrane. With these two restrictions, the quantity $J_j \Delta x/(u_j z_j F E_M)$ becomes a constant, and Equation 3–12 can be integrated from one side of the membrane (the outside, o) to the other (the inside, i). Since $\int_{x^o}^{x^i} dx$ equals Δx, this integration gives

$$\frac{z_j F E_M}{RT} = \ln \frac{\left(K_j c_j{}^o + \dfrac{J_j \Delta x}{u_j z_j F E_M} \right)}{\left(K_j c_j{}^i + \dfrac{J_j \Delta x}{u_j z_j F E_M} \right)} \tag{3-13}$$

After taking exponentials of both sides to put Equation 3–13 into a more convenient form, it becomes

$$K_j c_j{}^i\, e^{z_j F E_M / RT} + \frac{J_j \Delta x}{u_j z_j F E_M}\, e^{z_j F E_M / RT} = K_j c_j{}^o + \frac{J_j \Delta x}{u_j z_j F E_M} \tag{3-14}$$

A quantity of considerable interest appearing in Equation 3–14 is J_j, the net flux of species j. This equation can be readily solved for J_j, giving

$$J_j = J_j{}^{in} - J_j{}^{out} = \left(\frac{K_j u_j z_j F E_M}{\Delta x} \right)\left(\frac{1}{e^{z_j F E_M / RT} - 1} \right)(c_j{}^o - c_j{}^i\, e^{z_j F E_M / RT}) \tag{3-15}$$

where J_j^{in} is the influx of species j, J_j^{out} is the efflux, and thus their difference is the net flux. Although the mathematical manipulations necessary to go from Equation 3–11 to Equation 3–15 are lengthy and cumbersome, the resulting expression is of extreme importance for understanding both membrane potentials and passive fluxes of ions. It will be used to derive the Goldman equation, which describes the diffusion potential across membranes, and later will be invoked in the derivation of the Ussing-Teorell equation, a relation obeyed by certain passive fluxes.

Equation 3–15 shows how the passive flux of some charged species j depends on the internal and the external concentrations and on the electrical potential difference across the membrane. For most cell membranes, E_M is negative, i.e., the inside of the cell is at a lower electrical potential than the outside. For a cation ($z_j > 0$) and a negative E_M, the terms in the first two parentheses on the right-hand side of Equation 3–15 are both negative, and their product, therefore, is positive. For an anion ($z_j > 0$) and a negative E_M, on the other hand, both parentheses are positive, and their product is still positive (for $E_M > 0$, the product of the first two parentheses is also positive for both anions and cations). Thus, the sign of J_j depends on the value of c_j^o relative to that of $c_j^i\, e^{z_j F E_M / RT}$. When c_j^o is greater than $c_j^i\, e^{z_j F E_M / RT}$, the expression in the last parenthesis of Equation 3–15 is positive, and a net inward flux of species j occurs ($J_j > 0$). Such a condition may be contrasted with Equation 1–8, where the net flux in the absence of electrical effects was inward when c^o was simply larger than c^i, as would adequately describe the situation for neutral solutes. However, knowledge of the concentration difference alone is not sufficient to predict the magnitude or even the direction of the flux of ions; rather, the electrical potential difference between the two regions under consideration must also be taken into account.

Membrane Diffusion Potential—Goldman Equation. Passive ionic fluxes, which can each be described by Equation 3–15 and are caused by gradients in the chemical potentials of the various ions, create an electrical potential difference across a membrane that is known as the diffusion potential. This electrical potential difference can be determined by considering the contributions from all of the ionic fluxes across the membrane and the condition of electroneutrality although certain assumptions are needed to keep the equations manageable. Under usual biological situations, not all anions and cations can easily move through the membranes. For example, many divalent cations do not readily enter or leave plant cells passively, which means that their mobility in the membranes is small. Such ions usually do not make a large enough contribution to the fluxes into or out of plant cells to influence markedly the diffusion potentials across the membranes; thus they will be omitted in the present analysis, which nevertheless becomes rather complicated.

For many plant cells, the total ionic flux consists mainly of movements of K^+, Na^+, and Cl^-. These three ions are generally in fairly high concentrations in and near plant cells, and thus they would be expected to make substantial contributions to the overall ionic fluxes. It should be mentioned at the outset that in some cases there may also be a sizable flux of H^+ or OH^- as well as other ions, the restriction to three ions here being partially in the interest of algebraic simplicity. However, the real justification for considering only K^+, Na^+, and Cl^- is that the diffusion potentials that are calculated by using the passive fluxes of these three ions across biological membranes are often in very good agreement with the measured electrical potential differences. The previous electrical calculations have indicated that solutions are essentially neutral, a condition that will again be invoked here. (Because of the large effects resulting from small amounts of uncanceled charge, the microscopic net charge actually needed to cause the electrical potential difference across a membrane is negligible compared with the existing concentrations of ions.) Furthermore, the steady-state fluxes of the ions across the membrane will not change this condition of electrical neutrality, which means that no net charge is transported by the algebraic sum of the various charge movements across the membrane. When the bulk of the ionic flux consists of K^+, Na^+, and Cl^- movements, this important condition of electroneutrality can be described by equating the cationic fluxes ($J_K + J_{Na}$) to the anionic one (J_{Cl}), which leads to the following relation (as mentioned above, the various ions are indicated by using only their atomic symbols as subscripts):

$$J_K + J_{Na} - J_{Cl} = 0 \qquad (3\text{--}16)$$

Equation 3–16 describes the net ionic fluxes which lead to the electrical potential difference across the membrane. After substituting the expressions for the various J_j's into Equation 3–16, the resulting equation will be solved for the diffusion potential, E_M.

To obtain a useful expression for E_M in terms of measurable parameters, it is convenient to introduce a permeability coefficient for species j, P_j. In Chapter 1, a permeability coefficient, P, was defined as $DK/\Delta x$, where D is the diffusion coefficient, K is the partition coefficient, and Δx is the membrane thickness. Upon comparing Equation 3–7 with Equation 1–1, one can see that $u_j RT$ takes the place of the diffusion coefficient of species j, as was pointed out above. Analogous to the definition employed in Chapter 1, the quantity $K_j u_j RT / \Delta x$ can similarly be defined as the permeability coefficient, P_j, of species j for some particular membrane. In this way, the unknown mobility of species j in a given membrane, the unknown thickness of the membrane, and the partition coefficient for the solute can be replaced by one term to describe the permeability properties of that solute crossing the particular membrane under consideration.

With all the preliminaries out of the way, let us now determine the expression for the diffusion potential across a membrane for the case where most of the ionic flux is due to K^+, Na^+, and Cl^- movements. Using the permeability coefficients of the three ions and substituting the net flux of each species defined by Equation 3–15, Equation 3–16 becomes

$$P_K \left(\frac{1}{e^{FE_M/RT} - 1} \right) (c_K{}^\circ - c_K{}^i \, e^{FE_M/RT}) + P_{Na} \left(\frac{1}{e^{FE_M/RT} - 1} \right)$$

$$\times (c_{Na}{}^\circ - c_{Na}{}^i \, e^{FE_M/RT}) + P_{Cl} \left(\frac{1}{e^{-FE_M/RT} - 1} \right) (c_{Cl}{}^\circ - c_{Cl}{}^i \, e^{-FE_M/RT}) = 0$$

$$(3\text{–}17)$$

where z_K and z_{Na} have been replaced by 1 in Equation 3–17, z_{Cl} by -1, and FE_M/RT has been canceled from each of the terms for the three net fluxes. To simplify this rather unwieldly expression, the quantity $1/(e^{FE_M/RT} - 1)$ can be canceled from each of the three terms represented in Equation 3–17. $[1/(e^{-FE_M/RT} - 1)$ appearing in the last term is the same as $-e^{FE_M/RT}/(e^{FE_M/RT} - 1)$.] Equation 3–17 then assumes a much more manageable form:

$$P_K c_K{}^\circ - P_K c_K{}^i \, e^{FE_M/RT} + P_{Na} c_{Na}{}^\circ - P_{Na} c_{Na}{}^i \, e^{FE_M/RT}$$

$$- P_{Cl} c_{Cl}{}^\circ \, e^{FE_M/RT} + P_{Cl} c_{Cl}{}^i = 0$$

$$(3\text{–}18)$$

After solving Equation 3–18 for $e^{FE_M/RT}$ and taking logarithms, one obtains the following expression for the electrical potential difference across the membrane:

$$E_M = \frac{RT}{F} \ln \frac{(P_K c_K{}^\circ + P_{Na} c_{Na}{}^\circ + P_{Cl} c_{Cl}{}^i)}{(P_K c_K{}^i + P_{Na} c_{Na}{}^i + P_{Cl} c_{Cl}{}^\circ)} \qquad (3\text{–}19)$$

Equation 3–19 is known as the Goldman or constant field equation and gives the diffusion potential existing across a membrane. It has been derived by assuming independent passive movements of K^+, Na^+, and Cl^- across a membrane in which $\partial E/\partial x$, γ_j, J_j, and u_j are all constant. The driving force for the net flux of each ion was taken as the gradient of its chemical potential. Thus, Equation 3–19 gives the electrical potential difference arising from the different tendencies of K^+, Na^+, and Cl^- to *diffuse* across a membrane to regions of lower chemical potential. When other ions cross some particular membrane in appreciable amounts, they will also make a contribution to its membrane potential. However, the inclusion of divalent and trivalent ions in the derivation of an expression for E_M complicates the algebra considerably. Frequently, the fluxes of such ions are rather small and may be neglected, in which case Equation 3–19 may be adequate for describing the membrane potential.

Application of the Goldman Equation.   In certain cases, the terms appearing in Equation 3–19, viz., the permeabilities and the internal and the external concentrations of potassium, sodium, and chloride, can all be measured, and the validity of the Goldman equation can be experimentally checked. In other words, the predicted diffusion potential can be compared with the actual electrical potential difference existing across the membrane. As a specific example, the Goldman equation will be used here to evaluate the membrane potential across the plasmalemma of *Nitella translucens*.

The concentrations of K^+, Na^+, and Cl^- in the external bathing solution and in the cytoplasm of *Nitella translucens* are given in Table 3–1. E. A. C. MacRobbie found the ratio of the permeability of sodium to that of potassium, P_{Na}/P_K, to be about 0.18 for *Nitella translucens*. The plasmalemma of *Nitella* is much less permeable to chloride than it is to potassium, probably only 0.1% to 1% as much. Thus, for purposes of calculation, P_{Cl}/P_K can be taken as 0.003. In terms of permeabilities relative to that for potassium, P_K for *Nitella* then is 1.00, P_{Na} is 0.18, and P_{Cl} is 0.003. Using these relative permeability coefficients and the concentrations given in Table 3–1, the argument of the logarithm appearing in Equation 3–19, $(P_K c_K^\circ + P_{Na} c_{Na}^\circ + P_{Cl} c_{Cl}^i)/(P_K c_K^i + P_{Na} c_{Na}^i + P_{Cl} c_{Cl}^\circ)$, has the numerical value of $[(1.0)(0.1) + (0.18)(1.0) + (0.003)(65)]$ divided by $[(1.0)(119) + (0.18)(14) + (0.003)(1.3)]$, which is $(0.475)/(121.5)$ or 0.00391. Since ln is 2.303 log and 2.303 RT/F equals 58.2 mv at 20° (Appendix III), the Goldman equation predicts a membrane potential, E_M, of (58.2) log (0.00391) or -140 mv. Thus the cytoplasm is expected to be electrically negative with respect to the external bathing solution, as is indeed the case. In fact, the measured value of the electrical potential difference across the plasmalemma of *Nitella translucens* is -138 mv at $20°$ (Table 3–1). This excellent agreement between the observed electrical potential difference and that calculated from the Goldman equation supports the contention that the membrane potential is a diffusion potential. This point can be checked fairly easily by varying the external concentration of K^+, Na^+, and/or Cl^- and then seeing whether the membrane potential changes in accordance with Equation 3–19.

The different ionic concentrations on the two sides of the membrane set up the passive ionic fluxes creating the diffusion potential, but the actual magnitude of the contribution of a particular ionic species to E_M also depends on the ease with which that type of ion can cross the membrane. For instance, based on the relative permeabilities, the major contribution to the electrical potential difference across the plasmalemma of *Nitella* comes from the potassium and sodium fluxes, with chloride playing a secondary role. Specifically, if the chloride terms are omitted from Equation 3–19 (i.e., if P_{Cl} is set equal to zero), the membrane potential that is calculated is -153 mv, compared with -140 mv when chloride is included. This rather small difference between the two potentials is a reflection of the relatively low permeability coefficient for chloride crossing the plasmalemma of *Nitella*, and hence chloride fluxes have a lesser effect on E_M than do potassium or sodium fluxes.

It should be pointed out that changes in the amount of calcium in the external medium cause some deviations from the predictions of Equation 3–19 for the electrical potential difference across the plasmalemma of *Nitella*. Thus the diffusion potential is influenced by the properties of the particular membrane being considered, and ions other than potassium, sodium, and chloride may need to be included in specific cases. Nevertheless, restriction to these three ions has proved to be adequate for treating the diffusion potential across many membranes, and thus the Goldman or constant field expression in the form of Equation 3–19 has found widespread application.

Donnan Potential.   Another type of electrical potential difference encountered in biological systems and referred to as a Donnan potential is associated with immobile or fixed charges in some solid phase adjacent to an aqueous phase. Such an electrical potential difference arising from electrostatic interactions at a solid-liquid interface can be viewed as a special type of diffusion potential as will be indicated shortly. Two examples of solid phases adjacent to which Donnan potentials occur in plants are cell walls and membranes.

Pectin and other compounds in the cell wall have a large number of immobile carboxyl groups ($-COOH$) from which hydrogen ions dissociate,

Donnan phase

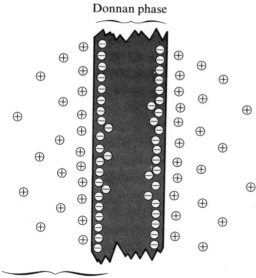

Figure 3–1. Distribution of positively charged ions ($\oplus$) occurring on either side of a Donnan phase in which are embedded immobile negative charges ($\ominus$).

Electrical double layer

which gives the cell wall a net negative charge, as mentioned in Chapter 1 This negativity electrostatically attracts cations such as Ca^{++} to the cell wall, and the overall effect is an exchange of H^+ with Ca^{++}. (Such an attraction of positively charged species to the cell wall increases the local concentration of solutes, and consequently a greater osmotic pressure generally exists in the cell wall than in the adjacent aqueous solutions.) The region containing the immobile charged particles, such as carboxyl groups in the case of the cell wall, is generally referred to as the Donnan phase. (See Fig. 3–1.) At equilibrium, a distribution of oppositely charged ions that are electrostatically attracted to the immobile charges occurs between the Donnan phase and the adjacent aqueous one, as is indicated in Figure 3–1; this sets up an electrical potential gradient and thus a Donnan potential. The sign of the electrical potential in the Donnan phase relative to the surrounding electrolyte solution is the same as the sign of the charge of the immobile ions. For instance, because of the presence of dissociated carboxyl groups, the electrical potential in the cell wall is negative with respect to the external solution or to the aqueous phase on the inner side of the wall. Donnan phases also occur in the cytoplasm, where the immobile charges are often due to proteins. These proteins are fixed in the sense that they are unable to diffuse across either the plasmalemma or the tonoplast.

When the immobile or fixed ions are in a planar layer, the mobile ions of opposite sign occur in an adjacent layer, the composite being referred to as an electrical double layer, which is shown in Figure 3–1. For instance, layers containing cations are often formed in the aqueous solutions on each side of biological membranes, which generally act as Donnan phases having a net negative charge. (Incidentally, the electrical potential changes or Donnan potentials on either side of the membrane, cf. Fig. 3–1, are in opposite directions and therefore are *assumed* to cancel out when calculating a diffusion potential across the membrane.) At equilibrium, no net movement of the ions occurs, and so the chemical potentials of each of the mobile ions (e.g., K^+, Na^+, Cl^-, Ca^{++}) have the same values up close to the Donnan phase as they do in the surrounding aqueous phase. The potential difference or Donnan potential across the electrical double layer can thus be calculated by equating the chemical potentials on the two sides of it. But this is exactly the same principle used to derive the Nernst potential $[E_{N_j} = E^{II} - E^I = (59.2/z_j) \log (a_j^I/a_j^{II})$ mv at 25° (Eq. 3–5)] between two aqueous compartments. In fact, since again the argument hinges on the constancy of the chemical potential, the distribution of any ion in equilibrium across the electrical double layer going from the Donnan phase to the aqueous phase that extends away from the barrier must satisfy the Nernst potential, E_{N_j}, for that particular ion. Thus from the ratio of the activities or concentrations, the electrical potential difference across the double layer can be calculated by using Equation 3–5.

The electrical potential difference known as the Donnan potential can also be viewed as a special case of a diffusion potential, as suggested above. To see why this is so, imagine that the mobile ions tend to diffuse away from the fixed immobile ions of the opposite sign. For instance, it could be assumed that initially the mobile ions were placed in the same region as the immobile ones, but in time the mobile ions would tend to diffuse away. This tendency based on thermal agitation causes a slight charge separation and thus sets up an electrical potential difference across the double layer. For the case of a single species of mobile cations and the anions fixed in the membrane (both assumed here to be monovalent), the diffusion potential across the electrical double layer can be described by Equation 3–10 $[E^{II} - E^I = 59.2 (u_- - u_+)/(u_+ + u_-) \log (c^{II}/c^I)$ mv at 25°], which was derived for diffusion toward regions of lower chemical potential in a solution. Fixed anions have zero mobility $(u_- = 0)$, and so $(u_- - u_+)/(u_+ + u_-)$ is here $-u_+/u_+$ or -1. Equation 3–10 then becomes $E^{II} - E^I$ equals $-59.2 \log (c^{II}/c^I)$ mv at 25°, which is simply the Nernst potential (Eq. 3–5) for monovalent cations $[-\log (c^{II}/c^I) = \log (c^I/c^{II})]$. Thus, the Donnan potential can also be viewed as a type of diffusion potential occurring as the mobile ions tend to diffuse away from the charges of opposite sign that remain fixed in the solid Donnan phase.

Active Transport

Active transport implies that energy derived from metabolic processes is somehow involved in moving a solute in the energetically uphill direction across a membrane. There are three different aspects to this description of active transport, viz., a supply of energy, movement, and an increase in chemical potential. By itself a difference in chemical potential of a certain species across a membrane does not necessarily imply active transport. For instance, if the solute does not penetrate the membrane, then the solute is unable to attain equilibrium across it, and μ_j would not be the same on the two sides. For ions actually moving across some membrane, the ratio of the influx to the efflux of a particular ionic species provides information which helps indicate whether or not active transport is taking place. Specifically, the Ussing-Teorell or flux ratio equation to be derived below will be satisfied for that species, if it moves passively and independently across the membrane. A very simple and often effective approach for determining whether fluxes are active or passive is to remove possible energy sources. For photosynthesizing plant tissue, this can mean comparing the fluxes in the light with those in the dark. (In addition, one should check whether the permeability of the membrane changes or other alterations occur.) Compounds or treatments which disrupt metabolism also can be useful for ascertaining whether metabolic energy is being used for the active transport of various solutes.

One of the possible consequences of actively transporting a certain ionic species into a cell or organelle is the development of an excess of electrical charge inside the membrane-surrounded entity. If the active transport process of that ionic species involves an accompanying ion of opposite charge or an equal release of a similarly charged ion, then the total charge in the cell or organelle is unaffected. However, if the charge of the actively transported ion is not directly compensated, the process is electrogenic, i.e., it tends to generate an electrical potential difference across the membrane. An electrogenic uptake of an ion which gives a net transport of charge into the cell or organelle will thus affect the membrane potential. Such an electrogenic process causes an adjustment of the passive fluxes across the membrane so that the net charge actively brought in is eventually electrically compensated for by appropriate passive movements of other ions into or out of the cell. The actual electrical potential difference across the membrane results from the diffusion potential caused by these new passive fluxes plus a contribution from the electrogenic process involving the active transport of some charged species.

In this section, we will compare the temperature dependencies of metabolic reactions with those for diffusion processes across a barrier to show that a marked enhancement of solute uptake caused by increasing the temperature does not necessarily indicate active transport. Next, we will consider a much more reliable criterion for deciding whether fluxes are passive or not, viz., the Ussing-Teorell or flux ratio equation. After examining a specific case where active transport is involved, we will discuss a relationship often invoked for describing the concentration dependence of ion uptake.

Q_{10}, a Temperature Coefficient. Most metabolic reactions have a fairly strong dependence on temperature compared with processes like diffusion in a free solution, which are often rather insensitive to temperature. Thus a doubling of the rate of ion uptake into a tissue when the temperature is raised by 10° centigrade has sometimes been thought to indicate that metabolic energy is being used in active transport, but the following discussion suggests that such a marked stimulation by a temperature increase could also occur for passive diffusion across a membrane. For many types of reactions, there is a minimum energy required before the process will take place. Therefore, to analyze the effect of temperature on the rate of reactions, an expression describing the distribution of energy among the molecules as a function of temperature is needed in order to determine what fraction of the molecules has the requisite energy for a particular process. In aqueous solutions, the relevant energy leading to the specific event being considered is generally the kinetic energy of motion of the species involved.

The range of kinetic energies possessed by molecules at equilibrium at a given temperature is closely approximated by a Boltzmann distribution. In the present case, such an energy distribution indicates that the number of molecules with kinetic energy U per molecule resulting from velocities in some particular direction is proportional to $(1/\sqrt{T})\, e^{-U/kT}$, where k is the Boltzmann constant [8.617 $\times$ 10^{-5} electron volts (ev)/°K, where 1 ev is the energy acquired by a particle of unit electronic charge when it moves through an electrical potential difference of 1 volt]. As mentioned above, a minimum kinetic energy, which can be represented by U_B, is often necessary to diffuse past some barrier or to cause some specific reaction. Thus any molecule with a kinetic energy of U_B or greater has sufficient energy for the particular process. For the Boltzmann energy distribution, the number of such molecules is proportional to $\int_{U_B}^{\infty} (1/\sqrt{T})e^{-U/kT}\, dU$, where infinity ($\infty$) has been taken as the theoretical upper limit for the kinetic energy. Upon integration, this quantity can be shown to equal $k\sqrt{T}\, e^{-U_B/kT}$, an expression to be used below. (These expressions having the factor $\sqrt{T}$ apply only to one-dimensional cases, e.g., for molecules diffusing across a membrane.)

In many studies, the effect of temperature on some particular process has been investigated to help see whether metabolic energy is involved. Using the above consideration of the Boltzmann energy distribution, the number of molecules having the requisite energy is proportional to $k\sqrt{T}\, e^{-U_B/kT}$, where U_B is the minimum kinetic energy needed to surmount the energy barrier involved in the process. At a temperature 10° higher, the number is proportional to $k\sqrt{(T+10)}\, e^{-U_B/[k(T+10)]}$. The ratio of these two quantities is called the Q_{10} or temperature coefficient of the process:

$$Q_{10} = \sqrt{\frac{T+10}{T}}\ e^{\frac{10U_B}{kT\,(T+10)}} \tag{3-20}$$

A Q_{10} near 1 is characteristic of some passive processes which have no energy barrier to surmount, i.e., where U_B equals 0. On the other hand, most enzymatic reactions take place only when the reactants have a considerable kinetic energy, and so such processes tend to be quite sensitive to temperature. A value of 2 or greater for Q_{10} is thus often taken to indicate the involvement of metabolism, such as occurs for active transport of a solute into a cell or organelle. However, Equation 3–20 indicates that any process having an appreciable energy barrier, U_B, can have a large temperature coefficient.

The value of the temperature coefficient Q_{10} for a particular process can be indicative of the minimum kinetic energy required, U_B, and vice versa. For instance, for the case of diffusion in a solution, U_B may be near zero, and Q_{10} can be taken to equal $\sqrt{(T+10)/T}$ by Equation 3–20. For a temperature T of 20° (293°K), Q_{10} is then $\sqrt{(303/293)}$ or 1.02. Such a temperature coefficient close to 1 has been observed for diffusion in a free solution. On the other hand, a membrane often represents an appreciable energy barrier to diffusion of charged solutes, and the U_B for passive ion movement across it can be 0.50 ev/molecule. Using Equation 3–20, this would lead to a temperature coefficient for T equaling 20° of $\sqrt{(303/293)}e^{(10)(0.50)/[(8.617\times10^{-5})(293)(303)]}$ or $1.02\, e^{0.654}$, which equals 1.96. In other words, the uptake of this particular ion would approximately double for only a 10° increase in temperature.

This example indicates that a passive process can have a rather high Q_{10}. A kinetic energy of 0.50 ev or greater is possessed by only a relatively few molecules in the Boltzmann energy distribution. [1 ev/molecule is 23.06 kcal/mole (Appendix III), and so 0.50 ev/molecule is 11.5 kcal/mole.] As T is raised, the number of such molecules in the high energy part of the Boltzmann distribution increases greatly; thus many more molecules have the requisite kinetic energy, U_B, and consequently can take part in the process being considered. Thus an appreciable energy barrier can lead to a large temperature coefficient for a passive diffusion process, indicating that a high Q_{10} does not necessarily imply active transport.

Ussing-Teorell Equation.   One of the most useful physicochemical criteria for deciding whether a particular ionic movement across a membrane is active or passive is the application of the Ussing-Teorell or flux ratio equation. For ions moving passively, this expression shows how the ratio of the influx to the efflux depends on parameters such as concentrations and the electrical potential difference across the membrane. If the Ussing-Teorell equation is satisfied, active transport of the ions need not be invoked. This expression can be readily derived by considering how the influx and the efflux could be separately determined experimentally, as the following arguments indicate.

For measuring the influx of a certain ion, J_j^{in}, the plant cell or tissue can be placed in a solution containing a radioactive isotope of species j. Initially, none of the radioisotope is inside the cells, and the internal concentration, c_j^i, for this isotope equals zero at the beginning of the experiment. Since none is inside, the initial efflux of the radioisotope, J_j^{out}, is zero, and the initial net flux (J_j) of the isotope thus reflects J_j^{in}. From equation 3–15, this influx of the radioisotope can be represented by $(K_j u_j z_j F E_M / \Delta x) [(1/(e^{z_j F E_M / RT} - 1)] c_j^o$. After the isotope has entered the cell, some of it will start coming out. Hence only the initial flux will give an accurate measure of the influx of the radioisotope of species j. Let us assume that once the radioactivity has built up inside to a substantial level, the radioisotope is removed from the outside solution. The flux of the isotope will then be from inside the cells to the external solution. In this case, c_j^o for the radioisotope equals zero, and c_j^i determines the net flux of the isotope. From Equation 3–15, this efflux of the isotope of species j differs in magnitude from the initial influx only by having the factor c_j^o replaced by $c_j^i e^{z_j F E_M / RT}$, as the quantities in the first two parentheses remain the same. (As for any radioisotope study, only some of the molecules of species j are radioactive. The particular fraction, known as the specific activity, needs to be determined for both $c_j{}^o$ and $c_j{}^i$ in the particular experiment just outlined.) Using the above approach, the ratio of these two fluxes, each of which can be determined separately, takes on the following relatively simple form:

$$\frac{J_j{}^{in}}{J_j{}^{out}} = \frac{c_j{}^o}{c_j{}^i \, e^{z_jFE_M/RT}} \qquad (3\text{--}21)$$

Equation 3–21 was derived independently by Ussing and by Teorell and is known both as the Ussing-Teorell equation and as the flux ratio equation. It is strictly valid only for ions moving passively, independently of each other, and without interacting with other substances that may also be moving across the membrane. The present derivation has made use of Equation 3–15, which gives the passive flux of some charged species across a membrane in response to differences in the chemical potential of that species across the barrier. The Ussing-Teorell equation can thus be used to determine whether the observed influxes and effluxes are the result of passive responses to the chemical potentials of the ions on the two sides of a membrane or whether additional factors such as active transport need to be invoked. After making one further comment about Equation 3–21, we will consider a specific example where the Ussing-Teorell equation can be used to evaluate membrane fluxes.

The ratio of the influx of species j to its efflux as given by Equation 3–21 can be readily related to the difference in chemical potential of the ion on the two sides of the membrane, $\mu_j{}^o - \mu_j{}^i$. This difference shows what causes the flux ratio to differ from unity, and also it will be returned to below to estimate the minimum amount of energy needed to actively transport that ionic species across the membrane. Upon taking logarithms of both sides of the Ussing-Teorell equation (Eq. 3–21) and multiplying by RT, we obtain the following equalities:

$$RT \ln \frac{J_j{}^{in}}{J_j{}^{out}} = RT \ln \frac{c_j{}^o}{c_j{}^i} - z_jFE_M$$

$$\qquad (3\text{--}22)$$

$$= RT \ln a_j{}^o + z_jFE^o - RT \ln a_j{}^i - z_jFE^i = \mu_j{}^o - \mu_j{}^i$$

To derive these relationships, the membrane potential, E_M, appearing in Equation 3–22 has been replaced by $E^i - E^o$ in keeping with the previous convention. The derivation is restricted to the case of constant γ_j ($\gamma_j{}^i = \gamma_j{}^o$), which means that $\ln (c_j{}^o/c_j{}^i)$ equals $\ln (a_j{}^o/a_j{}^i)$, which is $\ln a_j{}^o - \ln a_j{}^i$. Finally, the $\bar{V}_jP$ term in the chemical potential is ignored for the charged species, and μ_j is taken to be $\mu_j^* + RT \ln a_j + z_j FE$. Thus, $\mu_j^o - \mu_j^i$ is simply $RT \ln a_j^o + z_j FE^o - RT \ln a_j^i - z_j FE^i$, as indicated in Equation 3–22.

A difference in chemical potential of species j across the membrane would cause the flux ratio of the passive fluxes to differ from unity, a conclusion that follows directly from Equation 3–22. When μ_j^o equals μ_j^i, the influx would balance the efflux, and there is no net passive flux of species j across the membrane ($J_j = J_j^{in} - J_j^{out}$ by Eq. 3–15). This condition ($\mu_j^o = \mu_j^i$) is also described by Equation 3–4, which was used to derive the Nernst equation. In fact, the electrical potential difference across the membrane in such a case of equality of the chemical potentials is the Nernst potential, E_{Nj}, given by Equation 3–5 [$E_{Nj} = (RT/z_j F) \ln (a_j^o/a_j^i)$]. Thus when E_M equals E_{Nj} for some species, J_j^{in} equals J_j^{out}, and so no net passive flux of that ion is expected across the membrane and no energy is expended in moving the ion from one side of the membrane to the other. When Equations 3–21 and 3–22 are not satisfied for some species, such ions are not moving across the membrane passively or perhaps not moving independently from other fluxes. One of the ways this may occur is when the various fluxes are interdependent, a situation describable by irreversible thermodynamics, which will be introduced later in this chapter. Another way is to have active transport of the ions taking place, whereby energy derived from metabolism is used to move solutes to regions of higher chemical potential.

Example of Active Transport.   The principles discussed above for deciding whether or not active transport of certain ions is taking place can be illustrated by using data obtained with the large internodal cell of *Nitella translucens* (Table 3–1). For instance, all the parameters appearing in the Ussing-Teorell equation have been measured for sodium, potassium, and chloride. For experimental purposes, this fresh water alga is placed in a dilute aqueous solution containing 1 mM NaCl, 0.1 mM KCl, plus 0.1 mM $CaCl_2$ (this solution is not unlike the pond water in which *Nitella* grows), which thus indicates the values for the three c_j^o's. The concentrations of sodium, potassium, and chloride measured in the cytoplasm, c_j^i, are given in column 3 of Table 3–1. Assuming that activities can be replaced by concentrations, the Nernst potential across the plasmalemma can then be calculated from these concentrations for each ion by using Equation 3–5, $E_{Nj} = (58.2/z_j) \log (c_j^o/c_j^i)$ in mv (the numerical factor here is 58.2 since the measurements were at 20°). E_{Nj} for Na^+ is [(58.2)/(1)] log [(1.0)/(14)] or -67 mv; for K^+ it is -179 mv; and for Cl^- it is 99 mv (column 4). A direct measurement of the potential across the plasmalemma, E_M, gives -138 mv, as was mentioned above when discussing the Goldman equation. Since E_{N_j} differs from E_M in all three cases, none of these ions is in equilibrium across the plasmalemma of *Nitella*.

The physiological consequences of not being in equilibrium can be appreciated by considering the value of E_M relative to the E_{N_j} for a particular species. If the actual membrane potential is algebraically more positive than the calculated Nernst potential, then the chemical potential in the inner aqueous phase (here the cytoplasm) is higher for a cation but lower for an anion (cf. the electrical term in the chemical potential, $z_j FE$). Since E_M (-138 mv) is considerably less positive than $E_{N_{Na}}$ (-67 mv), sodium is at a much lower chemical potential in the cytoplasm than outside in the external solution. Reasoning in an analogous manner, potassium is seen to be at a higher chemical potential inside while chloride is at a much higher chemical potential inside. If these ions can move across the plasmalemma, this suggests an active transport of K^+ and Cl^- into the cell and an active extrusion of Na^+ from the cell.

Table 3–1: Concentrations, potentials, and fluxes of various ions for *Nitella* translucens in the light and the dark. The superscript o refers to the concentrations in the external bathing solution; i refers to the cytoplasm. The Nernst potentials, E_{N_j}, were calculated from Equation 3–5 by using concentration ratios and a numerical factor of 58.2 mv. The potential across the plasmalemma, E_M, was -138 mv and the temperature was 20°. A picomole is 10^{-12} mole (Appendix IV). The particular fluxes indicated for the dark refer to values soon after removing the illumination (about 1000 lux) from the cells.

Ion	c_j^o (mM)	c_j^i (mM)	E_{N_j} (mv)	$c_j^o/(c_j^i e^{z_j FE_M/RT})$	Light J_j^{in}	Light J_j^{out}	Dark J_j^{in}	Dark J_j^{out}
						(picomole/cm²-sec)		
Na^+	1.0	14	-67	17	0.55	0.55	0.55	0.10
K^+	0.1	119	-179	0.20	0.85	0.85	0.2	(0.85)
Cl^-	1.3	65	99	0.000085	0.85	0.85	0.05	—

Source: Data are taken from E. A. C. MacRobbie, *Journal of General Physiology* **45**, 861-78 (1962) and R. M. Spanswick and E. J. Williams, *Journal of Experimental Botany* **15**, 193–200 (1964); by permission.

Movement of the various ions into and out of *Nitella* can also be considered in terms of the Ussing-Teorell equation to help determine whether active transport need be invoked to explain the fluxes. The Ussing-Teorell equation predicts that the quantity appearing on the right-hand side of Equation 3–21, $c_j{}^o/(c_j{}^i \ e^{z_jFE_M/RT})$, should be the ratio of influx to efflux of the various ions—if the ions are moving passively in response to gradients in their chemical potential. Using the values given in Table 3–1, this ratio, $J_j{}^{in}/J_j{}^{out}$, is calculated for sodium as follows: the factor RT/F is 25.3 mv at 20° (Appendix III) and so $e^{z_jFE_M/RT}$ is $e^{(-138)/(25.3)}$ or $e^{-5.45}$ for an E_M of -138 mv; therefore $c^o{}_{Na}/c^i{}_{Na} \ e^{z_{Na}FE_M/RT}$ is $(1.0)/[(14)(e^{-5.45})]$, which equals 17. Using the same procedure, the expected flux ratio is calculated to be 0.20 for potassium and 0.000085 for chloride by Equation 3–21. (These values are given in column 5 of Table 3–1.) However, the observed influxes in the light equal the effluxes for each of these three ions (columns 6 and 7, Table 3–1). In other words, the flux ratios given by Equation 3–21 are not satisfied for sodium, potassium, or chloride. On the other hand, equal influxes and effluxes are quite reasonable for *Nitella*, which actually exists close to a steady-state condition in the present case, a mature cell. Active transport of the ions is reponsible for the marked deviations from the Ussing-Teorell equation for the three ions we have considered, probably using energy derived from some process related to photosynthesis, an aspect to be dealt with next.

As mentioned above, another approach for studying active transport is to remove the supply of energy. In the case of *Nitella*, cessation of illumination caused an appreciable decrease in sodium efflux, in potassium influx, and in chloride influx (columns 8 and 9, Table 3–1). But these are the three fluxes that are toward regions of higher chemical potential for the particular ions involved, and thus they are all reasonably expected to be active. On the other hand, some fluxes remain essentially unchanged by placing the cells in the dark. For instance, the Na influx and the K efflux are the same in the light as in the dark, i.e., neither of these unidirectional fluxes seems to depend on metabolism. In diffusing to regions of lower chemical potential, the ionic movement by such passive fluxes helps create the electrical potential difference across the membrane while active transport is instrumental in maintaining the asymmetrical ionic distributions which sustain the passive fluxes. Thus, the passive and active fluxes are interdependent in the ionic relations of cells.

The minimum amount of energy needed to move a mole of species j from the external solution on one side of some membrane to the aqueous phase on the other is the difference in chemical potential across it, $\mu_j{}^i - \mu_j{}^o$. As indicated when we were considering Equation 3–22 above, the quantity $\mu_j{}^o - \mu_j{}^i$ for ions is $RT \ln a_j{}^o + z_jFE^o - RT \ln a_j{}^i - z_jFE^i$. But the Nernst potential, E_{N_j}, is (RT/z_jF) ln (a_j^o/a_j^i), which is equal to (RT/z_jF) ln $a_j^o -$ (RT/z_jF) ln a_j^i (Eq. 3–5). Moreover, the potential across the membrane, E_M, is $E^i - E^o$. Thus the difference in chemical potential across the membrane can be expressed as follows:

$$\mu_j^i - \mu_j^o = z_jF\ (E_M - E_{N_j}) \tag{3–23}$$

The factor F appearing in Equation 3–23 is 0.02306 kcal/mole-mv (Appendix II).

Using the Nernst potentials of Na^+, K^+, and Cl^- for *Nitella translucens* and the value of E_M given in Table 3–1, $z_j(E_M - E_{N_j})$ in Equation 3–23 can be calculated in millivolts for transporting these ions across the plasmalemma of this alga. Such a quantity is $(-138) - (-67)$ or -71 mv for sodium, $+41$ mv for potassium, and $+237$ mv for chloride. These values for $z_j(E_M - E_{N_j})$ mean that sodium is at a higher chemical potential outside in the external bathing solution while potassium and chloride are at higher chemical potentials inside the cell, as was concluded above. From Equation 3–23, the minimum energy required to actively transport or "pump" 1 mole of sodium out across the plasmalemma of the *Nitella* cell equals F times the energy difference in millivolts, which is $(0.02306)(71)$ or 1.6 kcal in the case of sodium [F is 0.02306 kcal/mole-mv (Appendix II)]. Likewise, potassium requires 0.9 kcal/mole to be pumped inward. The active extrusion of sodium from certain algal cells may be linked to the active uptake of potassium, ATP being implicated as the energy source for this coupled exchange process. As will be discussed in Chapter 6, the hydrolysis of ATP under biological conditions usually releases at least 10 kcal/mole. This is sufficient energy per mole of ATP hydrolyzed to pump a mole of sodium out (1.6 kcal/mole) and one of potassium in (0.9 kcal/mole) for the case of a *Nitella* cell. The transport of chloride inward takes a minimum of $(0.02306)(237)$ or 5.5 kcal/mole according to Equation 3–23. This is a fairly large amount of energy. Neither the form of the energy used nor the actual mechanism involved in actively transporting chloride into *Nitella* or other plant cells is understood at the present time. As a final comment, it should be pointed out that the active uptake of potassium and chloride together with an active extrusion of sodium, which have been discussed for the specific case of *Nitella*, are actually fairly widespread phenomena among plant cells.

Ion Uptake, Carriers, and the Michaelis-Menten Formalism.   Although active transport clearly is of common occurrence, its actual mechanism, including the means whereby metabolic energy is used, remain uncertain. The possible involvement of a "carrier" molecule in such active transport of solutes across plant cell membranes was first suggested by W. J. V. Osterhout in the early 1930s. This carrier was proposed to bind selectively certain molecules and then to carry or ferry them across the membrane. Carriers could provide a cell with the specificity or selectivity needed to control the entry and exit of the various types of solutes encountered. Thus certain metabolites or vitamins can be specifically taken into the cell while photosynthetic and waste products can be selectively moved out across the membranes. Also, the active transport of certain nutrients into cells in the root allows a plant to obtain and accumulate these solutes from the soil. Even though the all-important mechanism for physically moving the solutes through the membrane is still unknown, the carrier concept has found widespread application in the interpretation of experimental observations.

Based primarily on results from competition studies, certain ions are described as being bound to or associated with a particular carrier. In other words, when an ion of some species is bound to a carrier, another similar ion (of the same or a different species) which competes for the same binding site cannot also be bound. For instance, the similar monovalent cations, potassium and rubidium, appear to bind in a competitive fashion to the same carrier. For some cells, one carrier might transport sodium out of the cell and potassium in, the so-called sodium-potassium pump alluded to above. Calcium and strontium may compete with each other for binding sites on another common carrier. Two other divalent cations, magnesium and manganese, are apparently transported by a particular carrier that is different from the one for calcium and strontium. The halides (Cl^-, I^-, and Br^-) may also be transported by a single carrier.

One of the most important variables used in the study of carrier-mediated uptake is the external concentration. As the external concentration of the solute increases, the rate of uptake generally reaches an upper limiting value. All of the binding sites on the carriers for that particular ion or neutral solute may then have become filled or saturated. Such saturation effects and the possibility for competitive inhibition mentioned previously are the two key features of the carrier model for active transport, and both of these properties are consistent with Equation 3–24, below. Although ions have been found to bind specifically to certain proteins isolated from cellular membranes, neither the chemical nature of any "carrier" nor of its binding site or sites is known as yet with any certainty. However, carriers have proved to be a useful operational concept for considering the competition effects and concentration dependence of solute uptake.

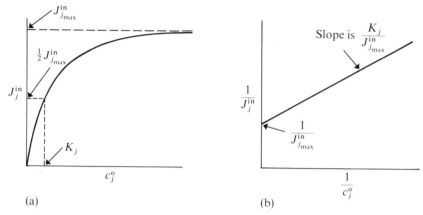

Figure 3–2. The relationship between the external solute concentration, $c_j{}^o$, and the rate of influx, $J_j{}^{in}$, for active uptake according to a Michaelis-Menten type of kinetics, as given by Equation 3–24: (a) linear plot, and (b) reciprocal plot.

The uptake of ions into plants is not only influenced by metabolism, but it also illustrates the competition and saturation effects generally attributed to the presence of specific carriers. In particular, the rate of active uptake of species j, $J_j{}^{in}$, is often proportional to the external concentration of that solute, $c_j{}^o$, over the lower range of concentrations and then levels off as $c_j{}^o$ is raised, eventually approaching a maximum or saturation rate for the influx. This kind of behavior can be described by the following equation:

$$J_j{}^{in} = \frac{c_j{}^o J_j{}^{in}{}_{max}}{K_j + c_j{}^o} \tag{3–24}$$

where $J_j{}^{in}{}_{max}$ is the maximum rate of active influx of species j while K_j is a constant characteristic of species j crossing a particular membrane and is expressed in the units of concentration. For the uptake of many ions into roots and other plant tissues, $J_j{}^{in}{}_{max}$ is 1 to 10 μmoles/g fresh weight-hour while the range for K_j is generally from 10 μM up to 20 mM.

The two most common ways of graphing data on solute uptake that fit Equation 3–24 are illustrated in Figure 3–2. Figure 3–2(a) indicates that when the external concentration of species j, $c_j{}^o$, is K_j, $J_j{}^{in}$ equals $\frac{1}{2}J_j{}^{in}{}_{max}$, as can also be directly seen from Equation 3–24, i.e., $J_j{}^{in}$ is then $K_j J_j{}^{in}{}_{max}/(K_j + K_j)$ or $\frac{1}{2}J_j{}^{in}{}_{max}$. Thus, K_j is the external concentration at which the rate of active uptake is half-maximal—in fact, the observed values of K_j have proved to be quite convenient parameters for comparing the characteristics of uptake of various species. As the concentration $c_j{}^o$ is increased, the uptake continuously rises and eventually approaches an upper limit, $J_j^{in}{}_{max}$, which is the asymptotic value for the active influx [Fig. 3–2(a)]. For many purposes, it is advantageous to plot the experimental data such that a linear relationship is obtained when Equation 3–24 is satisfied for the active uptake. For instance, when $1/J_j^{in}$ is plotted versus $1/c_j^o$ [Fig. 3–2(b)], Equation 3–24 takes the form of a straight line with an intercept on the ordinate of $1/J_j^{in}{}_{max}$ and a slope of $K_j/J_j^{in}{}_{max}$. This latter method of treating the experimental results has proved to be rather convenient and has found widespread application in studies of solute uptake by plant tissues, especially roots.

Equation 3–24 is similar in appearance to the Michaelis-Menten equation used for describing enzyme kinetics in biochemistry. The substrate concentration in the latter relation is analogous to c_j^o in Equation 3–24 and the enzyme reaction velocity to J_j^{in}. The term in the Michaelis-Menten equation equivalent to K_j in Equation 3–24 is the substrate concentration for half-maximal velocity of the reaction (the Michaelis constant). The analogy between enzyme kinetics and active uptake can be pressed even further. The lower the enzymatic Michaelis constant, the greater is the affinity of the enzyme for the substrate. Likewise, a low value for K_j is taken to mean that the ion or other solute is more readily bound to some substance in the membrane such as a "carrier" molecule. The physiological consequence of a low K_j is that species j can be efficiently bound, even when its external concentration is relatively low, which means that such a species is actually favored or selected for active transport into the cell.

It should be pointed out that the basis for the mathematical form of Equation 3–24 for describing uptake is the competitive binding of solutes to sites on a limited number of carriers. In other words, active processes involving metabolic energy do not necessarily have to be invoked. If a solute were to diffuse across the membrane only when bound to a carrier, then the expression for the influx could also be Equation 3–24. This passive entry of a solute that is mediated by a carrier is termed *facilitated diffusion*.

Under usual biological conditions, both active and passive fluxes across the cellular membranes occur concomitantly, these movements depending on concentrations in rather different ways. For passive diffusion, J_j^{in} should be simply proportional to c_j^o, as is indicated by Equation 1–9 for neutral solutes $[ds/dt = PA(c^o - c^i)]$ and Equation 3–15 for ions. This proportionality strictly applies only over the range of external concentrations for which the permeability coefficient for that solute is constant, and moreover, the membrane potential must not be affected in the case of charged solutes (it generally is to some extent). Nevertheless, passive influxes do tend to be proportional to the external concentration while an active influx or facilitated diffusion described by a Michaelis-Menten type of formalism shows saturation effects at the higher concentrations.

Principles of Irreversible Thermodynamics

To interpret correctly the many experimental observations on the ion and water relations of plants, certain theoretical refinements are necessary for the equations which have been used up to this point to describe the relationship between fluxes and forces. For instance, water, ions, and other solutes moving through a membrane can exert a frictional drag on each other, and thus the magnitude of the flux of a solute may depend on whether water is also flowing. In other words, the fluxes of various species across a membrane are interdependent. More formally, the flux of a solute is not only dependent on its own chemical potential gradient, which has been considered to be the sole driving force on it up to now, but also is influenced by the gradient in chemical potential of water as well.

A quantitative description of interdependent fluxes is given by irreversible thermodynamics, a subject which treats nonequilibrium situations such as those actually occurring under biological conditions. (Nonequilibrium and irreversible are related, since a system in a *nonequilibrium* situation that is left isolated from external influences will spontaneously and *irreversibly* move toward equilibrium.) In this brief introduction to irreversible thermodynamics, emphasis will be on certain underlying principles and on the derivation of the reflection coefficient, a parameter important in plant physiology. In order to keep the analysis in a manageable form, attention will be restricted to isothermal conditions, which approximate most biological situations where fluxes of water and solutes are considered.

Fluxes, Forces, and Onsager Coefficients. In the previous discussion of fluxes, the driving force leading to the flux of species j (J_j) was the gradient in its chemical potential, $\partial \mu_j / \partial x$. As just indicated, irreversible thermodynamics takes a more general view. Namely, the flux of species j depends not only on $\partial \mu_j / \partial x$ but can also be affected by *any* other force occurring in the system, such as the gradient in chemical potential of some other species. A particular force, X_k, can likewise influence the flux of any species. Thus, the various fluxes become interdependent or coupled since they can respond to changes in any of the forces. Another premise used in irreversible thermodynamics is that J_j is linearly dependent on the various forces. Even with such a simplification, the algebra often becomes rather cumbersome owing to the coupling of the various forces and fluxes.

Using a linear combination of all the forces, we find that the flux of species j is

$$J_j = \sum_k L_{jk} X_k = L_{j1} X_1 + L_{j2} X_2 + \ldots + L_{jj} X_j + \ldots \quad (3\text{--}25)$$

where the summation in Equation 3–25, $\sum_k$, is over all the forces (X_k's), and the L_{jk}'s are referred to as the Onsager coefficients or the phenomenological coefficients. The first subscript on these coefficients, e.g., j on L_{jk}, identifies the flux and the second subscript (i.e., k on L_{jk}) designates the force. Thus each term, $L_{jk} X_k$, is like the partial flux of species j due to the particular force, X_k. The individual Onsager coefficients in Equation 3–25 are therefore the proportionality factors indicating what contribution the force X_k makes to the flux of species j, J_j.

The reciprocity relation, L_{jk} equals L_{kj}, considerably simplifies equations like 3–25 describing the fluxes of various species. This equality of cross coefficients was derived by Onsager from statistical considerations which utilized the principle of "detailed balancing." In words, the Onsager reciprocity relation means that the proportionality coefficient relating the flux of species k caused by the force on species j equals the proportionality coefficient giving the flux of j due to the force on k. (Strictly speaking, conjugate forces and fluxes must be used, as will be the case below.) Stated another way, L_{jk} being the same as L_{kj} corresponds to having equal action and reaction. For instance, the frictional drag exerted by a moving solvent back on the solute is equal to the drag exerted by the moving solute on the solvent. The pairwise equality of cross coefficients given by the Onsager reciprocity relation reduces the number of coefficients needed to describe the interdependence of forces and fluxes in irreversible thermodynamics and, consequently, leads to a simplification in solving the sets of simultaneous equations.

Water and Solute Flow. As a specific application of the principles just introduced, the important coupling of water and solute flow will be considered in some detail. The driving forces for the fluxes are the gradients in chemical potential, which will be represented by the differences in chemical potential across some barrier, here considered to be a membrane. The development will be for a single nonelectrolyte to help keep the algebra relatively simple. The fluxes are across a membrane permeable both to water (w) and to the solute (s), thereby removing the assumption made in Chapter 2 where membranes that are permeable to water only were the ones considered (except for Eq. 2–23). From Equation 3–25, the fluxes can be represented as a linear combination of the differences in chemical potential as follows:

$$J_w = L_{ww}\Delta\mu_w + L_{ws}\Delta\mu_s \qquad (3\text{–}26)$$

$$J_s = L_{sw}\Delta\mu_w + L_{ss}\Delta\mu_s \qquad (3\text{–}27)$$

Equations 3–26 and 3–27 indicate that each of the fluxes depends on the differences in both of the chemical potentials, $\Delta\mu_w$ and $\Delta\mu_s$. Four phenomenological coefficients are used in these two equations. By the Onsager reciprocity relation, L_{ws} equals L_{sw}. Thus, three different coefficients (L_{ww}, L_{ws}, and L_{ss}) are needed to describe the relationship of these two fluxes to the two driving forces. This is in marked contrast to Equation 3–6 [$J_j = u_j c_j(-\partial\mu_j/\partial x)$], where each flux depends on but one force, and so only two coefficients would be involved in describing J_w and J_s.

To obtain more convenient formulations for the fluxes of water and the solute, the differences in chemical potentials are generally expressed in terms of the osmotic and hydrostatic pressures, π and P. This is a straightforward matter for $\Delta\mu_w$, the only possible ambiguity arising in deciding the algebraic sign. In particular in Equations 3–26 and 3–27, fluxes are considered positive when directed inward, as is the usual convention. The difference in chemical potential of water, $\Delta\mu_w$, is therefore the chemical potential of water on the outside minus that on the inside. From Equation 2–12 ($\mu_w = \mu_w{}^* - \bar{V}_w\pi + \bar{V}_w P$), $\Delta\mu_w$ is given by

$$\Delta\mu_w = -\bar{V}_w\Delta\pi + \bar{V}_w\Delta P \qquad (3\text{–}28)$$

To convert $\Delta\mu_s$ to a similar form, the activity term, $RT \ln a_s$, in the chemical potential of the neutral solute [$\mu_s = \mu_s{}^* + RT \ln a_s + \bar{V}_s P$ (Eq. 2–4)] needs to be expressed in terms of the osmotic pressure, π, in order to be consistent with Equation 3–28 where $\Delta\mu_w$ is so expressed. To do this, consider the differential $RT\, d(\ln a_s)$, which equals $RT\, da_s/a_s$ or $RT\, [d(\gamma_s c_s)/\gamma_s c_s]$. When γ_s is constant, this latter term becomes simply $RT\, dc_s/c_s$. From Equation 2–10 ($\pi_s = RT \sum_s c_s$), $RT\, dc_s$ can be shown to equal $d\pi$ for a dilute solution. Hence, $RT\, d(\ln a_s)$ can be replaced by $d\pi/c_s$ as a useful approximation. To express the difference in chemical potential across a membrane, interest is in macroscopic changes, not in the infinitesimal changes given by differentials. To go from differentials to differences (Δ), $RT\,d(\ln a_s)$ becomes $RT\,\Delta \ln a_s$ and $d\pi/c_s$ can be replaced by $\Delta\pi/\bar{c}_s$, where $\bar{c}_s$ is essentially the mean concentration of solute s, in this case across the membrane. (Alternatively, $\bar{c}_s$ can simply be taken as the definition of that concentration for which $RT\,\Delta \ln a_s$ exactly equals $\Delta\pi/\bar{c}_s$.) Therefore, the term $RT\,\Delta \ln a_s$ appearing in $\Delta\mu_s$ can be replaced by the equivalent term, $\Delta\pi/\bar{c}_s$. From Equation 2–4, the difference in chemical potential of the neutral solute across the membrane then becomes

$$\Delta\mu_s = \frac{1}{\bar{c}_s}\Delta\pi + \bar{V}_s\Delta P \tag{3–29}$$

The two expressions representing the driving forces, $\Delta\mu_w$ (Eq. 3–28) and $\Delta\mu_s$ (Eq. 3–29), are thus expressed as functions of the same two pressure differences, $\Delta\pi$ and ΔP.

Volume Flow, L$_P$, and σ. Now that the chemical potential differences of water and the solute are expressed appropriately, attention will be directed to the fluxes. The fluxes J_w and J_s are the moles of water and solute, respectively, moving across one cm^2 of membrane surface in a second. A quantity of considerable interest in plant physiology is the volume flow, J_v, which is the rate of movement of the total volume of both water and solute across unit area of the membrane. J_v has the units of volume per unit area per unit time, e.g., cm^3/cm^2-sec which is cm/sec. The molar flux of some species j (J_j) in moles/cm^2-sec times the volume occupied by each mole of it ($\bar{V}_j$) in cm^3/mole gives the volume flow for that component in cm/sec. For solute and water both moving across the membrane, the total volume flow J_v is the volume flow of water plus that of solute, which in the case of a single solute can be represented as follows:

$$J_v = \bar{V}_w J_w + \bar{V}_s J_s \tag{3–30}$$

It is generally simpler and more convenient to measure the total volume flux, such as that given in Equation 3–30, than one of the component volume fluxes ($\bar{V}_j J_j$).

Although straightforward, the algebraic substitution necessary to incorporate the various forces and fluxes into the volume flow leads to a rather cumbersome expression. However, insight is thereby provided—albeit in symbols—into the way in which the reflection coefficient arises, a quantity to be considered in detail. When the fluxes of water and solute given by

Equations 3–26 and 3–27, respectively, are substituted into the expression for the volume flow (Eq. 3–30), the following relation is obtained:

$$J_v = (\bar{V}_w L_{ww} + \bar{V}_s L_{sw})\Delta\mu_w + (\bar{V}_w L_{ws} + \bar{V}_s L_{ss})\Delta\mu_s \qquad (3\text{–}31)$$

As mentioned above, L_{sw} equals L_{ws}, and so only the symbol L_{ws} needs to be retained. Next, the chemical potential differences across the membrane for water and for the solute as given by Equations 3–28 and 3–29, respectively, will be incorporated into Equation 3–31. Upon rearrangement, J_v is then given by

$$J_v = (\bar{V}_w{}^2 L_{ww} + 2\bar{V}_s\bar{V}_w L_{ws} + \bar{V}_s{}^2 L_{ss})\Delta P -$$

$$(\bar{V}_w{}^2 L_{ww} - \bar{V}_w\frac{1}{\bar{c}_s}L_{ws} - \bar{V}_s\frac{1}{\bar{c}_s}L_{ss} + \bar{V}_s\bar{V}_w L_{ws})\Delta\pi \qquad (3\text{–}32)$$

Equation 3–32 is the desired relationship giving the dependence of the total volume flow on the hydrostatic and osmotic pressure differences across some membrane permeable to both water and the solute.

The quantities multiplying ΔP and $\Delta\pi$ in Equation 3–32 are rather cumbersome, and so it has proved convenient to define some new parameters. The factor multiplying the difference in hydrostatic pressure, ΔP, is called the hydraulic conductivity coefficient, L_P. From Equation 3–32, this hydraulic conductivity coefficient has the following value:

$$L_P = \bar{V}_w{}^2 L_{ww} + 2\bar{V}_s\bar{V}_w L_{ws} + \bar{V}_s{}^2 L_{ss} \qquad (3\text{–}33)$$

Such a coefficient describes the membrane conductivity since the larger L_P is, the greater is J_v for a given hydrostatic pressure difference across the membrane. In an analogous manner, the other unwieldly factor appearing in Equation 3–32, viz., the parenthesis multiplying $\Delta\pi$, is incorporated into the reflection coefficient, σ. It turns out to be advantageous to define σ as the ratio of the coefficient of $\Delta\pi$ divided by the coefficient of ΔP in the expression for the volume flow (Eq. 3–32). Using the definition of L_P (Eq. 3–33), σ is therefore given by

$$\sigma = \frac{\bar{V}_w{}^2 L_{ww} - \bar{V}_w\frac{1}{\bar{c}_s}L_{ws} - \bar{V}_s\frac{1}{\bar{c}_s}L_{ss} + \bar{V}_s\bar{V}_w L_{ws}}{L_P} \qquad (3\text{–}34)$$

The quantity defined by Equation 3–34 is perhaps the most important parameter introduced by irreversible thermodynamics into the fluxes relevant to plant physiology. In the absence of a hydrostatic pressure difference across the membrane, the volume flow J_v equals $-L_P\sigma\Delta\pi$ by Equation 3–32. Thus the magnitude of σ determines the volume flow expected in response to a difference in osmotic pressure across the membrane. The properties of reflection coefficients will be discussed below, after further consideration of the expression for volume flow.

Using L_P and σ defined by Equations 3–33 and 3–34, respectively, the expression for the total volume flow (Eq. 3–32) can be rewritten in the following convenient form:

$$J_v = L_P(\Delta P - \sigma\Delta\pi) \qquad (3\text{--}35)$$

Equation 3–35 indicates that the osmotic contribution to the volume flow across the membrane is changed by the factor σ, which is less than 1 when the solute and water can both cross the membrane. This point was stated without proof in Chapter 2 (Eq. 3–35 is identical to Eq. 2–23) and will be returned to shortly.

Many different solutes can penetrate a given biological membrane under usual conditions. Each such species j can be characterized by its own reflection coefficient, σ_j, for that particular membrane. The volume flow across the membrane given by Equation 3–35 can then be generalized to

$$J_v = L_P(\Delta P - \sum_j \sigma_j\Delta\pi_j) \qquad (3\text{--}36)$$

where $\Delta\pi_j$ is the osmotic pressure difference across the membrane for the individual solute j (e.g., $\Delta\pi_j = RT\Delta c_j$ by Eq. 2–10). Although interactions with water are still taken into account, the generalization represented by Equation 3–36 has introduced the assumption that the solutes do not interact with each other as they penetrate the membrane. (Strictly speaking, J_v given by Eq. 3–36 also refers only to the movement of neutral species.) Nevertheless, the total volume flow in Equation 3–36 provides a useful approximation to the actual situation describing the multi-component solutions encountered by plants and will be used below as the starting point for the general consideration of solute movement across membranes. Before discussing such movement, let us consider the range of values that can be taken on by reflection coefficients.

Values of Reflection Coefficients.   A reflection coefficient characterizes some particular solute interacting with a specified membrane. In addition, σ depends on the solvent, as the subscripts w for water that appear in Equation

3–34 clearly indicate. Two extreme conditions that describe the passage of solutes are impermeability—which will be considered below—and non-selectivity. In the latter case, the membrane does not distinguish or select between solute and solvent molecules, and the reflection coefficient is zero. A σ of 0 can describe a solute moving across a very coarse membrane (one with large pores) or may refer to the passage through the barrier of a molecule very similar in size to water itself.

Impermeability describes the limiting case where water can cross the membrane, but the solute cannot. When the solute does not penetrate the membrane, J_s remains zero for any and all values of $\Delta\mu_w$ and $\Delta\mu_s$. Since J_s equals $L_{sw}\Delta\mu_w + L_{ss}\Delta\mu_s$ (Eq. 3–27), the only way in which J_s will always be zero is for both L_{ss} and L_{ws} to be zero. Therefore, when the membrane is impermeable to the particular solute under consideration, both L_{ss} and L_{ws} are zero. Putting these zero values for L_{ss} and L_{ws} into Equations 3–33 and 3–34 results in $L_P = \bar{V}_w{}^2 L_{ww}$ (Eq. 3–33) and $\sigma = \bar{V}_w{}^2 L_{ww}/L_P$ (Eq. 3–34), and so σ equals $\bar{V}_w{}^2 L_{ww}/\bar{V}_w{}^2 L_{ww}$, which is 1. A reflection coefficient of unity thus signifies that the solute does not cross the membrane. Rather, all the solute is "reflected" from the membrane, and the reflection coefficient has its maximum value. For the case where the solute can penetrate, L_{ss} takes on a positive value, i.e., the force on solute s causes a flux of it across the membrane. The $-L_{ss}\bar{V}_s/\bar{c}_s$ term then causes the numerator of the expression for σ (Eq. 3–34) to decrease as L_{ss} increases while the denominator [L_P (see Eq. 3–33)] tends to increase as the ability of the solute to penetrate goes up. As a consequence, the reflection coefficient becomes less than 1 when the solute can cross the membrane.

A relatively simple condition for which σ equals 0 can be readily understood from Equation 3–35 [$J_v = L_P(\Delta P - \sigma\Delta\pi)$]. Consider the situation where ΔP is zero across the membrane, and the volume flow across the membrane, J_v, is simply $-L_P\sigma\Delta\pi$ by Equation 3–35. For a solute having a reflection coefficient equal to zero for that particular membrane, the volume flow would then also be zero. By Equation 3–30, a zero J_v implies that $\bar{V}_w J_w$ equals $-\bar{V}_s J_s$. In words, the volume flow of water must be equal and opposite to the volume flow of the solute in order to get no net volume flow. It thus follows that when ΔP is zero but $\Delta\pi$ is nonzero, the absence of a net volume flow J_v across a membrane that is permeable to both water and the single solute indicates that the reflection coefficient for that solute is zero. This condition of σ equaling zero occurs when the volume of water flowing toward the side with the higher π is balanced by an equal volume of solute diffusing across the membrane in the opposite direction toward the side where the solute is less concentrated (lower π). Such a situation of zero volume flow anticipates the concept of a "stationary state," to be introduced in the next section.

Most solutes moving across biological membranes exhibit properties between the extremes of impermeability ($\sigma = 1$) and nonselectivity ($\sigma = 0$). Substances which are retained in or excluded from plant cells have reflection coefficients rather close to unity for the cellular membranes. For instance, the σ for sucrose is usually near 1.0 for plant cells. Methanol and ethanol enter cells very readily and have reflection coefficients of approximately 0.3 for giant algal cells. On the other hand, σ can essentially equal zero for solutes that are crossing porous barriers, such as those presented by cell walls, or for molecules that are penetrating very readily across membranes, D_2O being an example of the latter type.

For most neutral solutes not going through aqueous channels in the membrane, the reflection coefficient is correlated with the partition coefficient, K, for that substance. For instance, when K for nonelectrolytes is less than about 10^{-3}, σ is generally close to 1. Thus compounds which do not readily enter the lipid phase of the membrane (low K) also do not cross the membrane easily (σ near 1). When the partition coefficient is 1 or greater, the solutes can enter the membrane in appreciable amounts, and σ is generally close to zero. Considering the intermediate case, the reflection coefficient can be near 0.5 for small nonelectrolytes having a K of about 0.1, although individual molecules differ depending on their molecular weight, branching, and atomic composition. Neglecting the frictional effects with other solutes, we see that the intermolecular interactions affecting the partition coefficient are similar to those governing the value of the reflection coefficient, and thus there is somewhat of a correlation between the permeability coefficient of a solute ($P_j = D_j K_j / \Delta x$) and its reflection coefficient for the same membrane. In the next section, some of the consequences of reflection coefficients which differ from unity will be specifically considered for solutes crossing organelle and cellular membranes.

Solute Movement Across Membranes and in the Phloem

Certain aspects of the movement of solutes into and out of plant cells and organelles discussed previously can profitably be reexamined by using the more general equations developed from irreversible thermodynamics. One particularly important situation amenable to a rather uncomplicated analysis is when the total volume flow J_v is zero, an example of a "stationary state." This stationary state in which the volume of the cell or organelle is not changing can be brought about by having the volume flow of water in one direction across the membrane equal to the volume flow of solutes in the opposite direction. Thus a stationary state is not the same as a steady state or an equilibrium condition for the cell or organelle but rather represents a situation occurring at a particular time or under some special experimental arrangement. The restriction to cases of zero volume flow for the present discussion considerably simplifies the algebra and emphasizes the role played by reflection coefficients. Moreover, a stationary state often characterizes the experimental situation under which the Boyle-Van't Hoff relation (Eqs. 2–15 and 2–18) or the expression describing incipient plasmolysis (Eq. 2–19) is invoked. Thus the derivation of both of these relationships will be reconsidered in terms of irreversible thermodynamics and the implications of reflection coefficients discussed. This chapter will be concluded by a brief description of solute movement in the phloem—the vascular system primarily concerned with the distribution of organic substances throughout the plant.

Extension of the Boyle-Van't Hoff Relation.   In Chapter 2, the Boyle-Van't Hoff relation was derived, assuming equality of the water potential across the cellular or organelle membrane under consideration. Thus equilibrium conditions were imposed on water, and furthermore, it was implicitly assumed that the membrane was impermeable to the solutes. Such a derivation is really for the case of zero water flow ($J_w = 0$) across the membrane whereas zero volume flow ($J_v = 0$) is actually a better description of the experimental situation where the Boyle-Van't Hoff relation is applied. This condition of not having the membrane-bounded volume change ($J_v = 0$) during the measurement is a good example of a stationary state, and so the Boyle-Van't Hoff relation will be reexamined from the point of view of irreversible thermodynamics. In this way, both of the previous restrictions, equilibrium and impermeability, can be removed.

The stationary state condition of zero net volume flow appropriate to the Boyle-Van't Hoff relation follows directly from Equation 3–36 $[J_v = L_P(\Delta P - \sum_j \sigma_j \Delta \pi_j)]$. The osmotic pressures referred to in that equation are for the effect of solutes on water activity, as interfacial phenomena have been ignored. In the general case, both osmotic contributions from solutes (π_s) and matric pressures resulting from the presence of interfaces (τ) are involved. The appropriate volume measurements for osmotic studies where the Boyle-Van't Hoff relation is invoked are generally made when the external solution is at atmospheric pressure ($P^o = 0$) and when there are no external interfaces ($\tau^o = 0$). From Equation 3–36 and replacing $\Delta\pi_j$ by $\pi_j{}^o - \pi_j{}^i$, the condition that the volume flow equals zero then gives

$$\sum_j \sigma_j\pi_j{}^o = \sum_j \sigma_j\pi_j{}^i + \tau^i - P^i \qquad (3\text{–}37)$$

where the possibility of interfacial interactions and hydrostatic pressures within the cell or organelle has been explicitly recognized by the inclusion of τ^i and P^i in Equation 3–37. The quantity π_j is simply that part of the osmotic pressure caused by species j in the phase indicated (inside or outside) and can be replaced by $RT\gamma_jc_j$ in many cases (Eq. 2–10). Equation 3–37 describes the stationary state of zero volume flow when the external solution is at atmospheric pressure (and $\tau^o = 0$) and when the solutes are capable of crossing the membrane, as occurs for molecules interacting with real, not idealized, biological membranes.

When molecules can cross the membranes bounding the cells or organelles, the reflection coefficients for both internal and external solutes must be included in the Boyle-Van't Hoff relation. It is convenient to characterize the external solutes by an average reflection coefficient, σ^o, taken so that $\sum_j \sigma_j\pi_j{}^o$ equals $\sigma^o\pi^o$, where π^o is the total external osmotic pressure of all the solutes present there. Since σ^o is less than 1 if the external solutes can penetrate, the effect of the external osmotic pressure is reduced. Likewise, the reflection coefficients for solutes within the cell or organelle will lessen the contribution of the internal osmotic pressure of each solute. Replacing $\sum_j \sigma_j\pi_j{}^o$ by $\sigma^o\pi^o$ and $\pi_j{}^i$ by $RT\gamma_j{}^in_j{}^i/(\bar{V}_wn_w{}^i)$ (Eq. 2–10), Equation 3–37 leads to the following Boyle-Van't Hoff relation for the stationary state condition ($J_v = 0$ in Eq. 3–36):

$$\pi^o = RT\frac{\displaystyle\sum_j \sigma_j\gamma_j{}^in_j{}^i}{\sigma^o\ \bar{V}_wn_w{}^i} + \frac{\tau^i - P^i}{\sigma^o} \qquad (3\text{–}38)$$

The reflection coefficients of the membrane for solutes both internal and external are seen to enter into this extension of the expression relating volume and external osmotic pressure. As mentioned in Chapter 2, the quantity $V - b$ in the conventional Boyle-Van't Hoff relation [$\pi^o(V - b) = RT\sum_j \varphi_jn_j$ (Eq. 2–15)] can be identified with $\bar{V}_wn_w{}^i$. Upon comparison with Equation 3–38, it is evident that the osmotic coefficient of species j, φ_j in Equation 2–15, can be equated to $\sigma_j\gamma_j{}^i/\sigma^o$ as an explicit recognition of the activity coefficient and the permeation properties of specific solutes, both internal and external.

As discussed in Chapter 2, the volume of pea chloroplasts responds linearly to $1/\pi^o$ (Fig. 2–3), indicating that $\tau^i - P^i$ is negligible in such plastids compared with the external osmotic pressures used. Replacing $\bar{V}_w n_w^i$ by $V - b$, Equation 3–38 can be rewritten as follows in this special case:

$$\pi^o(V - b) = \frac{RT}{\sigma^o} \sum_j \sigma_j \gamma_j^i n_j^i \qquad (3\text{–}39)$$

Equation 3–39 is a form of the Boyle-Van't Hoff relation appropriate when solutes can cross the limiting membranes.

When the refinements introduced by reflection coefficients are taken into account, osmotic responses of cells and organelles can be used to provide information on their membranes. For instance, using data from Figure 2–3, it was found that $\sigma_j \gamma_j^i$ averaged about 0.8 for pea chloroplasts both in the light and the dark. Since the activity coefficient γ_j^i would be less than 1, 0.8 is a lower limit for the mean reflection coefficient of the solutes in pea chloroplasts. Thus, the limiting membranes around these organelles can effectively control what enters or leaves the chloroplasts, which consequently act like intracellular compartments, as mentioned in Chapter 1. Moreover, once $\sum_j \sigma_j \gamma_j^i n_j^i$ has been determined, the osmotic responses of the chloroplasts or other membrane-bounded bodies can be utilized to obtain information on various σ^o's by making use of Equation 3–39. In other words, V can be plotted versus $1/\pi^o$ for a number of different substances, and the slopes used to give the values of σ^o for a particular solute entering the specific cell or organelle whose osmotic responses are under consideration.

The Influence of Reflection Coefficients on Incipient Plasmolysis. The condition for incipient plasmolysis [$\pi^o_{\text{plasmolysis}} = \pi^i$ (Eq. 2–19)] that is reached when the internal pressure P^i inside a plant cell just becomes zero was derived in Chapter 2 using classical thermodynamics. As in the treatment of the Boyle-Van't Hoff relation in the previous chapter, the derivation was made assuming equilibrium of water (i.e., equal water potential) across a membrane impermeable to solutes. Measurements can be made when there is zero volume flow ($J_v = 0$) and for a simple external solution at atmospheric pressure, in which case Equation 3–37 would be the underlying expression from irreversible thermodynamics, instead of the less realistic condition of no water flow ($J_w = 0$), which was used previously. Using Equation 3–37, one obtains the following expression describing incipient plasmolysis ($P^i = 0$) for the case where the solutes can cross the cell membrane:

$$\sigma^\circ \pi^\circ_{\text{plasmolysis}} = \sum_j \sigma_j \pi_j^i + \tau^i \tag{3-40}$$

where $\sum_j \sigma_j \pi_j^\circ$ has been replaced by $\sigma^\circ \pi^\circ$, as was done above.

Since the value of σ° depends on the external solutes, Equation 3–40 indicates that the osmotic pressure (π°) at incipient plasmolysis varies from solute to solute placed in the solution surrounding the plant cells. Suppose that solute i cannot penetrate the membrane and that σ_i therefore equals 1, a situation often true for sucrose. Consider another solute, species j, which can penetrate into the cells ($\sigma_j < 1$), as is the general case for many small nonelectrolytes encountered by plant cells. The external osmotic pressure due to any species k, π_k°, can be represented by $RT\gamma_k^\circ c_k^\circ$ (cf. Eq. 2–10) as a useful approximation. Thus when the condition for incipient plasmolysis given by Equation 3–40 is separately satisfied for two different solutes (i and j) in the external solution, the properties of the two solutes are related as follows:

$$\sigma_i RT\gamma_i^\circ c_i^\circ{}_{\text{plasmolysis}} = \sigma_j RT\gamma_j^\circ c_j^\circ{}_{\text{plasmolysis}} \tag{3-41}$$

But solute i was chosen as one for which the membrane is impermeable ($\sigma_i = 1$). Assuming that γ_i° equals γ_j°, Equation 3–41 can therefore be rewritten to give the following simple expression for the reflection coefficient of species j:

$$\sigma_j = \frac{c_i^\circ{}_{\text{plasmolysis}}}{c_j^\circ{}_{\text{plasmolysis}}} \tag{3-42}$$

Equation 3–42 not only suggests a rather straightforward way of evaluating a specific reflection coefficient, but also it provides insight into the consequences of having σ's less than 1. Since by supposition species j can cross the cell membrane, σ_j must be less than 1. By Equation 3–42, therefore, $c_j^\circ{}_{\text{plasmolysis}}$ is greater than $c_i^\circ{}_{\text{plasmolysis}}$, where the latter refers to the concentration of the impermeable solute at the point of incipient plasmolysis. In words, a higher external concentration or osmotic pressure is needed to cause plasmolysis, if that solute is able to enter the plant cell. Experimentally, it is difficult to replace one external solution by another with no changes in the tissue taking place or with none of the previous solution adhering to the cell. Also, although easy in principle and involving only the use of a light microscope, the determination of just when the plasmalemma begins to pull away from the cell wall is a rather subjective judgment. Never-theless, the use of Equation 3–42 provides a simple way of measuring individual reflection coefficients for various solutes entering plant cells.

The incorporation of reflection coefficients modifies some of the equations describing solute and water movement in plants and unifies others. In particular, the role of osmotic pressure can be stated more precisely and uniformly. For Poiseuille flow, which can adequately describe water flow in the xylem, the water potential gradient ($\partial \Psi / \partial x = \partial P / \partial x - \partial \pi / \partial x$ by Eq. 2–13) was replaced by the hydrostatic pressure gradient (cf. Eq. 2–24). An alternative way of viewing the same situation is that σ equals zero for the solutes; then osmotic pressures need have no effect on the movement described by Poiseuille's law. The real importance of reflection coefficients comes when $0 < \sigma < 1$, i.e., for those cases intermediate between non-selectivity and impermeability. Then the volume flow does not depend on the full osmotic pressure difference across the barrier, but it would also be invalid to completely ignore the osmotic contribution.

When solutes can cross membranes, the following extension of Equations 3–41 and 3–42 is a convenient definition for σ:

$$\sigma = \frac{\text{effective osmotic pressure}}{\text{theoretical osmotic pressure}} \qquad (3\text{–}43)$$

The theoretical osmotic pressure indicated in Equation 3–43 is the maximum that can be exerted and is defined either by Equation 2–7 [$\pi = -(RT/\bar{V}_w)$ ln a_w] or by Equation 2–10 ($\pi_s = RT \sum_j \gamma_j c_j$, when activity coefficients are included). This maximum osmotic pressure occurs experimentally when the membrane is impermeable to the solute, in which case σ equals 1, i.e., the apparent osmotic pressure equals that which is expected theoretically only when the solutes cannot penetrate the membrane. The apparent or effective osmotic pressure takes into consideration the fact that most solutes can move across biological membranes, and so the $\Delta \pi$ effective in leading to a net volume flow is reduced from its maximum value [cf. 3–35, $J_v = L_P(\Delta P - \sigma \Delta \pi)$]. As Equation 3–43 indicates, the reflection coefficient is a measure of how effectively the osmotic pressure of a given solute can be exerted across a particular membrane. Since osmotic pressures play a large role in plant physiology, σ is an important parameter for quantitatively describing the ion and water relations of plants.

Phloem. Any discussion of solute movement into and out of plant cells would not be complete without at least a brief consideration of the transport of substances in the phloem. Solute movement in this vascular tissue involves cooperative interactions between many different types of cells embedded within the plant. Furthermore, the conducting cells of the phloem generally have a high internal hydrostatic pressure, which often leads to artifacts during cytological investigations. Due in part to the observational difficulties, there is a lack of agreement as to the actual mechanism for solute movement in the phloem. The present brief treatment will be primarily concerned with certain anatomical features of the phloem cells and an overall description of flow; a comprehensive physicochemical analysis must await future research.

The conducting cells of the phloem are the sieve cells (the main phloem conduction pathway in gymnosperms) and the phylogenetically more advanced sieve-tube members (Fig. 1–3), which are generally joined end-to-end to form the sieve tubes. Both types of cells are collectively called sieve elements. Mature sieve elements have often lost their nuclei and apparently have no large central vacuole, but unlike the conducting elements of the xylem, the analogous phloem cells are alive. The sieve elements generally vary from 0.1 to several millimeters in length and tend to be somewhat longer in gymnosperms than in angiosperms. Typical cross-sectional areas of the conducting cells are about 1000 μm^2, indicating radii of approximately 15 to 20 μm. The end walls between two sequential sieve-tube members generally have many large pores, the assemblage being referred to as a sieve plate (Fig. 1–3). The pores range in diameter from about 0.5 to 5 μm and usually have strands of protoplasm passing through them. Most solutes translocated in the phloem cross the sieve plate in these strands of cytoplasm that are apparently continuous from one cell to the next. Cells adjacent to the sieve elements (see Fig. 1–3) accumulate sugars and other solutes, which then either passively diffuse or are actively transported into the conducting elements of the phloem.

A rather elegant way of studying the contents of certain sieve elements is by means of aphid stylets. The aphid feeds on the phloem by inserting its stylet into an individual sieve element. After the aphid has been anesthetized and its body removed, the remaining mouth part forms a tube that leads the phloem solution from the sieve element to the outside. Over 90% of the solutes in the sieve element are thereby found to be carbohydrates, mainly sucrose and some other oligosaccharides. The concentration of sucrose is generally from 0.2 to 0.5 M, values near 0.3 M being typical. The types and the concentrations of the various solutes exhibit diurnal and seasonal variations and also depend on the tissues that the phloem is flowing toward or away from. For instance, the solution in the phloem moving out of senescent leaves is low in sucrose but contains an appreciable concentration of amino acids and amides. The movement of ions from the soil to the root and then throughout the plant occurs mainly in the xylem (as discussed in Chapter 2), but some movement of ions also takes place in the phloem, such as the movement of mineral nutrients out of leaves just before abscission.

Solutes can rapidly move in either direction in the phloem. Photosynthetic products move from the leaves to storage tissues in the root while sugars, produced from the hydrolysis of starch, move in the opposite direction from such storage tissue to meristematic areas at the top of the plant. The velocity of solute movement can be about 100 cm/hour, the actual rate varying considerably with the plant species, among other things. Although a particular solute generally moves in the phloem in the direction of a decrease in its concentration, diffusion is not involved. First, the rate of solute movement far exceeds that possible by diffusion. (See Chapter 1.) Second, the solute moves with a rather constant velocity (distance moved is proportional to time) while for a diffusional process, distance moved is proportional to the square root of time $[x_e^2 = 4Dt$ (Eq. 1–6)].

What causes solute movement in the phloem? Due to the observational and experimental difficulties alluded to above, this question has proved hard to answer. Water may readily enter and leave the various types of cells in the phloem as well as those of the surrounding tissue; thus the phloem cannot be viewed as an isolated independent system. For instance, when the water potential in the xylem decreases, as occurs during rapid transpiration, the velocity of fluid movement in the phloem generally becomes less. Some water may move upward in the xylem and later downward in the phloem, but this is not the whole story as movement in the phloem can be in either direction. Two general hypotheses on the causative agent for movement in the phloem have been proposed. In one, the force is a hydrostatic pressure gradient, which leads to fluid movement analogous to that in the xylem as described by Poiseuille's law (Eq. 2–24). Although precise information on possible pressure gradients along the conducting cells of the phloem is lacking, the solution in the sieve elements has been found to be under a hydrostatic pressure of up to 20 bars. The other type of "force" proposed to cause movement in the phloem is protoplasmic streaming, in which the solution moves as a unit or plug. The actual energetic basis for such motion is poorly understood although it is clear that the solution must somehow be propelled at the wall. Thus the wall of the tube is the site for the maximum velocity in the case of plug flow, in marked distinction to Poiseuille flow.

For the latter flow, the velocity profile across the cylinder is parabolic, the maximum velocity occurring in the center of the tube, while due to friction the fluid at the walls is stationary. Determination of the velocity profile across the sieve elements and an unambiguous answer to the question of the causative force for movement in the phloem remain for future research.

Problems

3–1. At the beginning of this chapter, we calculated that an average concentration of 1 μM excess monovalent anions can lead to a -100 mv potential drop across the surface of a spherical cell 30 μm in radius. (a) If the same total amount of charge were all concentrated in a layer 30 Å thick at the surface of the sphere, what would be its average concentration there? (b) If 10^7 sulfate ions are added inside the sphere, what is the new potential difference across the surface? (c) Approximately how much electrical work in joules is required to transport the 10^7 sulfate ions across the surface of the cell?

3–2. Consider a cell with a membrane potential of -118 mv (inside negative) at 25°. The external solution contains 1 mM KCl, 0.1 mM NaCl, and 0.1 mM $MgCl_2$, and the internal concentration of K^+ is 100 mM, of Ca^{++} is 1 mM, and of Mg^{++} is 10 mM. Except for (d), assume that activity coefficients are unity. (a) Are K^+ and Mg^{++} in equilibrium across the membrane? (b) If Na^+ and Ca^{++} are in equilibrium, what are their concentrations in the two phases? (c) If Cl^- is 177 mv away from equilibrium such that the passive driving force on it is outward, what is its internal concentration? (d) For the purposes of calculation, assume that the external solution is 1 mM KCl and the internal solution is 100 mM KCl. If K^+ were in equilibrium across the membrane and mean activity coefficients for monovalent ions are calculated from Equation 3–3, what would be the membrane potential?

3–3. Suppose that a 10 mM KCl solution at 25° is placed outside a cell formerly bathed in 1 mM KCl. (a) Assuming that some of the original solution adheres to the cell and the ratio of mobilities, u_{Cl}/u_K, is 1.04, what diffusion potential would be present? (b) After a sufficient lapse of time, assume that equilibrium is reached in the bathing solution. The membrane may contain many carboxyl groups ($-COOH$) whose H^+'s will dissociate. The ensuing negative charge will attract K^+, and its concentration near the membrane may reach 200 mM. What type and how large a potential would be associated with this situation? (c) Suppose that 10 mM NaCl is also in the external solution (with the 10 mM KCl) while internally there is 100 mM K^+, 10 mM Na^+, and 100 mM Cl^-. Assume that P_{Na}/P_K is 0.20 and P_{Cl}/P_K is 0.01. What diffusion potential would be expected across the membrane? (d) What would E_M be if P_{Cl}/P_K were 0.00? If P_{Na}/P_K and P_{Cl}/P_K were both 0.00? Assume that other conditions are as in (c).

3–4. Consider an illuminated spherical spongy mesophyll cell that is 40 μm in diameter and that contains 50 spherical chloroplasts that are 4 μm in diameter. (a) Suppose that some monovalent cation produced by photosynthesis has a net flux out of the chloroplasts of 1 picomole/cm²-sec. If this product is not changed in any of the cellular compartments, what is the net passive flux out of the cell? (b) If the passive influx of the above substance into the cell at 25° is 0.1 picomole/cm²-sec, what is the difference in its chemical potential across the cellular membrane? (c) Suppose that when the cell is placed in the dark, the influx and the efflux both become 0.01 picomole/cm²-sec. If the plasmalemma potential is -118 mv (inside negative) and the same concentration occurs on the two sides of the membrane, what can be said about the energetics of the two fluxes? (d) If 1 ATP is required per ion transported, what is the rate of ATP consumption in (c)? Express your answer in $\mu moles/sec$ per liter of cellular contents.

3–5. Consider a cell whose membrane has a hydraulic conductivity coefficient, L_P, of 10^{-4} cm/sec-bar. When placed in a solution having the following composition, initially no net volume flow occurs: sucrose ($\pi_j{}^\circ = 2$ bars, $\sigma_j = 1.00$), ethanol (1 bar, 0.30), and glucose (1 bar, 0.80). The external solution is at atmospheric pressure while P^i is 5 bars. Inside the cell, the osmotic pressure caused by glucose is 2 bars, sucrose and ethanol are initially absent, and other substances that have an osmotic pressure of 10 bars are present. (a) What is the mean reflection coefficient for the external solution? (b) What is the mean reflection coefficient for the internal solutes other than glucose? (c) Suppose that some treatment makes the membrane nonselective for all solutes present. Is there then a net volume flow? (d) If another treatment makes the membrane impermeable to all solutes present, what is the net volume flow?

3–6. Consider a cell that is at the point of incipient plasmolysis for 0.3 molal sucrose, an impermeable solute. The concentration of glycine that just causes plasmolysis is 0.4 molal. Assume that no water enters or leaves the cell during the plasmolytic experiments. (a) What is the reflection coefficient of glycine for the cellular membrane? (b) Suppose that chloroplasts isolated from such a cell have the same osmotic responses as in Problem 2–4. What is the volume of such chloroplasts *in vivo*? Assume that activity coefficients are unity and that the temperature is 20°. (c) Suppose that chloroplasts are isolated in 0.3 molal sucrose, which has a reflection coefficient of 1.00 for the chloroplasts. If 0.1 mole of glycine is then added per liter of isolation medium and the chloroplast volume is 23 μm^3, what is the reflection coefficient of glycine for the chloroplast membranes?

References

Briggs, G. E., A. B. Hope, and R. N. Robertson. 1961. *Electrolytes and Plant Cells*, Davis, Philadelphia.

Crafts, A. S. 1961. *Translocation in Plants*, Holt, Rinehart, and Winston, New York.

Dainty, J. 1962. Ion transport and electrical potentials in plant cells. *Annual Review of Plant Physiology* **13**, 379–402.

Diamond, J. M., and E. M. Wright. 1969. Biological membranes: the physical basis of ion and nonelectrolyte selectivity. *Annual Review of Physiology* **31**, 581–646.

Gutknecht, J., and J. Dainty. 1968. Ionic relations of marine algae. *Oceanography and Marine Biology, An Annual Review* **6**, 163–200.

Katchalsky, A., and P. F. Curran. 1967. *Nonequilibrium Thermodynamics in Biophysics*, Harvard University Press, Cambridge, Mass.

Kedem, O., and A. Katchalsky. 1958. Thermodynamic analysis of the permeability of biological membranes to nonelectrolytes. *Biochimica et Biophysica Acta* **27**, 229–46.

Spanner, D. C. 1964. *Introduction to Thermodynamics*, Academic Press, New York.

Vorobiev, V. N. 1967. Potassium ion activity in the cytoplasm and the vacuole of cells of *Chara* and *Griffithsia*. *Nature* **216**, 1325–27.

Also see references for Chapter 2.

Chapter 4

Light

Not only does the sun maintain a habitable temperature on the earth, but it is also the ultimate source of the energy needed to sustain life. The energy from solar radiation is converted to storable forms by photosynthesis, a process to be discussed in some detail in the next chapter. Furthermore, sunlight regulates the activities of many plants and animals by acting as a switch or trigger. The energy to carry out such control or switching responses is supplied by dark metabolism, not by the light itself. Examples where light acts as a trigger are phototaxis, vision, and the control by phytochrome of certain processes in plants.

The conversion of radiant energy to other forms of energy that are important to plants will be the primary concern of the remainder of this book. In the present chapter, we will consider the physical nature of light and the mechanism of light absorption by molecules, followed by a critique on how the molecular states so excited can power endergonic (energy-requiring) reactions or be dissipated by other types of de-excitation processes. In the final two chapters, the primary events of photosynthesis will be considered in detail followed by a discussion of bioenergetics, a topic dealing with chemical and electrical energy in biological systems, especially from the standpoint of the energy conversion taking place in organelles.

In 1666 Newton showed that a prism could divide white light into many colors, indicating that such radiation consisted of a large number of components. Soon thereafter, Huygens proposed that the propagation of light through space was by wave motion while in the early 1800s, Young attributed interference properties to the wave character of light. However, a wave theory of light was not generally accepted until about 1850 when Foucault demonstrated that light travels more slowly in a dense medium such as water than in a rare medium such as air, one of the predictions of the wave theory. In 1887, Hertz discovered that light striking the surface of a metal could cause the release of electrons from the solid. He also found, however, that light above a certain wavelength could not eject any electrons at all, a result contradictory to the accepted wave theory of light. In an important departure from the wave theory, Planck in 1901 proposed that radiation was discontinuous or particle-like, i.e., light was describable as discrete packets or quanta instead of as a continuous wave. In 1905, Einstein explained the photoelectric effect of Hertz as a special example of the particle nature of light, indicating that the absorption of a light quantum by an electron in the metal could supply enough energy to cause the ejection or release of that electron. Since then the intriguing wave-particle duality of light has become understood through the development of quantum mechanics. Both the wave and the particle attributes of light are necessary for a complete description of radiation, and both will be considered in this chapter.

Wavelength and Energy

Light is often defined as radiation perceived by the human eye. Although such a definition may be strictly correct, the word *light* usually refers to a larger class of electromagnetic waves. In this section, we will focus our attention on the range of electromagnetic radiation that is important in plant physiology, including the subdivisions into various wavelength intervals. The wavelength of light will be related to its energy. After mentioning the units for light intensity, we will briefly consider some of the characteristics of solar radiation reaching the earth.

Light Waves. *Wave* is a term used to describe the periodic variation of some physical quantity that is propagating or traveling in a certain medium. Of particular concern here are the regular repetitive changes in the intensity of the minute electric and magnetic fields which indicate the passage of a light wave. Light can be propagated in a solid (e.g., glass), in a liquid (e.g., water), in a gas (e.g., air), and even in a vacuum (e.g., between the sun and the earth's atmosphere). One of the ways of characterizing light is by its wavelength, which is the separation in space between points of the same phase, such as between two successive peaks of a wave train. Thus a wavelength is the distance per cycle of the wave. One unit for wavelengths is the Ångstrom (Å), which equals 10^{-8} cm or 10^{-10} m (Appendix III). For plant physiology as well as for biology in general, wavelengths have commonly been expressed in millimicrons. The term *millimicron* is being replaced by nanometer (nm), which also is 10^{-9} m, nanometer being the unit to be used in this text (1 nm = 10 Å).

The wavelength regions of major interest in biology are the ultraviolet, the visible, and the infrared (Table 4–1). Wavelengths below about 400 nm are referred to as ultraviolet (UV), meaning on the other side of or beyond violet in the sense of having a shorter wavelength. The visible region extends from approximately 400 to 740 nm and is subdivided into various bands such as blue, green, or red (Table 4–1), these divisions being based on the subjective color experienced by humans. The region having wavelengths longer than for the red end of the visible spectrum is known as the infrared (IR), for which an upper limit of approximately 40 μm may be set.

Besides its wavelength, a wave phenomenon can also be characterized by its frequency of vibration or change, ν, and by a velocity of propagation, v. These three quantities are related as follows:

$$\lambda \nu = v \qquad (4\text{--}1)$$

where λ is the wavelength. The speed of light in a vacuum is a constant, generally designated as c, which experimentally equals 299,792 ± 1 km/sec or approximately 3.00×10^8 m/sec. Light passing through a medium other than a vacuum has a velocity less than c. For example, light having a wavelength of 589 nm in a vacuum is decreased in speed 0.03% by air, 25% by water, and 40% by dense flint glass. The wavelength undergoes a decrease in magnitude equal to the decrease in the speed of light in these various media since the unchanging property of a wave propagating through different media is its frequency.

For light, $\lambda_{\text{vacuum}} \nu$ equals c by Equation 4–1. Therefore, the frequency can be calculated if the wavelength in a vacuum is known. In fact, the wavelengths given for light generally refer to the values in a vacuum, as is the case for columns 2 and 3 in Table 4–1 (λ's in air differ only slightly from the magnitudes listed). As a specific example, let us consider a wavelength in

Table 4–1: Definitions and characteristics of the various wavelength regions of light. The frequencies and energies refer to the particular wavelengths indicated in column 3 for each wavelength interval. The magnitudes for the wavelengths are the values in a vacuum.

Color	Approximate wavelength range (nm)	Typical wavelength (nm)	Frequency (cycles/sec) (Hertz)	Energy (ev per quantum)	Energy (kcal/"mole" of quanta)
Ultraviolet	below 400	254	11.80×10^{14}	4.88	112.5
Violet	400–424	410	7.31×10^{14}	3.02	69.7
Blue	424–491	460	6.52×10^{14}	2.70	62.2
Green	491–550	520	5.77×10^{14}	2.39	55.0
Yellow	550–585	580	5.17×10^{14}	2.14	49.3
Orange	585–647	620	4.84×10^{14}	2.00	46.2
Red	647–740	680	4.41×10^{14}	1.82	42.1
Infrared	above 740	1400	2.14×10^{14}	0.88	20.4

the blue region of the spectrum, e.g., 460 nm. The corresponding frequency equals c/λ_{vacuum} or $(3.00 \times 10^8)/(460 \times 10^{-9})$, which is 6.52×10^{14} cycles/sec for such blue light. Since ν is constant or unchanging from medium to medium, it is often desirable to describe light by its frequency, as has been done in column 4 of Table 4–1.

Energy of Light.   In addition to having wave characteristics, light can also exhibit particle-like properties, as in the photoelectric effect mentioned above. This means that light can act as if it were divided or quantized into discrete units, which are termed quanta or photons. The light energy, E, carried by a photon or a quantum is

$$E = h\nu = hc/\lambda_{vacuum} \tag{4–2}$$

where h is a fundamental physical quantity called Planck's constant. Since frequency has the units of reciprocal time, Equation 4–2 indicates that Planck's constant is in energy $\times$ time, the appropriate energy unit depending on the particular application. For instance, h is equal to 6.626×10^{-27} erg-sec, 0.4136×10^{-14} ev-sec, or 1.584×10^{-37} kcal-sec (Appendix II). By Equation 4–2, a quantum of light has an energy proportional to its frequency and inversely proportional to its wavelength. The direct proportionality between E and ν is another reason why electromagnetic radiation is often described by its frequency.

For many purposes, the energies of individual quanta are most conveniently expressed in electron volts. Blue light of 460 nm has a frequency of 6.52×10^{14} cycles/sec (Table 4–1); from Equation 4–2, a quantum of such light has an energy $h\nu$ of $(0.4136 \times 10^{-14})(6.52 \times 10^{14})$ or 2.70 ev. Using Equation 4–2 and the appropriate numerical value of hc, we can also calculate energies in electron volts from the wavelengths of light. Since hc is equal to 1240 ev-nm (Appendix III), blue light of 460 nm (strictly speaking, this is the wavelength in a vacuum) has an energy of $(1240)/(460)$ or 2.70 ev. Column 5 of Table 4–1 gives the energy in ev/quantum at various wavelengths in the ultraviolet, visible, and infrared.

The customary energy unit for chemical reactions is the kcal/mole, and it is often advantageous to express light energy in a comparable way. The unit analogous to moles but used for radiation is the Einstein, which has Avogadro's number (6.023×10^{23}), N, of photons. Although not strictly correct, a "mole" of quanta is often used to refer to 6.023×10^{23} photons. Using Equation 4–2 and the appropriate numerical value of h, we can calculate that the energy of an Einstein or mole of blue photons of wavelength 460 nm is $Nh\nu$ or $(6.023 \times 10^{23})(1.584 \times 10^{-37})(6.52 \times 10^{14})$, which equals 62.2 kcal. Equivalently, since Nhc equals 28,600 kcal/mole-nm (Appendix III), the energy of such blue photons can also be calculated using their vacuum wavelength, which gives $(28,600)/(460)$ or 62.2 kcal/mole in the present case. The energies of various wavelengths of light are presented in kcal/mole in column 6 of Table 4–1.

Quanta of visible light carry relatively large amounts of energy. The hydrolysis of ATP, the main currency for chemical energy in biology, yields about 10 to 14 kcal/mole under physiological conditions. (See Chapter 6.) By comparison, blue light has about five times as much energy per Einstein. Quanta of ultraviolet light possess even higher energies than for visible light, e.g., 254 nm photons have 113 kcal of radiant energy/mole (Table 4–1). This is greater than the carbon-carbon bond energy of 83 kcal/mole or the oxygen-hydrogen bond energy of 111 kcal/mole. The high energy of UV radiation underlies its mutagenic and bactericidal action since it is energetic enough to cause disruption of certain covalent bonds.

Absorption of radiation by an atom or molecule leads to a more energetic state of the absorbing species. Energetic states can also be produced by collisions resulting from the random thermal motion of the molecules. The higher the temperature, the greater is the average kinetic energy of the atoms and molecules, and, consequently, the greater the probability of achieving a given excited state by collision. The number of molecules having a particular kinetic energy can often be approximated by the Boltzmann energy distribution (see p. 100). At equilibrium, the fraction of atoms or molecules having a kinetic energy of U or greater is proportional to the Boltzmann factor, $e^{-U/kT}$, where k is the Boltzmann constant [8.617×10^{-5} ev/°K (Appendix II)]. Therefore, the number of molecules with kinetic energy in excess of U at a given temperature exponentially decreases with increasing values of U. Energies of molecules are generally of the order of magnitude of kT, which equals $(8.617 \times 10^{-5})(298)$ or 0.026 ev at a room temperature of 25° (298°K). For instance, the average kinetic energy of molecules in a gas is $(3/2)kT$, which equals 0.039 ev at 25°.

Next, we will use the Boltzmann energy distribution to estimate the fraction of the molecules that have certain minimum kinetic energies, namely, 0.1 ev or 2.70 ev at 25°. For a U of 0.1 ev at 25°, the Boltzmann factor equals $e^{-(0.1)/(0.026)}$ or $e^{-3.8}$, which is 0.022. Therefore, only a relatively few molecules would have a kinetic energy of at least 0.1 ev at room temperature resulting from thermal collisions. On the other hand, the absorption of infrared radiation could lead to an excited state of the same energy. In particular, since the energy E for radiation equals $hc/\lambda_{\text{vacuum}}$ (Eq. 4–2) where hc is 1240 ev-nm (Appendix III), 0.1 ev corresponds to a photon with a wavelength of $(1240)/(0.1)$ or 12,400 nm (12.4 μm), which is in the IR. Absorption of such infrared radiation can increase the rate of certain reactions because molecules having a higher energy are usually more reactive. As an example of excitation energies corresponding to visible light, consider a kinetic energy U of 2.70 ev. In this case, $e^{-U/kT}$ is only 4×10^{-46} at room temperature! In other words, the chance of a molecule's gaining 2.70 ev or more of energy by means of thermal collisions is extraordinarily small. From Table 4–1, 2.70 ev corresponds to blue light of 460 nm. The absorption of such visible light leads to energetic states that otherwise would simply not occur at room temperature. Using the relatively high energy of light to attain very improbable energetic states is a key feature of photobiology.

Light Intensity. For many purposes in studying plant physiology, it is desirable to know the light intensity. The two most common systems of units used for measuring light intensity are the photometric units, which are related to the wavelength sensitivity of the human eye, and the radiometric units, which depend on the energy of the radiation.

By definition, photometric devices do not respond appreciably to radiation in the infrared or the ultraviolet since they are "light" meters in the sense applied to human vision. They often read directly in footcandles or lux. The candle is a unit of luminous intensity, originally based on a standard candle or lamp. The present international unit is called a candela (often, however, referred to as a candle) which is 1/60 of the light intensity emitted from 1 cm² of a blackbody radiator (one that radiates maximally) at the melting temperature of pure platinum (2042°K). The total light emitted in all directions by a source of 1 candela is 4π lumens. One footcandle is simply 1 lumen/ft² while one lux is 1 lumen/m² (hence the lux is a metric unit). To convert footcandles to lux, the number of footcandles is multiplied by the square feet per square meter, 10.76. Measurement in lux is adequate for certain purposes, particularly where human vision is involved. Since chlorophyll absorbs in the visible region (see p. 170), photometric units are often employed to describe light intensities that are used for photosynthesis. However, such a description can be misleading if the light source or its wavelength distribution is not indicated. For instance, at the same light intensity measured in lux, a fluorescent lamp produces about three times as much blue light as a tungsten lamp does.

Radiometric devices are sensitive to radiation in the ultraviolet and the infrared as well as in the visible. The readings are expressed in energy units such as ergs/cm²-sec or perhaps μwatts/cm² [a watt = 1 joule/sec (Appendix III)] and cannot be converted to photometric units. If the light intensity at a specified wavelength is measured in radiometric units, the value can be converted to a quantum flux (quanta/cm²-sec) by using the energy of an individual quantum given by Equation 4–2.

Essentially all the energy for life originates in the form of electromagnetic radiation from the sun; therefore we will consider some of the characteristics of its light intensity incident on the earth. On a cloudless day, sunlight can reach an intensity of 100,000 lux on the surface of the earth. In radiometric units, the intensity of solar radiation incident on the earth's atmosphere averages 2.00 cal/cm²-min. (This number, which is often referred to as the solar constant, will be considered in Chapter 6 in terms of both the temperatures of radiating bodies and also the annual photosynthetic yield.) The total daily amount of radiant energy from the sun reaching the earth's surface is about 900 cal/cm² on a cloudless day in the summer (the actual amount varies with latitude). About 41% of the quanta at the earth's surface are in the infrared region, 7% in the ultraviolet, and the rest are in the visible region.

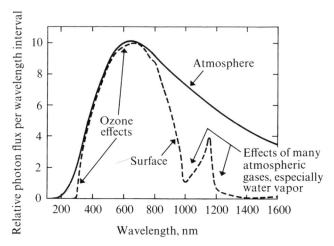

Figure 4–1. Wavelength distributions of the sun's photons incident on the earth's atmosphere and the surface of the earth.

Figure 4–1 shows the relative number of the sun's photons that impinge on the earth's atmosphere and that reach the surface as a function of wavelength. Most of the ultraviolet fraction of sunlight incident on the atmosphere is prevented from reaching the surface of the earth by ozone (O_3) present in the upper atmosphere. Ozone absorbs some visible radiation (especially near 600 nm) and effectively screens out the shorter ultraviolet rays by absorbing strongly below 300 nm. Much of the infrared from the sun is absorbed by atmospheric water vapor (cf. Fig. 4–1). Water absorbs strongly from 900 to 1100 nm and above 1200 nm, having a major infrared absorption band at 1400 nm (1.4 μm). Although the amount of water vapor in the air varies with latitude and season, the mean vapor concentration is equivalent to a path of liquid water 2.6 cm thick.

The wavelength distribution of photons reaching the earth's surface profoundly influences life. For instance, the strong absorption of ultraviolet by ozone reduces the potential hazard of mutagenic effects caused by the short wavelength radiation. The broad peak near 680 nm for photons that reach the earth's surface (Fig. 4–1) coincides with the red absorption band of chlorophyll. Vision also utilizes the wavelength region where most of the sunlight reaches the earth. Evolutionary competition evidently gave a selective advantage to species having photochemical systems utilizing visible light.

Absorption of Light by Molecules

In this discussion of light utilization by plants, we will first consider the actual absorption process, which must occur whether radiant energy is to be stored or light simply used as a trigger. In fact, only absorbed light is effective in producing a chemical change, a principle embodied in the Grotthus-Draper law of photochemistry. Another important principle of photochemistry is the Stark-Einstein law, which specifies that each absorbed photon activates but one molecule. Einstein further postulated that all the energy of the light quantum is transferred to a single electron during the absorption event, resulting in the movement of this electron to a higher energy state. To help understand light absorption, we must therefore first consider some of the properties of electrons. The fate of the excited electron will be discussed in the next section.

Role of Electrons in Absorption Event. From a classical viewpoint, an electron is a charged particle that moves in some orbit around a nucleus. The energy of the electron depends both on the location of the orbit in space and also on how fast the electron moves in the orbit. In classical language, the increase in energy of an electron upon absorbing a photon can be used to transfer that electron into an orbit which lies at a higher energy than the original orbit or to cause the electron to move more rapidly about the nucleus than it did before the light arrived. The locations of various possible electronic orbits and the speeds for electrons moving in them are both limited to certain discrete or "allowed" values, a phenomenon that has been interpreted by quantum mechanics. This means that an electron can take on only specific energies, and consequently the total electronic energy of an atom or molecule occurs in discrete levels or magnitudes. Only light of certain wavelengths will have the proper energy to cause the electron to move from one possible state to another. Therefore, for light absorption to occur, the photon energy given by Equation 4–2 must equal the difference in energy between some allowed excited state of the atom or molecule and the initial state, the latter usually being the ground or lowest energy state.

During light absorption, an interaction occurs between the electromagnetic field of the light and some electron in matter. Because electrons are charged particles, they will experience a force when in an electric field. Light consists of periodic variations in both the local electric and magnetic fields in the medium through which it is passing. It is the oscillating electric field of light which represents a periodic driving force acting on the electrons in matter.

This electric field, which is a vector quantity—meaning that it has a certain direction in space—causes or induces electrons to move. If the frequency of the electromagnetic radiation is such as to cause a large sympathetic oscillation or beating of some electron, that electron is said to be in resonance with the light wave. Such a resonating electron corresponds to a so-called electric dipole in the molecule, as the electron is displaced first in a certain direction and then in the opposite one in response to the oscillating electric field of the light. (An electric dipole is simply the local separation of positive and negative charge.) The direction and magnitude of the induced electric dipole will depend on the resisting or restoring forces on the electron that are provided by the rest of the molecule. These restoring forces depend on the other electrons and the atomic nuclei in the molecule and, consequently, are not the same in different types of molecules. Thus the actual electric dipoles that can be induced in a particular molecule are characteristic of that molecule, which underlies the unique absorption spectrum (to be discussed below) of a given molecular species.

The probability for light absorption depends both on its wavelength and the relative orientation of its electromagnetic field with respect to the electrons in the molecules. Absorption of photons can take place only if the following two conditions exist: (1) the light has the proper energy to get to a discrete excited state of the molecule (i.e., a specific wavelength, cf. Eq. 4–2), and (2) the electric field vector associated with the photon has a component parallel to the direction of the potential electric dipole in order that the electron can be induced to oscillate. In fact, the probability for absorption is proportional to the square of the cosine of the angle between the electric field vector of light and the direction of the induced electric dipole in the molecule. When these conditions on the wavelength and orientation are met, the light energy can be captured by the molecule, placing it in an excited state.

Electron Spin and State Multiplicity. Light absorption is affected by the arrangement of electrons in an atom or molecule, which depends among other things on a property of the individual electrons known as their "spin." Each electron can be considered to be a charged particle spinning about an axis in much the same way as the earth spins about its axis. Such a rotation has associated with it an intrinsic angular momentum or spin. The magnitude of the spin of all electrons is the same, but since spin is a vector quantity, it can be in different directions in space. For an electron, only two orientations are found, viz., the spin of the electron can be aligned either parallel or antiparallel to the local magnetic field. (Even in the absence of an external magnetic field such as that of the earth or some electromagnet, there is a local internal magnetic field provided by the moving charges in the nucleus and by the motion of the electrons.) For reasons which need not be discussed here, it has proved convenient to express the spin of electrons in units of $h/2\pi$, where h is Planck's constant. In these units, the projection along the magnetic field of the spin for a single electron is either $+\frac{1}{2}$, e.g., when it is parallel to the local magnetic field, or $-\frac{1}{2}$, when it is in the opposite direction. The total spin of the atom or molecule is the vector sum of the spins of all the electrons, each individual electron having a spin of either $+\frac{1}{2}$ or $-\frac{1}{2}$. The magnitude of this total spin is given the symbol, S, and is an extremely important quantity in spectroscopy.

The spin "multiplicity" of an electronic state is defined as $2S + 1$, where S is the magnitude of the net spin for the whole atom or molecule. For example, if S equals 0—which means that the spin projections of all the electrons taken along the magnetic field cancel each other—then $2S + 1$ is 1, and the state is called a *singlet*. On the other hand, if S equals 1, the state is a *triplet* ($2S + 1$ then equals 3). Singlets and triplets are the two most important spin multiplicities encountered in biological systems and will be considered in further detail below. When referring to an absorbing species, the spin multiplicity is generally indicated by S for singlet and T for triplet, the convention that will be adopted here.

As mentioned above, electrons are found only in certain "allowed" regions of space, the particular locus in which some electron can move being referred to as its *orbital*. In the 1920s, W. Pauli observed that when an electron having a spin in some direction was in a given atomic orbital, a second electron having its spin in the same direction was excluded from that orbital. This led to the enunciation of the Pauli exclusion principle of quantum mechanics, which requires that when two electrons are in the same orbital, their spins must be in opposite directions. When a molecule has all its electrons paired in orbitals with their spins in opposite directions, the total spin of the molecule is zero ($S = 0$), and the molecule is in a singlet state ($2S + 1 = 1$). The ground or unexcited state of most molecules is such a singlet, i.e., all the electrons are in pairs in the lower energy orbitals. When some electron is excited to an unoccupied orbital, two spin possibilities exist. The spins of the two electrons, which are now in different orbitals, may be in opposite directions, as they were when paired in the ground state. This electronic configuration is still a singlet state. On the other hand, the two electrons may have their spins in the same direction, which gives a triplet state (since the electrons are in different orbitals, their spins can be in the same direction without violating the Pauli principle). An important rule, first enunciated by Hund based on empirical observations and later explained using quantum mechanics, is that the level with the greatest spin multiplicity has the lowest energy. Thus, an excited triplet state is lower in energy than the corresponding excited singlet state, as will be illustrated below for the specific case of the chlorophyll molecule.

Molecular Orbitals.   When discussing the light absorption event involving the interaction of the electromagnetic wave with some electron, it was easiest to visualize the electron as a small point located at some specific position in the atom or molecule. When discussing the energy of an electron, we can consider the electron as moving in some fixed trajectory or orbit about the nucleus. However, to describe the role of electrons in the binding together of atoms to form a molecule, it is most convenient to imagine that the electron is spatially distributed like a cloud of negative charge surrounding the nuclei of adjacent atoms in the molecule. In this last description, which involves probability considerations introduced by quantum mechanics, the electrons are said to be located in molecular orbitals.

To discuss adequately the absorption of light by chlorophyll, carotenoids, and other pigments in plants, the electronic states of molecules need to be described using the language of molecular orbitals. These descriptions of the locations of electrons are based on the probability of finding an electron at various positions in space and are an extension of the concept of atomic orbitals. In atomic theory, there are s, p, d, . . . orbitals. An electron in an s orbital is referred to as an s electron. Such s electrons have zero orbital angular momentum, and their probability distributions in space are spherically symmetric about their respective atomic nuclei; p electrons have one unit of orbital angular momentum. By definition, a molecule contains more than one atom, certain of the electrons being able to move between the atoms. However, it still proves possible to describe the spatial localization of electrons in molecules by using suitable linear combinations of various atomic orbitals that are centered about the nuclei involved.

Some of the electrons in molecules are localized about a single nucleus while others are *delocalized* or shared between nuclei. In the latter case, the spatial overlap of the various atomic orbitals that are used to describe the molecular orbitals of the delocalized electrons leads to a finite probability of finding the atomic electrons moving between the adjacent nuclei. This sharing of electrons is responsible for the chemical bonds that prevent the molecule from separating into its constituent atoms, i.e., the negative elec-

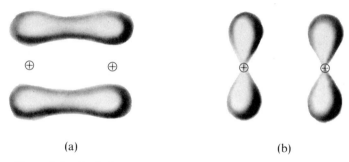

(a)   (b)

Figure 4–2. Typical π and π^* orbitals, indicating the spatial distribution about the nuclei ($\oplus$) where the greatest probability of finding the electrons occurs: (a) π orbital (bonding), and (b) π^* orbital (antibonding).

trons moving between the positive nuclei hold the molecule together by attracting nuclei in different atoms. Moreover, these delocalized electrons are the ones usually involved in light absorption by molecules.

The lowest energy molecular orbital is a σ orbital, which is analogous in symmetry properties to the s atomic orbital. Nonbonding or lone-pair electrons contributed by atoms like oxygen or nitrogen occur in n orbitals and retain their atomic character in the molecule. In other words, these n electrons are essentially physically separate from the other electrons in the molecule and do not take part in the bonding between nuclei. Most attention will be devoted here to electrons in π molecular orbitals, which are the equivalent of p electrons in atoms. Such π electrons are delocalized in a bond joining two or more atoms and since they are of such importance in light absorption, we will next consider the properties of π electrons in a little detail.

As just indicated, most photochemical reactions and spectroscopic properties of biologically important molecules result from the absorption of light quanta by π electrons. The excitation by light of a π electron can lead to an excited state of the molecule where the electron moves into a π^* orbital (the asterisk refers to an excited high-energy molecular orbital). The probability distributions for electrons in both π and π^* orbitals are indicated in Figure 4–2 (the circumscribed regions show where the electrons are most likely to be found). The left-hand side of this figure shows a π orbital delocalized between two nuclei, both of which as a consequence are electrostatically attracted by the same cloud of negative charge. Thus, the presence of electrons in the π orbital helps join the atoms together, and so this type of molecular orbital is referred to as a bonding one. As indicated in Figure 4–2(b), electrons in π^* orbitals do not help join atoms together but rather tend to decrease the bonding between the atoms in the molecule since the clouds of negative charge in adjacent atoms are then in a position to repel each other. Therefore, a π^* orbital is referred to as an antibonding one. The decrease in bonding in going from a π to a π^* orbital results in a less stable (higher energy) electronic state for the molecule, and so a π^* orbital is at a higher energy than a π orbital.

In photochemistry, the increase in energy in moving an electron from the attractive or bonding π orbital to the antibonding π^* orbital is achieved by the absorption of a photon. For the cases of highly conjugated molecules like chlorophylls and carotenoids to be considered below, the π^* orbitals are often only a few electron volts higher in energy than the corresponding π orbitals. Therefore, the absorption of visible light, which corresponds to photons with energies from 1.7 to 3.1 ev (Table 4–1), can lead to the excitation of π electrons into the π^* orbitals in such molecules.

Light Absorption by Chlorophyll.   Certain terms introduced above to describe the absorption of light by molecules will be illustrated by a specific consideration of chlorophyll, whose principal energy levels and electronic transitions are presented in Figure 4–3. (Chlorophyll will be considered in more detail in Chapter 5.) In the ground state, chlorophyll is a singlet as are essentially all pigments of importance in biological systems. Upon the absorption of a photon, some π electron is excited to a π^* orbital (cf. the two types of orbitals indicated in Fig. 4–2). When this excited state is a singlet, it is represented by $S_{(\pi,\pi^*)}$. The first symbol in the subscript is the type of electron (here a π electron) which has been excited to the antibonding orbital indicated by the second symbol (here π^*). The ground state will be represented by $S_{(\pi,\pi)}$, indicating that no electrons are then in excited or antibonding orbitals. If the orientation of the spin of the excited π electron had become reversed during excitation, it would be in the same direction as the spin of the electron which remained in the π orbital. (Each filled orbital contains two electrons whose spins are in opposite directions, as mentioned above.) In this case, the net spin of the molecule in the excited state would be 1, which is known as a triplet. The excited triplet state of chlorophyll is represented by $T_{(\pi,\pi^*)}$ in Figure 4–3.

Chlorophyll has two principal excited singlet states which differ considerably in energy. One of these states, designated $S^a_{(\pi,\pi^*)}$ in Figure 4–3, can be excited by red light such as that having a wavelength of 680 nm. The

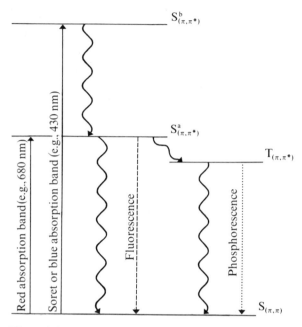

Figure 4–3. Energy level diagram indicating the principal electronic states and transitions of chlorophyll. Straight vertical lines represent the absorption of light while wavy lines indicate radiationless transitions and broken lines indicate those de-excitations that are accompanied by radiation.

other state, $S^b_{(\pi, \pi^*)}$, lies higher in energy and is excited by blue light (e.g., 430 nm). The electronic transitions caused by the absorption of photons are indicated by solid vertical arrows in Figure 4–3 while the vertical distances approximately correspond to the differences in energy involved. Excitation of a singlet ground state to an excited triplet state usually is only about 10^{-5} times as probable as going to an excited singlet state, and so the transition from $S_{(\pi, \pi)}$ to $T_{(\pi, \pi^*)}$ has not been indicated for chlorophyll in Figure 4–3. To go from $S_{(\pi, \pi)}$ to $T_{(\pi, \pi^*)}$, both the energy of the electron must be substantially increased and the orientation of the electron spin must simultaneously be reversed. Since the coincidence of these two events is rather improbable, very few chlorophyll molecules are directly excited to $T_{(\pi, \pi^*)}$ from the ground state by the absorption of light. The various transitions originating from the excited states, such as fluorescence, phosphorescence, and those which are radiationless, will be considered in the next section.

De-excitation

The primary processes of photochemistry involve the light absorption event together with the subsequent de-excitation reactions. Such transitions can be portrayed on an energy level diagram, such as Figure 4–3 for chlorophyll. One of the important features that distinguishes between the various excitation and de-excitation processes is the time that the individual transitions take. The amount of time necessary for the absorption of a photon can be roughly estimated from the time required for one complete oscillation of the electromagnetic field of the light wave. This amount of time is simply the reciprocal of the frequency ν. To be specific, consider blue light having a wavelength of 460 nm in a vacuum. From Table 4–1, the time for one cycle is $1/(6.52 \times 10^{14})$ or 1.5×10^{-15} sec. Light absorption is an extremely rapid event!

Times for de-excitation reactions are usually expressed in terms of "lifetimes." A lifetime is the time required for the number of molecules in a given state to decrease by 63%. This number is not as arbitrary is it may appear since the 37% remaining equals $1/e$ of the initial number. Lifetimes are therefore extremely convenient for describing first-order processes because the initial species in such processes decay or disappear exponentially with time. A "half-time," the time necessary for the number of species in a given state to decrease by 50%, is occasionally used to describe de-excitation processes (for an exponential decay, one half-time is ln 2 or 0.693 times the size of a lifetime).

Fluorescence, Phosphorescence, and Radiationless Transitions.   As would be expected, the excess energy of the excited state can be dissipated by a number of competing reactions. One of the ways in which de-excitation can occur is by the emission of light known as fluorescence and indicated by a dashed straight line in Figure 4–3 for the principal transitions of chlorophyll. Specifically, fluorescence is energy emitted as electromagnetic radiation when a molecule goes from an excited singlet state to a singlet ground state. Fluorescent lifetimes for most organic molecules are from 10^{-9} to 10^{-6} sec. The properties of chlorophyll fluorescence are extremely important for an understanding of the primary events of photosynthesis and will also be considered in Chapter 5.

De-excitation of an excited state often occurs without the emission of any radiation. Such transitions are termed nonradiative or radiationless and are indicated by wavy lines in Figure 4–3. For a radiationless transition to a lower energy excited state or back to the ground state, the energy of the absorbed photon is converted to heat that is passed on by collisions with the surrounding molecules. Radiationless transitions can be extremely rapid from one excited singlet state to a lower energy excited singlet state in the same molecule. For example, the radiationless transition from $S^b_{(\pi,\pi*)}$ to $S^a_{(\pi,\pi*)}$ indicated for chlorophyll in Figure 4–3 takes about 10^{-12} sec. This transition is so rapid that hardly any fluorescence has a chance to be emitted from $S^b_{(\pi,\pi*)}$, and so no fluorescent emission is indicated in Figure 4–3 from the upper excited singlet state of chlorophyll. The excited singlet state lying at the lower energy, $S^a_{(\pi,\pi*)}$, can decay to the ground state by a radiationless transition. As another alternative, $S^a_{(\pi,\pi*)}$ can go to $T_{(\pi,\pi*)}$ also by a radiation-less transition (Fig. 4–3). In fact, excited triplet states in molecules are mainly formed by radiationless transitions from excited singlet states having higher energies. The de-excitation of $T_{(\pi,\pi*)}$ to $S_{(\pi,\pi)}$ can be radiationless or by radiation known as phosphorescence (dotted straight line in Fig. 4–3), which will be considered next.

Phosphorescence accompanies the transition of a molecule from an excited triplet state to a ground state singlet, and so the net spin of the molecule must change during the emission of this electromagnetic radiation. The lifetimes for phosphorescence are usually from 10^{-3} to 10 sec, which are long compared with those for fluorescence (10^{-9} to 10^{-6} sec). These long times for de-excitation result because the transition is from one electronic state to another, and, simultaneously, the electron spin must be reversed, the coinci-dence of these two events being rather improbable. In fact, the low probability of forming $T_{(\pi,\pi*)}$ from $S_{(\pi,\pi)}$ by light absorption that was mentioned above has the same physical basis as the long lifetime for the de-excitation of the excited triplet state back to the ground state by emitting phosphorescence. The excited triplet state of chlorophyll has not been unambiguously demon-strated *in vivo*, e.g., the expected phosphorescence is not apparent although phosphorescence by chlorophyll *in vitro* has been shown.

Competing Pathways for De-excitation. Each excited state has not only a definite energy but also a specific lifetime which depends on the particular processes competing for its de-excitation. In addition to fluorescence, phosphorescence, and the radiationless transitions discussed above, the excitation energy can also be transferred to another molecule, causing this second molecule to go to an excited state while the originally excited molecule returns to its ground state. As an example of yet another type of de-excitation process, the excited or energetic electron may actually leave the molecule that absorbed the photon, which indeed occurs for certain excited chlorophyll molecules (to be discussed later). The excited state that appears to be of pivotal importance in photosynthesis is the lower excited singlet state of chlorophyll, indicated by $S^a_{(\pi,\pi*)}$ in Figure 4–3. This will be taken as a specific example to indicate some of the possible competing reactions leading to the de-excitation of an excited singlet state, $S_{(\pi,\pi*)}$.

The absorbed quantum can be reradiated as electromagnetic energy, $h\nu$, causing the excited molecule $[S_{(\pi,\pi*)}]$ to drop back to the ground state, $S_{(\pi,\pi)}$:

$$S_{(\pi,\pi*)} \xrightarrow{\ k_1\ } S_{(\pi,\pi)} + h\nu \qquad (4\text{–}3)$$

Such fluorescence decays away exponentially with time after the exciting light is removed, indicating a first-order process having a rate constant given by k_1 in Equation 4–3. The fluorescent lifetime of $S_{(\pi,\pi*)}$ is $1/k_1$, which typically is about 10^{-8} sec as indicated above. This would be the lifetime of $S_{(\pi,\pi*)}$, if no other competing de-excitation processes occurred. (Lifetimes and rate constants will be considered again below.) It is important to point out that when the energy of the absorbed quantum is dissipated as fluorescence, no photochemical work can be done. Therefore, the fluorescent lifetime is essentially the upper time limit in which any biologically useful reactions can be driven by the lowest excited singlet state of a molecule.

The next de-excitation processes we will consider are the radiationless transitions by which $S_{(\pi,\pi*)}$ dissipates its excess electronic energy as heat.

$$S_{(\pi,\pi*)} \xrightarrow{\ k_2\ } S_{(\pi,\pi)} + \text{heat} \qquad (4\text{–}4)$$

$$S_{(\pi,\pi*)} \xrightarrow{\ k_3\ } T_{(\pi,\pi*)} + \text{heat} \qquad (4\text{–}5)$$

Radiationless transitions like those indicated in Equations 4–4 and 4–5 involve de-excitation by collisions; the radiant energy of the absorbed light is eventually converted into thermal energy. As is the case for fluorescence, such radiationless transitions also obey first-order kinetics. Although the dissipation of excitation energy as heat in a transition to the ground state (Eq. 4–4) is wasteful photochemically in that no biological work is performed, the transition to $T_{(\pi,\pi*)}$ indicated by Equation 4–5 can be quite useful. The lowest excited triplet state usually lasts 10^4 to 10^8 times longer than does $S_{(\pi,\pi*)}$, which allows time for many more intermolecular collisions. Since each collision increases the opportunity for a given reaction to occur, $T_{(\pi,\pi*)}$ can be an important excited state in photobiology.

The absorption of light can lead to a photochemical reaction initiated by a molecule other than the one which actually absorbed the photon. Such a phenomenon suggests that electronic excitation can be transferred from molecule to molecule, resulting in the excitation of one and de-excitation of the other. For instance, the excitation energy of $S_{(\pi,\pi*)}$ might be transferred to a second molecule, represented in the ground state by $S_{2(\pi,\pi)}$:

$$S_{(\pi,\pi*)} + S_{2(\pi,\pi)} \xrightarrow{k_4} S_{(\pi,\pi)} + S_{2(\pi,\pi*)} \qquad (4\text{--}6)$$

This second molecule thereby becomes excited, indicated by $S_{2(\pi,\pi*)}$ in Equation 4–6, while the molecule which absorbed the quantum becomes de-excited and is returned to the ground state. Such transfer of electronic excitation from molecule to molecule underlies the energy migration among the pigments involved in photosynthesis.

As another type of de-excitation process, $S_{(\pi,\pi*)}$ can directly take part in a photochemical reaction, this process representing the biologically most important way of disposing of excess electronic energy. For example, the excited $\pi*$ electron can be donated to a suitable acceptor. In the following equation, this ejected electron is represented by $e*$:

$$S_{(\pi,\pi*)} \xrightarrow{k_5} S_{(\pi)} + e* \qquad (4\text{--}7)$$

The electron ejected from $S_{(\pi,\pi*)}$ is replaced by another one donated from some other compound; $S_{(\pi)}$ in Equation 4–7 then goes back to the original ground state, $S_{(\pi,\pi)}$. (Electron energy and donation will be considered in Chapters 5 and 6.) Photochemical reactions of the form of Equation 4–7 serve as the crucial link in the conversion of radiant energy into chemical or electrical energy. Moreover, Equation 4–7 can be used to represent the photochemical reaction taking place at special chlorophyll molecules (to be discussed later). In that case, $e*$ could be the electron removed from a type of chlorophyll known as P_{700}, this electron being replaced by one coming from a reduced cytochrome or other electron donor.

Lifetimes and Quantum Yields.   Equations 4–3 through 4–7 represents five competing pathways for the de-excitation of the excited singlet state, $S_{(\pi,\pi*)}$, which must all be considered when predicting its lifetime. Assuming that each of these various dissipative processes is a first-order one, we find that the disappearance of the excited singlet state satisfies the following relation:

$$-\frac{dS_{(\pi,\pi*)}}{dt} = (k_1 + k_2 + k_3 + k_4 + k_5)S_{(\pi,\pi*)} \qquad (4\text{--}8)$$

where the various k_j's appearing in Equation 4–8 are the rate constants for the five individual decay reactions indicated (Eqs. 4–3 through 4–7). Upon integration of Equation 4–8, the following expression for the time dependence of the number of molecules in the excited singlet state is obtained:

$$S_{(\pi,\pi^*)_t} = S_{(\pi,\pi^*)_0} e^{-(k_1 + k_2 + k_3 + k_4 + k_5)t} \qquad (4\text{–}9)$$

where $S_{(\pi,\pi^*)_0}$ represents the number of molecules in the excited singlet state when the illumination is ceased ($t = 0$) and $S_{(\pi,\pi^*)_t}$ is the number of excited singlet states remaining at a subsequent time t. Equations like 4–9 showing the disappearance of some state with time are extremely important for describing processes that have first-order rate constants.

As was mentioned above, the lifetime of an excited state is the time required for the number of excited molecules to decrease to $1/e$ of the initial value. Thus, $S_{(\pi,\pi^*)_t}$ in Equation 4–9 equals $(1/e)$ $S_{(\pi,\pi^*)_0}$ when t equals the lifetime τ, which leads to the following relationship:

$$(k_1 + k_2 + k_3 + k_4 + k_5)\tau = 1 \qquad (4\text{–}10)$$

Equation 4–10 indicates that the greater the rate constant for *any* particular de-excitation process, the shorter will be the lifetime of the excited state. Equation 4–10 can be generalized to include all competing reactions, which gives the following expression for the lifetime:

$$\frac{1}{\tau} = \sum_j k_j = \sum_j \frac{1}{\tau_j} \qquad (4\text{–}11)$$

where k_j is the first-order rate constant for the jth de-excitation process and τ_j is its lifetime ($\tau_j = 1/k_j$, which can be derived from Eq. 4–10 or Eq. 4–11 by considering that only the jth de-excitation pathway is available). Equations 4–10 and 4–11 indicate that when more than one de-excitation process is possible, τ is less than the lifetimes for any of the competing reactions. In other words, the observed rate of decay of an excited state is faster than the deactivation by any single competing reaction acting alone. If the rate constant for one particular reaction is much larger than for its competitors, the excited state will become de-excited predominantly by that process.

A quantum efficiency or yield, Φ, is often used to describe de-excitation processes such as those which occur in the primary events of photosynthesis. Specifically, the quantity Φ_i indicates the fraction of the molecules in some excited state reached by the absorption of light which will decay by the ith de-excitation reaction:

$$\Phi_i = \frac{\text{number of molecules undergoing } i^{th} \text{ reaction}}{\text{number of quanta absorbed}} = \frac{k_i}{\sum\limits_{j} k_j} = \frac{\tau}{\tau_i} \quad (4\text{--}12)$$

The competition between the various reactions, expressed by $k_i / \sum\limits_j k_j$ in Equation 4–12, determines the fraction of the molecules in a given excited state that will use the ith de-excitation pathway. In other words, the rate constant for a particular pathway determines what share of the excitations is dissipated by that process and thus determines the quantum yield for that de-excitation pathway. From Equation 4–11 and the definition of τ_j given above, such competition among pathways can also be indicated by lifetimes (cf. Eq. 4–12). The shorter the lifetime τ_j for a particular de-excitation pathway, the larger will be the fraction of the molecules using that pathway and hence the higher will be its quantum yield.

To illustrate the use of Equation 4–12, let us consider the quantum yield for chlorophyll fluorescence, Φ_{Fl}. The fluorescent lifetime τ_{Fl} of the lowest excited singlet state of chlorophyll in ether is 1.5×10^{-8} sec while the observed lifetime τ for de-excitation of this excited state in ether has been measured to be 0.5×10^{-8} sec. By Equation 4–12, the expected quantum yield for fluorescence would be $(0.5 \times 10^{-8})/(1.5 \times 10^{-8})$ or $1/3$, which is consistent with the observed Φ_{Fl} of 0.33 for the fluorescent de-excitation of chlorophyll in ether.

Absorption Spectra and Action Spectra

As has been discussed above, the absorption of radiation causes a transition from the ground state to some excited state where one of the electrons is in an orbital that lies at a higher energy. Both the ground state and the various excited states have so far been considered to occur at specific energy levels, as was indicated by the horizontal lines in Figure 4–3 for the case of the electronic states of chlorophyll. In other words, it might appear that only a very limited number of wavelengths could be absorbed, e.g., 430 and 680 nm for the chlorophyll molecule indicated in Figure 4–3. However, each electronic energy level is actually divided or split into various sublevels which differ in energy. The largest splitting is due to the vibrational sublevels, which play an important role in determining the absorption properties of molecules. The vibrational sublevels are caused by the atoms in a molecule vibrating back and forth with respect to each other, this vibration affecting the distribution of the electrons about the nuclei and consequently influencing the electronic energy. It has proved convenient to describe this atomic oscillation by the accompanying change in the internuclear distance. Therefore, we will consider an energy level diagram that indicates the range of positions (trajectories) taken on by the vibrating nuclei. The energies and trajectories of such nuclear vibrations are quantized, meaning that only specific values occur, as was the case for the quantization of angular momenta of electrons mentioned previously. As a consequence of this quantization of the trajectories for the vibrating nuclei, only discrete energies are possible for the vibrational sublevels of a given electronic state. (Further splitting of the vibrational sublevels will be considered later in this section.)

At temperatures normally encountered by plants, essentially all molecules are in the ground or unexcited state. Moreover, these molecules are nearly all in the lowest vibrational sublevel of the ground state. This condition of having most of the molecules in the lowest possible energy level is a consequence of the Boltzmann energy distribution. The absorption of a photon causes a transition of the molecule from the lowest vibrational sublevel of the ground state to one of the vibrational sublevels of the excited electronic state. The actual sublevel reached depends on the energy of the absorbed quantum. For reasons that will become clear as we discuss the vibrational sublevels, the probability of a photon's being absorbed also depends on its energy. Consideration of this absorption *probability* as a function of wavelength leads to an absorption spectrum for that particular molecule. The *effect* of light absorption as a function of wavelength is handled by an action spectrum, which will be considered at the end of this section for a phytochrome-mediated reaction.

Vibrational Sublevels and the Franck-Condon Principle.   Various vibrational sublevels of a representative ground state and an excited state are schematically indicated in Figure 4–4. The abscissa is the distance between a pair of nuclei which are vibrating back and forth with respect to each other, i.e., the x-axis is the nuclear separation obtained by imagining one nucleus to be situated at the origin of the coordinate system while the position of the other nucleus is recorded relative to this origin. The ordinate represents the total energy of the molecule in relative units. Figure 4–4 shows the excited state at the higher energy and also the splitting of both electronic states into many vibrational sublevels which differ in energy. Such an energy level

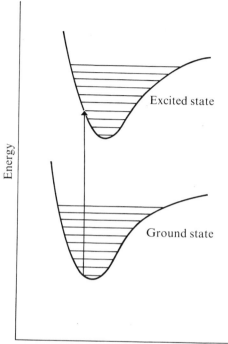

Energy

Nuclear separation

Figure 4-4. Energy curves for the ground and the excited states showing the various vibrational sublevels. The vertical arrow represents an electronic transition which is caused by the absorption of a photon and is consistent with the Franck-Condon principle.

diagram is extremely useful for predicting which electronic transitions are most likely to accompany the absorption of light.

Due to the balance of the internuclear repulsive forces against the electrostatic attraction between the nuclei and the shared electrons, only a certain range of internuclear separations occurs in a molecule. Specifically, as the separation between the nuclei decreases, they repel each other more and more, and thus the energy of the molecule increases. This is indicated by the steep rise of the energy curves in Figure 4-4 as the nuclear separation becomes less and less (left-hand side of the figure). On the other hand, the delocalized or bonding electrons shared by the two nuclei resist the unlimited increase in nuclear separation, this increase in distance between the nuclei corresponding to a stretching of the chemical bond. Thus the energy curve in Figure 4-4 also rises as the internuclear distance becomes greater and greater (right-hand side of the figure). Because of these two opposing tendencies, the range of possible nuclear separations is confined to an energy trough. It is within these troughs, one for the ground state and another for the excited state, that the trajectories of the nuclear vibrations occur.

The horizontal lines in Figure 4–4 are the actual range of nuclear separations corresponding to a given vibrational sublevel, which means that the nuclei vibrate back and forth along the distance indicated by the horizontal lines. As is evident in the figure, both the ground state and also the excited state have many vibrational sublevels which differ in energy. For the upper vibrational sublevels of a given electronic state, the nuclei vibrate over longer distances (more extensive range of nuclear separations in Fig. 4–4), which also corresponds to higher vibrational energies. Since the excited state has an electron in an antibonding orbital, it usually has a greater mean internuclear separation than does the ground state. This is shown in Figure 4–4 by a slight displacement to greater nuclear separations (i.e., to the right) for the upper curve.

Because the direction of nuclear motion is reversed at the extremities of the vibrational pathways (indicated by horizontal lines in Fig. 4–4), the velocity of the nuclei must be zero at these turning points. As the turning point at either end of the oscillation range is approached, the nuclei begin to slow down, and consequently they spend most of their time at or near the extreme ends of their trajectory. Therefore, a photon is most likely to arrive at the molecule when the nuclei are at or near the extremes of their vibrational range. Because of this probability consideration, the vertical arrow in Figure 4–4 indicating the electronic transition resulting from the absorption of a photon has been initiated from one of the ends of the nuclear oscillation range for the lowest vibrational sublevel of the ground state. (Based on the Boltzmann energy distribution, nearly all of the ground state molecules are in the lowest vibrational sublevel at the temperatures encountered in plants.)

The vibrational sublevels of the excited state that are most likely to be involved in the electronic transitions accompanying light absorption can be predicted using the Franck-Condon principle. This principle states that the nuclei do not change their position or their velocity during those transitions for which the absorption of a photon is most probable. Since a vertical line in Figure 4–4 corresponds to no change in nuclear separation, the absorption of a photon has been indicated by a vertical arrow. This condition of constant internuclear distance during absorption is statistically easiest to satisfy when the nuclei are moving slowly or actually stopped at the extremes of their oscillation range. Thus the origin of the arrow indicating the electronic transition in Figure 4–4 is at one of the turning points of the lowest vibrational sublevel of the ground state while the tip is drawn to an extremity of one of the vibrational sublevels in the excited state, this being the fourth vibrational sublevel for the particular case illustrated. The other condition embodied in the Franck-Condon principle is that a quantum has the greatest chance of being absorbed when the velocity (a vector) of the vibrating nuclei does not change. In other words, absorption is maximal when the nuclei would be moving in the same direction and at the same speed in both the ground state and the excited state. Again, this condition has the greatest statistical probability of being met when the nuclei are moving slowly or not at all as occurs at the turning points for the nuclear oscillation. Therefore, the most probable electronic transition represented in a diagram like Figure 4–4 is a vertical line, which originates from one of the ends of the horizontal line that represents the range of nuclear separations for the lowest vibrational sublevel of the ground state and which goes to the end of the vibrational trajectory for some sublevel of the excited state.

Another way of viewing the constancy of internuclear distance during light absorption as predicted by the Franck-Condon principle is to consider that the light absorption event is so rapid that the nuclei do not have a chance to move during it. As indicated above, the absorption of a photon requires about 10^{-15} sec. On the other hand, the period for one nuclear vibration back and forth along an oscillation range like those indicated by horizontal lines in Figure 4–4 is about 10^{-13} sec. Thus the nuclei are not able to move any appreciable distance during the time necessary for the absorption of a photon, especially when the nuclei are moving relatively slowly near the ends of their vibrational trajectory.

Since the frequency of nuclear oscillations has been introduced, another aspect having far-reaching consequences should be mentioned. Specifically, as the nuclei oscillate back and forth along their trajectories, they can have collisions with other nuclei, these encounters making possible the transfer of energy from nucleus to nucleus. Thus, the approximate time for one cycle of a nuclear vibration, 10^{-13} sec, is an estimate of the time in which excess vibrational energy can be dissipated as heat by collisions with other nuclei. As excess energy is exchanged by such processes, the molecule soon attains the lowest vibrational sublevel of the excited state, these transitions within the same electronic state usually being complete in about 10^{-12} sec. The fluorescent lifetime generally is of the order of 10^{-8} sec as indicated above, and so an excited singlet state gets to its lowest vibrational sublevel before appreciable de-excitation can occur by fluorescence. Meanwhile, the rapid dissipation of excess vibrational energy causes some of the energy of the absorbed photon to be released as heat. Therefore, fluorescence is generally of lower energy (longer wavelength) than the absorbed light, as will be specifically shown for chlorophyll in the next chapter.

The Franck-Condon principle predicts the most likely electronic transition that is caused by the absorption of light, but others do indeed occur. These other transitions become statistically less probable the further the conditions are from no change in nuclear position or velocity during the absorption of the photon. Since electronic transitions to higher and lower vibrational sublevels in the excited state occur to a lesser extent than to the optimal one, the absorption of light is not as great at the wavelengths that excite the molecule to such vibrational sublevels. Also, some transitions will begin from an excited vibrational sublevel of the ground state. (The fraction of the ground state molecules in the various vibrational sublevels can be calculated from the Boltzmann energy distribution.) The various vibrational sublevels of both the ground and the excited states are approximately 0.1 ev apart. An energy difference of 0.1 ev between two photons corresponds to a difference in wavelength of about 25 nm near the middle of the visible region of the spectrum (green or yellow, Table 4–1). As the wavelength of incident light is increased or decreased from that for the most intense absorption, transitions involving other vibrational sublevels become important, e.g., at approximately 25 nm intervals in the green or yellow region. In summary, the amount of light absorbed will be maximal at a certain wavelength that corresponds to the most probable transition predicted by the Franck-Condon principle. Transitions from other vibrational sublevels of the ground state and to other sublevels of the excited state occur less frequently and help lead to an absorption spectrum that is characteristic of a particular molecule.

Absorption Bands and Absorption Coefficients.   The above discussion of light absorption has been primarily concerned with transitions from the ground state energy level to those of the excited states, expanded to include the occurrence of vibrational sublevels of the electronic states. In addition, the vibrational sublevels are actually divided into numerous rotational and translational energy levels. The rotational energy increments are about 0.01 ev or approximately 3 nm in wavelength in the visible region. The broadening of absorption lines because of translational energies is generally much less, often about 0.001 ev. Moreover, interactions with the solvent or other neighboring molecules can affect the electronic distribution in a particular molecule and consequently can shift the position of the various energy levels.

The quanta that can be absorbed in a specific electronic transition— including the range of energies possible because of the various vibrational sublevels and other shifts, such as those due to rotational and translational subdivisions—give rise to an absorption band. This is a range of wavelengths that can be absorbed for the electronic transition from the ground state to some excited state. A plot of the relative efficiency for light absorption as a function of wavelength is an absorption spectrum, which may include more than one absorption band. The smoothness of the absorption bands of most pigment molecules indicates that a great number of different photon energies can correspond to the transition of an electron from the ground state to some excited state.

The absorption at a specific wavelength by a certain type of molecule is quantitatively described using an absorption coefficient, ϵ (also referred to as an extinction coefficient). Because of its descriptive usefulness in plant physiology, an expression involving ϵ will now be derived. Let us consider a parallel monochromatic beam of light of intensity I_o (monochromatic means of a single wavelength). While passing through a solution, some of the light may be absorbed, and so the emerging beam will generally have a lower intensity, I (scattering and reflection losses are assumed to be negligible). In a small path length dx along the direction of the beam, the light intensity decreases by an amount dI due to absorption. The quantity of light absorbed is directly proportional to the light intensity I and to the concentration c of the species absorbing the light, which leads to the following expression:

$$-dI = KIcdx \qquad (4\text{--}13)$$

where K is a proportionality constant and the minus sign occurs in Equation 4–13 because the light intensity is decreased by absorption. After dividing both sides of Equation 4–13 by I, integration across a solution of a given concentration leads to

$$-\ln \frac{I}{I_o} = Kcb \qquad (4\text{--}14)$$

where I in Equation 4–14 is the intensity of the beam after traversing a distance b through the solution. The natural logarithm appearing in Equation 4–14 can be replaced by the common logarithm [ln = 2.303 log (Appendix III)] and $K/2.303$ by the absorption coefficient, ϵ, which gives

$$A = \log \frac{I_o}{I} = \epsilon cb \qquad (4\text{--}15)$$

where A in Equation 4–15 is the absorbance (colloquially, the "optical density") of the solution being considered. Equation 4–15 is referred to as Beer's law (sometimes called the Beer-Lambert or Lambert-Beer law).

According to Beer's law, the absorbance at some particular wavelength is independent of the light intensity but is proportional to the concentration of the absorbing species and to its absorption coefficient at that wavelength. In many absorption studies performed in the laboratory using solutions of biological pigments, the optical path length b is 1 cm, and the absorbing species is dissolved in a solvent that does not absorb light at the wavelengths under consideration. The concentration of the absorbing species, c, is usually expressed in moles/cm^3 or moles/liter, and so the absorption coefficient ϵ is in cm^2/mole or liters/mole-cm, respectively. When expressed in liters/mole-cm, ϵ is called the molar absorption coefficient (often referred to as the molar extinction coefficient). Values of ϵ for organic compounds range from less than 1 to over 10^5 liters/mole-cm in the UV and the visible. If ϵ at a specified wavelength is known for a particular molecule, its concentration can be determined from the measured absorbance by using Beer's law, Equation 4–15.

Applying Beer's law, we will roughly estimate the average chlorophyll concentration in leaf cells. The palisade and spongy mesophyll cells in the leaf section portrayed in Figure 1–2 correspond to an average thickness of chlorophyll-containing cells of about 200 μm (0.02 cm). The maximum molar absorption coefficient, ϵ, in the red or blue bands of chlorophyll (cf. Fig. 4–3 and the discussion in Chapter 5) is close to 10^5 liters/mole-cm. At the peaks of the absorption bands, about 99% of the incident red and blue light can be absorbed by chlorophyll in a leaf section such as that illustrated in Figure 1–2. This corresponds to having an emergent intensity, I, equal to 1% of the incident intensity, I_o, and so the absorbance, A, in Equation 4–15 equals log (100/1) or 2. Using Beer's law (Eq. 4–15), we find that the average chlorophyll concentration, c, is $(2)/[(10^5)(0.02)]$ or 1×10^{-3} mole/liter, a value characteristic of the average chlorophyll concentration in the photo-synthesizing cells in many different types of leaves. Chlorophyll is located only in the chloroplasts, which in turn occupy about 4% or 1/25 of the volume of a mesophyll cell in the leaf of a higher plant. Therefore, the average concentration of chlorophyll in chloroplasts is about twenty-five times higher than the above estimate of chlorophyll in a leaf and so is 25 mM. A typical light path through a chloroplast (cf. Fig. 1–7) is about 3 μm $(3 \times 10^{-4}$ cm). Again using Beer's law [$A = \epsilon c b$ (Eq. 4–15)], we find that the absorbance of a single chloroplast in the red or blue bands is thus $(10^5)(25 \times 10^{-3})(3 \times 10^{-4})$ or 0.75. This means that I_o/I equals 5.6 (using log table in Appendix V), and so I is only about 18% of I_o. Therefore, up to approximately 82% of the incident red or blue light at the peak of the absorption bands is absorbed by a single chloroplast, which explains why individual chloroplasts appear green under a light microscope.

Conjugation.   As mentioned in our discussion of molecular orbitals, light absorption by molecules generally involves electronic transitions of π electrons to excited states where the electrons are in π^* orbitals. These π electrons that take part in the absorption of photons occur in double bonds. The number of double bonds in conjugation determines the effectiveness of a particular molecule in absorbing electromagnetic radiation, where the term *conjugation* refers to the alternation of single and double bonds (e.g., C—C=C—C=C—C=C—C) along some part of the molecule. When the number of double bonds in the conjugated system is increased, the absorption bands are shifted to longer wavelengths, and they become more intense. The absorption coefficient, ϵ, increases with the number of double bonds in the molecule since there are then more delocalized (shared) π electrons capable of interacting with the light.

   The effect of the number of double bonds in conjugation on the wavelength position for an absorption band can be made plausible by considering the shifts in energy for the various orbitals as the number of π electrons in the conjugated system is changed. The various π orbitals in a conjugated system occur at different energy levels, the average energy remaining about the same as for the π orbital in an isolated double bond which is not part of a conjugated system (Fig. 4–5). In particular, the more double bonds there are in the conjugated system, the more π orbitals there are in the conjugated system, and the greater is the energy range from the lowest to the highest energy π orbital, as is illustrated in Figure 4–5. Since the average energy of the π orbitals in a conjugated system does not appreciably depend on the number of double bonds, the energy of the highest energy π orbital increases as the number of double bonds in conjugation increases. The π^* orbitals are similarly split into various energy levels, as is diagrammed in Figure 4–5. Also, the range of energy levels about the mean for these π^* orbitals increases as the number of double bonds in the conjugated system increases. Consequently, the more π^* orbitals there are available in the conjugated system, the lower in energy will be the lowest of these. Hence, a transition from the highest energy π orbital to the lowest energy π^* orbital requires less energy the more delocalized π electrons there are in the conjugated system. This is illustrated in Figure 4–5 by a decrease in the length of the vertical arrow that

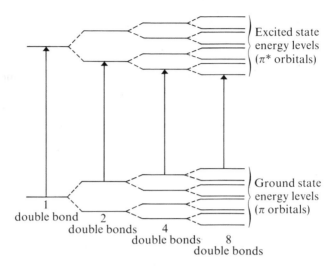

Figure 4–5.   Effect on the energy levels of π and π^* orbitals as the number of double bonds in conjugation increases. The vertical arrows represent electronic transitions caused by the absorption of photons, the energy required becoming less and less as the extent of conjugation increases.

represents an electronic transition as the number of double bonds in conjugation increases.

The decrease in energy separation between the π and the π^* orbitals as the number of double bonds in conjugation increases underlies the accompanying shift of the peaks of the absorption bands toward longer wavelengths. An isolated double bond (C—C=C—C) absorbs maximally near 185 nm in the ultraviolet and has a maximum absorption coefficient of nearly 10^4 liters/mole-cm. For two double bonds in conjugation (C—C=C—C=C—C), the absorption coefficient doubles and the wavelength position for maximum absorption shifts to about 225 nm, i.e., toward the visible region and longer wavelengths. As the number of double bonds in conjugation in straight-chain hydrocarbons increases from 3 to 5 to 7 to 9, the center of the absorption band for these hydrocarbons that are dissolved in hexane is shifted from approximately 265 to 325 to 375 to 415 nm, respectively. Concomitantly, the absorption coefficient increases nearly proportionally to the number of double bonds in the conjugated system and hence is almost 10^5 liters/mole-cm for the hydrocarbon containing 9 double bonds in conjugation. For molecules to absorb strongly in the visible region, a fairly extensive conjugated system of double bonds is generally necessary, as is indeed the case for pigments like the chlorophylls and the carotenoids to be discussed in the next chapter.

Action Spectra.   The relative *effectiveness* of various wavelengths in producing a specified response is of basic importance in photobiology and is called an action spectrum. An action spectrum is complementary to an absorption spectrum, the latter being the relative probability of different wavelengths being *absorbed*. In a biological system having many different types of pigments, the action spectrum for a particular response can differ greatly from the absorption spectrum of the entire system. However, the Grotthus-Draper law (i.e., only absorbed light leads to a photochemical reaction) implies that the action spectrum should correspond to the absorption spectrum of the particular molecule absorbing the light responsible for the specific effect or action being considered.

One way to obtain an action spectrum for some particular response is to expose the system to the same number of photons per unit area per unit time at each of a series of wavelength intervals and to measure the effect or action; the responses that are obtained are then plotted as a function of their respective wavelength intervals to see which wavelengths are most effective (cf. Fig. 5–8). Another way to obtain an action spectrum is to plot the reciprocal of the number of quanta required in the various wavelength intervals to give a particular response; if twice as many photons are needed at one particular wavelength compared with another, the action spectrum would have half the height at the former wavelength, and thus the effectiveness of various wavelengths can be readily presented (cf. Fig. 4–8). Using the latter approach, we find that since the light intensity is varied until the response is the same at each wavelength interval, such an action spectrum is independent of any nonlinearity with light intensity. This is an important point since to be a true action spectrum, the action or effect measured must be linear with light intensity at each of the wavelength intervals that is used, e.g., it must not be approaching light saturation.

One compares an action spectrum with the absorption spectra of the pigments that are suspected of being involved in order to see whether one type of pigment can be singled out as being responsible. If the measured action spectrum closely resembles the known absorption spectrum of some molecule, then light absorbed by that molecule may be leading to the particular action being considered. Examples where the use of action spectra have been important in understanding the photochemical aspects of plant physiology include the study of photosynthesis (Chapter 5) and investiga-

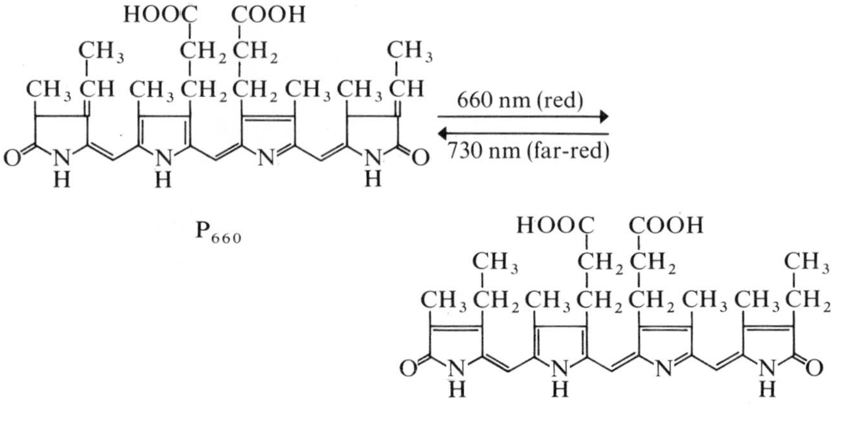

Figure 4–6. Tentative structures of the two interconvertible forms of phytochrome which absorb strongly in the red region (P_{660}) and in the far-red (P_{730}). [These structures are taken from H. W. Siegelman, D. J. Chapman, and W. J. Cole, in *Porphyrins and Related Compounds*, Biochemical Society Symposium No. 28, T. W. Goodwin, ed., Academic Press, London, 1968, pp. 107–20; by permission.]

tions on the responses mediated by the pigment phytochrome, which will now be considered.

Absorption and Action Spectra of Phytochrome.   Applications of action and absorption spectra will be illustrated by a specific consideration of phytochrome. This important plant pigment is responsible for the regulation of many aspects of plant growth and development such as seed germination, formation of certain carotenoids, stem elongation, leaf expansion, and photoperiodism. In the following paragraphs, attention will be directed first to the proposed structures of two of the forms of phytochrome and then to their absorption spectra. The absorption spectra will subsequently be compared with the action spectra obtained for the promotion as well as for the inhibition of seed germination.

The tentative structures for two interconvertible forms of phytochrome are given in Figure 4–6. Strictly speaking, the term phytochrome applies to the phytochrome pigment or chromophore (Fig. 4–6) plus the protein to which it is attached, but commonly the chromophore or light-absorbing part is itself loosely referred to as phytochrome. Phytochrome is a tetrapyrrole, as are the chlorophylls and the bile pigments associated with photosynthesis. (Pyrrole consists of a five-membered ring having 4 carbons, 1 nitrogen, and

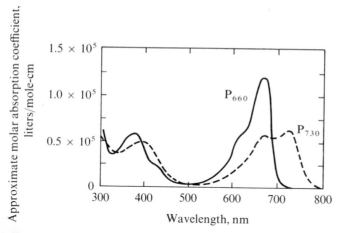

Figure 4–7. Absorption spectra for the red (P_{660}) and the far-red (P_{730}) absorbing forms of phytochrome. [Data are replotted from W. L. Butler, S. B. Hendricks, and H. W. Siegelman, in *Chemistry and Biochemistry of Plant Pigments*, T. W. Goodwin, ed., Academic Press, London, 1965, pp. 197–210; by permission.]

2 double bonds,   .) Both the form of phytochrome that is designated

P_{660} and that termed P_{730} are highly conjugated, as the structures in Figure 4–6 indicate (P stands for pigment). The P_{660} form has 7 double bonds in conjugation. (Not all the double bonds in P_{660} are in the conjugated system since only those alternating with single bonds along the molecule are part of the conjugation.) The P_{730} form given in the right-hand side of Figure 4–6 has a total of 10 double bonds in the conjugated system, including the 2 double bonds in the carbonyl groups on either end of the chromophore. Based on the extent of conjugation, we would expect that phytochrome absorbs in the visible region.

The absorption spectra of two forms of phytochrome (structures in Fig. 4–6) are presented in Figure 4–7. The structure having the greater extent of conjugation, P_{730}, has its absorption bands shifted toward longer wavelengths than for the other form, P_{660}. This would be predicted from the effect of the number of conjugated double bonds on the wavelength position for maximum absorption, as discussed in the preceding section. The term P_{660} is used since that form of phytochrome has a peak absorption in the red near 660 to 665 nm (Fig. 4–6). However, the absorption band is rather broad, and so many different wavelengths of light can be absorbed by P_{660}.

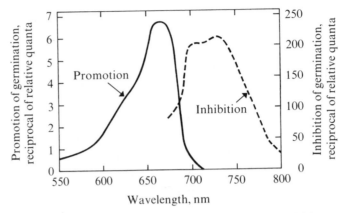

Figure 4–8. Action spectra for the promotion and the inhibition of lettuce seed germination. [Data are replotted from S. B. Hendricks and H. A. Borthwick, in *Chemistry and Biochemistry of Plant Pigments*, T. W. Goodwin, ed., Academic Press, London, 1965, pp. 405–36; by permission.]

The other form of phytochrome under consideration has a broad band extending into the near infrared (Fig. 4–7). Absorption is maximal near 725 to 730 nm, and therefore the structure is designated as P_{730}. As indicated in Figure 4–7, the maximum molar absorption coefficients are about 10^5 liters/mole-cm for both P_{660} and P_{730}. Such high values of ϵ are also found for the plant pigments to be considered in the next chapter.

Next, we will consider action spectra for seed germination responses (Fig. 4–8) with respect to the known absorption properties of phytochrome. In green tissues, chlorophyll absorption in the red region markedly affects the amount of light actually incident on phytochrome, making the evaluation of action spectra more difficult. As a result, seed germination has been chosen as an example of a possible phytochrome-mediated reaction. Figure 4–8 indicates that a pigment absorbing in the red region promotes the germination of lettuce seeds. Upon comparing this action spectrum with the absorption spectra given in Figure 4–7, the pigment absorbing the light which promotes seed germination is indicated to have an absorption spectrum essentially identical to that of the P_{660} form of phytochrome. This enhancement of seed germination by red light can be abolished by subsequent irradiation of the seeds with far-red light. In other words, the potential promotion of seed germination by red light can be stopped or at least inhibited by using various longer wavelengths for irradiation immediately following the red illumination. The action spectrum for such inhibition of lettuce seed germination is also presented in Figure 4–8. This inhibition induced by far-red light requires fewest quanta at wavelengths near 725 to 730 nm, similar to the position of the peak in the absorption spectrum of P_{730} (Fig. 4–7). The promotion of seed germination as well as its inhibition are apparently controlled by two forms of phytochrome, P_{660} and P_{730}, which can be reversibly interconverted by light.

The physiological significance of phytochrome interconversions is that P_{730} is found to be the active form. Thus, light absorbed by P_{660} converts it to P_{730}, and this latter form somehow promotes the germination of the lettuce seeds. If far-red light is incident on the tissue, then its absorption by P_{730} converts phytochrome to the inactive P_{660} form, and the germination is not promoted. The interconversion of phytochrome indicated in a simplified fashion in Figure 4–6 is actually a multistep process involving a number of intermediates whose structures and absorption characteristics are under investigation. Another important aspect of the role of phytochrome in plants is that the P_{730} form reverts spontaneously to P_{660} over a period of hours in the dark. Thus, the length of the night becomes an important variable for photoperiodic responses which are affected by P_{730}. In particular, phytochrome interconversions provide a plant with a timing mechanism for distinguishing between long nights compared with short nights, and consequently certain physiological responses regulated by the P_{660}-P_{730} system can be initiated at the appropriate time or season during the year. As yet, the electronic transitions and the biochemical mechanism of action of phytochrome are not fully understood.

Problems

4–1. Let us consider electromagnetic radiation that has the indicated wavelengths in a vacuum. (a) If λ is 4000 Å, how much energy in ev is carried by 10^5 photons? (b) If an Einstein of 1800 nm photons is absorbed by a liter of water at 0°, what would be the final temperature? (c) A certain filter, which passes all wavelengths below 600 nm and absorbs all those above 600 nm, is placed over a radiometric device. If the meter indicates 100 ergs/cm²-sec, what is the maximum flux in quanta/cm²-sec? (d) What is the intensity in (c) expressed in lux (lumens/m²)?

4–2. Consider electromagnetic radiation that has a frequency of 0.9×10^{15} cycles/sec. (a) Suppose that the velocity of the radiation is 2.0×10^8 m/sec in dense flint glass. What are the wavelengths in a vacuum, in air, and in such glass?

(b) Can such radiation cause an $S_{(\pi,\pi)}$ ground state to go directly to $T_{(\pi,\pi*)}$?
(c) Can such radiation cause the transition of a π electron to a π^* orbital in a molecule having six double bonds in conjugation? (d) Electromagnetic radiation is often expressed in "wave numbers," which is simply the frequency divided by the velocity of light. What is the wave number in cm^{-1} in the present case?

4–3. Assume that some excited singlet state can become de-excited by three competing processes: (1) fluorescence (lifetime $= 10^{-8}$ sec), (2) a radiationless transition to an excited triplet state (5×10^{-9} sec), and (3) a radiationless transition to the ground state (10^{-8} sec). (a) What is the lifetime of the excited singlet state? (b) What is the maximum quantum yield for de-excitations that emit electromagnetic radiation? (c) Suppose that the above molecule is inserted into a membrane, which adds a de-excitation pathway involving intermolecular transfer of energy from the excited singlet state (rate constant $= 10^{12}$ sec^{-1}). What is the new lifetime of the excited singlet state?

4–4. (a) Suppose that the spacing in wave numbers (see Problem 4–2) between vibrational sublevels for the transition depicted in Figure 4–4 is 1200 cm^{-1} and that the most probable absorption predicted by the Franck-Condon principle occurs at 500 nm (the main band). What are the wavelength positions of the satellite bands which occur for transitions to the vibrational sublevels that are just above and just below the one for the most probable transition?
(b) Suppose that the main band has a maximum molar absorption coefficient of 5×10^4 liters/mole-cm while each satellite band has an ϵ one-fifth as large. If 20% of the incident light is absorbed at the wavelengths of either of the satellite bands, what percentage is absorbed at the main band wavelength?
(c) When the pigment is placed in a cuvette (a glass cell used in a spectrophotometer) with an optical path length of 1 cm, the maximum absorbance is 0.6. What is the concentration?

References

Clayton, R. K. 1965. *Molecular Physics in Photosynthesis*, Blaisdell, New York.

Richardson, J. A. 1964. *Physics in Botany*, Pitman, New York.

Scientific American, **219** (3), September 1968, Scientific American, New York.

Seliger, H. H., and W. D. McElroy. 1965. *Light: Physical and Biological Action*, Academic Press, New York.

Turro, N. J. 1967. *Molecular Photochemistry*, Benjamin, New York.

Also see references for Chapter 5.

Photosynthesis

Photosynthesis is a sine qua non for plant and animal life, being in fact the largest scale synthetic process on earth. About 5×10^{16} g (50 billion tons) of carbon are fixed into organic compounds in photosynthetic organisms per year, much of this by phytoplankton living near the surface of the oceans. Such a large number is difficult to visualize but corresponds to a rectangular amount of photosynthetic product with a base of 1 km^2 and a height of slightly over 100 km! The carbon source used in photosynthesis is the 0.03 % CO_2 contained in the air and the CO_2 or HCO_3^- dissolved in lakes and oceans. In addition to the organic compounds, another extremely important product of photosynthesis essential for all respiring organisms is oxygen. The entire atmospheric content of oxygen could be evolved by photosynthesis in a few thousand years.

Photosynthesis is not a single reaction but rather is composed of a great number of individual steps that work together at a remarkably high overall efficiency. The process can be divided into three stages: (1) the photochemical steps (the primary concern of this chapter), (2) electron transport to which is coupled the formation of ATP (to be considered in both this and the next chapter), and (3) the many synthetic reactions involving the incorporation of CO_2 into carbohydrates. To introduce the relative amounts of the various reactants and products involved in photosynthesis, the following rather oversimplified summary of the chemical reactions may prove helpful:

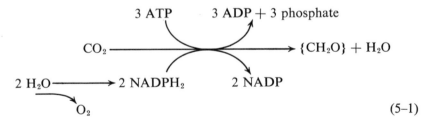

$$(5\text{--}1)$$

where {CH_2O} represents carbohydrate. As we will discuss in this chapter, $NADPH_2$ and ATP are the products of or closely linked to the electron transport steps, which in turn result from the photochemical reactions, the latter often being referred to as the primary events of photosynthesis.

Using Equation 5–1 and ignoring for the moment the various intermediates, we see that the overall net chemical reaction describing photosynthesis is carbon dioxide plus water yields carbohydrate plus oxygen. It is instructive to indicate the energy for each of the chemical bonds in these compounds, which leads to the following representation for the net photosynthetic reaction:

$$
\underset{\text{H}}{\overset{111}{\rule{0pt}{0pt}}}\rule{0pt}{0pt}\underset{}{\overset{111}{-\text{O}-}}\text{H} + \underset{}{\overset{192\quad192}{\text{O}=\text{C}=\text{O}}} \rightarrow \overset{99}{\text{H}}\;\begin{matrix}\overset{83/2}{|}\\ \overset{86}{-\text{C}-\text{O}}\\ |\\ \underset{83/2}{} \end{matrix}\overset{111}{-\text{H}} + \overset{119}{\text{O}=\text{O}}
$$

$$(5\text{--}2)$$

This formulation of photosynthesis belies the complexity and mechanisms of the reactions, but it is useful for estimating the energy that is stored. We can obtain the actual amount of energy storage by considering the energy indicated in kcal/mole adjacent to each of the chemical bonds in Equation 5–2. (A C—C bond, which occurs at either end of the carbon in {CH_2O}, has a value of 83 kcal/mole, and so 83/2 has been indicated in the appropriate places in Eq. 5–2.) The total bond energy of the reactants in Equation 5–2 is 606 kcal/mole ($111 + 111 + 192 + 192 = 606$) while it is 498 kcal/mole for the products ($99 + 83 + 86 + 111 + 119 = 498$). This means that the reactants are more stable, over 100 kcal of energy/mole being necessary to convert them to {CH_2O} plus O_2. Such energy, which is needed to transform H_2O plus CO_2 to products that are chemically less strongly bound, is provided by the light-dependent reactions of photosynthesis. Equation 5–2 also emphasizes that oxygen is a photosynthetic product, and thus energy is not simply stored in the form of carbohydrates but rather is used for the changes in chemical bonds occurring in the overall reaction describing photosynthesis.

The combustion of glucose in the presence of oxygen releases 114 kcal/mole of carbon atoms when the products are CO_2 and H_2O. This is generally taken to be the amount of energy stored by photosynthesis, which is the reverse of combustion in terms of reactants and products. (Actual energies per C depend somewhat on the particular carbohydrate being considered.) As we will discuss below, about eight quanta are required in photosynthesis to reverse the combustion reaction. Red light at 680 nm corresponds to 42.1 kcal/mole (Table 4–1), and so eight moles of such quanta have 337 kcal of radiant energy. Using this as the energy input and 114 kcal/mole as the amount of energy stored, the efficiency of energy conversion by photosynthesis is (114/337)(100) or 34%. Actually, slightly more than 8 quanta may be required per CO_2 fixed. Furthermore, the energy for wavelengths that are less than 680 nm, which are also used in photosynthesis, is higher than 42.1 kcal/mole. Both of these considerations lead to a calculated maximum efficiency somewhat less than 34%. Nevertheless, photosynthesis is an extremely efficient energy conversion process considering all the steps involved, each with its inherent energy losses.

Nearly all the enzymes involved in the synthetic reactions of photosynthesis are also found in nonphotosynthetic tissue. Thus the most unique feature of photosynthesis is the conversion of radiant energy into chemical and electrical energy, the subject of the rest of this text. Specifically, the present chapter will emphasize the light absorption and excitation transfer aspects of photosynthesis. We will consider the structures and the absorption characteristics of photosynthetic pigments and the means by which radiant energy is trapped, transferred, and eventually used. Thus, stress will be on the "photo" part of photosynthesis. In the next chapter, we will discuss energy conversion in a broader context, particular attention being paid to ATP and $NADPH_2$.

Chlorophyll—Chemistry and Spectra

The principal class of pigments responsible for light absorption in photosynthesis is chlorophyll. There are a number of different types of chlorophyll

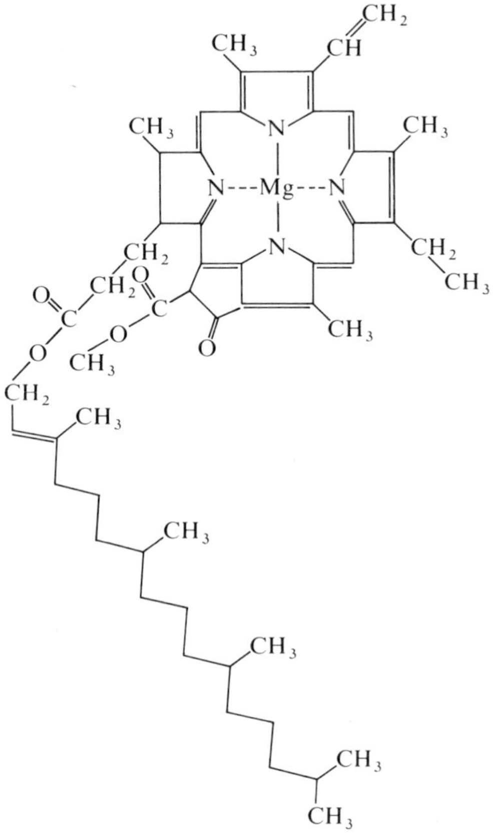

Figure 5-1. Structure of chlorophyll *a* indicating the highly conjugated porphyrin ring to which is attached a phytol tail.

as M. Tswett demonstrated in 1908 using adsorption chromatography. Some form of chlorophyll is found in all photosynthetic organisms, approximately 1 mg of the chlorophylls designated *a* and *b* being present per gram of fresh weight of green leaves. The empirical formulas were first given by R. Willstätter while the structures of various chlorophylls were clarified by H. Fischer. We will consider the structure of chlorophyll *a*, then the all-important absorption properties of the chlorophylls together with their fluorescence characteristics.

Types and Structures.   The various types of chlorophyll are identified by letters or by the taxonomic group in which they occur. One of the most important ones is chlorophyll *a*. It has a molecular weight of 893.5 and the structure given in Figure 5-1. Chlorophyll *a* is found in all photosynthetic organisms except bacteria, i.e., in all species where oxygen evolution accompanies photosynthesis. It is a tetrapyrrole having a relatively flat porphyrin head about 15 Å by 15 Å in the center of which a magnesium atom is covalently bound. Attached to the head is a long-chain terpene alcohol, phytol, which is like a tail about 20 Å in length and containing 20 carbon atoms. This tail provides a nonpolar anchor which is probably important in situating the chlorophyll molecules in the lamellar membranes in the proper relation to each other and to the other components with which they interact. However, the phytol part makes no appreciable contribution to the optical properties of chlorophyll in the visible region. The system of rings in the porphyrin head of the chlorophyll a molecule is highly conjugated, having nine double bonds in conjugation (plus three other double bonds occurring in branches to the main conjugated system). These alternating single and double bonds of the porphyrin ring provide many delocalized π electrons which can take part in light absorption.

A number of other forms structurally similar to chlorophyll a occur in nature. Chlorophyll b differs from chlorophyll a only by having a formyl group (—CHO) in place of a methyl group (—CH$_3$) on one of the pyrrole rings (the one with the ethyl group). Chlorophyll b is found in most land plants (including ferns and mosses), the green algae, and the Euglenophyta, the ratio of chlorophyll a to chlorophyll b in these organisms usually being close to three. Chlorophyll b is not essential for photosynthesis since a barley mutant is known which contains only chlorophyll a and yet carries out photosynthesis quite satisfactorily. Two other types of chlorophyll are chlorophyll c, which occurs in the dinoflagellates, cryptomonads, diatoms, and the brown algae; and chlorophyll d, which is found in some red algae. For convenience, chlorophyll a, which is the pigment of principal interest in this text, will henceforth be abbreviated to Chl a.

The common chlorophyll of bacteria is called bacteriochlorophyll while a modification of this pigment occurring in *Chlorobium* is known as chlorobium chlorophyll. These pigments differ from green plant chlorophylls in containing two more hydrogens in the porphyrin ring than does Chl a. Moreover, they have different substituents around the periphery of the porphyrin ring than do the other chlorophylls while in addition chlorobium chlorophyll has the alcohol farnesol in the place of phytol. Two classes of chlorobium chlorophyll occur in the green photosynthetic bacteria together with a type of bacteriochlorophyll, and two forms of bacteriochlorophyll are identified in the purple photosynthetic bacteria.

Absorption and Fluorescence Emission Spectra.   The absorption spectra of chlorophylls generally have two major bands in the visible region. The band

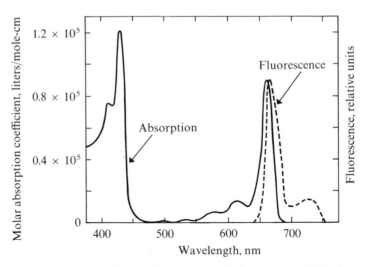

Figure 5-2. Absorption and fluorescence emission spectra of Chl *a* in ether. [Data are from A. S. Holt and E. E. Jacobs, *American Journal of Botany* **41**, 710–17 (1954); by permission.]

in the blue part of the spectrum has a peak at 430 nm for Chl *a* in ether (Fig. 5–2). This band is known as the Soret band and occurs in the upper UV, the violet, or the blue region for all tetrapyrroles. The wavelength position for a local maximum of the absorption coefficient in an absorption band can be designated as λ_{max}. Using this convention, the λ_{max} for the Soret band of Chl *a* in ether is said to occur at 430 nm. The molar absorption coefficient at this λ_{max} for the Soret band of Chl *a* is just over 1.2×10^5 liters/mole-cm (Fig. 5–2), such a high value being a consequence of the large number of double bonds in the conjugated system of the porphyrin ring. Chl *a* also has a major band in the red region, which has a λ_{max} at 662 nm when the pigment is dissolved in ether (Fig. 5–2). It is the absorption of light by the blue and red bands that leads to the characteristic green color of Chl *a*. Chl *a* dissolved in ether has a small absorption band at 615 nm, which is 47 nm on the short wavelength side of the main red band (Fig. 5–2). Absorption of light of 615 nm wavelength leads to an electronic transition requiring 0.14 ev more energy than for the main band at 662 nm. This extra energy is similar to the energy spacing between vibrational sublevels. Therefore, this small band on the shorter wavelength (higher energy) side of the red band may correspond to electrons going to the vibrational sublevel in the excited state immediately above the sublevel for the λ_{max} at 662 nm, a point that will be returned to shortly. (See Fig. 4–4 for indication of vibrational sublevels.)

The fluorescence emission spectrum of Chl *a* in ether is also presented in Figure 5–2. Although chlorophyll absorbs strongly in both the red and the blue, it is evident that the fluorescence is essentially all in the red region. This restriction on the wavelengths for fluorescence occurs since the upper singlet state of chlorophyll excited by blue light [$S^b_{(\pi,\pi*)}$ in Fig. 4–3] is extremely unstable and goes to the lower excited singlet state in about 10^{-12} sec, i.e., before any appreciable blue fluorescence can take place. Due to this rapid energy degradation by a radiationless transition, quanta absorbed by the Soret band of chlorophyll are no more effective for photosynthesis than are the lower energy quanta that are absorbed in the red region. One can readily demonstrate the red fluorescence of chlorophyll accompanying light absorption by the Soret band, e.g., when a green leaf is illuminated with blue light in a darkened room, a red glow is observed. With a light microscope, fluorescence emanating from individual chloroplasts in the cells of a leaf can be seen when using blue or shorter wavelengths for the exciting light.

With the discussion in the previous chapter as a basis, it is reasonable to suppose that the electronic transition having a λ_{max} at 662 nm in the absorption spectrum for Chl *a* dissolved in ether corresponds to the excitation of an electron from the lowest vibrational sublevel of the ground state to some vibrational sublevel of the excited state. It was also argued in Chapter 4 that fluorescence generally occurs from the lowest vibrational sublevel of the excited singlet state. In other words, any excess vibrational energy is dissipated before the energy of the absorbed quantum can be reradiated as fluorescence. But Figure 5–2 clearly shows that the wavelength region for most of the fluorescence is about the same as the red band in the chlorophyll absorption spectrum. This indicates that the transition from the lowest vibrational sublevel of the ground state to the excited state (the red band) has the same energy as a transition from the lowest vibrational sublevel of the excited state to the ground state (fluorescence). The only way for this to occur is to have the lowest vibrational sublevels of both the ground and the excited states involved in both the transitions, i.e., the red absorption band corresponds to a transition of the chlorophyll molecule from the lowest vibrational sublevel of the ground state to the lowest vibrational sublevel of the excited state.

This point that the lowest vibrational sublevels of the ground and the excited states of Chl *a* are involved in the main red band can also be appre-

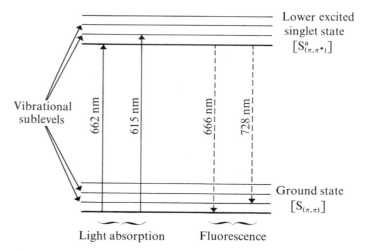

Figure 5–3. Energy level diagram indicating the vibrational sublevels of the ground state [$S_{(\pi,\pi)}$] and the lower excited singlet state [$S^a_{(\pi,\pi*)}$] of Chl *a*. Straight vertical lines indicate absorption of light by Chl *a* in ether while dashed lines represent fluorescence at the specified wavelengths. The lengths of the arrows are proportional to the amounts of energy involved in the various transitions.

ciated by comparing the bands at 662 and 615 nm in the absorption spectrum with the two bands in the fluorescence emission spectrum. The shorter wavelength (higher energy) absorption band at 615 nm corresponds to a transition to the first excited vibrational sublevel in the excited state while de-excitations to excited vibrational sublevels of the ground state would correspond to fluorescence at wavelengths greater than 700 nm. In fact, a small band near 730 nm in the fluorescence emission spectrum of Chl *a* (Fig. 5–2) occurs about 60 nm on the long wavelength side of the main fluorescence band, indicating an electronic transition having 0.15 ev less energy. This band most likely corresponds to fluorescence emitted as the chlorophyll molecule goes from the lowest vibrational sublevel of the excited state to the first excited vibrational sublevel of the ground state. Figure 5–3 sums up the various vibrational sublevels and electronic transitions that have been discussed for light absorption and fluorescence emission by Chl *a* in ether.

Absorption Bands in vivo.   Chl *a* exists in a number of differently absorbing forms *in vivo*, each type being described by the λ_{max} of its red band. One type has a peak from 670 to 673 nm and will be referred to as Chl a_{670}.

Another type of Chl a has a λ_{max} from 680 to 683 nm and will be designated as Chl a_{680}. A special Chl a (1 in approximately 450 chlorophylls) has a λ_{max} near 700 nm and is termed P_{700} (P indicating pigment). The various values of λ_{max} for Chl a *in vivo* result from interactions between the chlorophylls and the surrounding molecules, such as the proteins and lipids in the lamellae. All of the forms of Chl a occurring *in vivo* have their red bands shifted to longer wavelengths than for Chl a dissolved in ether (λ_{max} at 662 nm), stressing the pronounced effect that the solvent or other neighboring molecules can have in determining the positions of the electronic energy levels. For instance, P_{700} is apparently located in an environment where neighboring molecules strongly interact with it, thereby markedly influencing the electron distribution within this type of chlorophyll and consequently altering its absorption properties compared with other Chl a's. For completeness, it should be mentioned that the red absorption band of Chl b *in vivo* occurs as a shoulder on the low wavelength side of the Chl a red band, usually near 650 nm.

The bandwidth of an absorption band is conveniently given by the difference in energy between photons on the two sides of the band at wavelengths where the absorption has dropped to half of that for λ_{max}. C. S. French has found that such bandwidths of the red absorption bands of the various Chl a's *in vivo* are actually fairly narrow—about 15 nm. At 680 nm, a bandwidth of 15 nm is equivalent to 0.04 ev in energy, i.e., a photon having a wavelength of 673 nm has an energy which is 0.04 ev greater than a photon with a wavelength 15 nm longer (688 nm). An energy of 0.04 ev is somewhat smaller than the usual energy difference between vibrational sublevels, the spacing of vibrational sublevels being about 0.14 ev for Chl a, as indicated above. Thus a bandwidth of 0.04 ev results mainly from the rotational and translational broadening of an electronic transition to but one vibrational sublevel of the excited state of Chl a.

The absorption band for bacteriochlorophyll corresponding to the red band of Chl a occurs at much longer wavelengths. Specifically, bacteriochlorophyll dissolved in ether shows an absorption band centered at 770 nm compared with 662 nm for Chl a in ether. As is the case for Chl a, the wavelength positions of the absorption band are markedly influenced by the environment of the pigment molecules. *In vivo*, the 770 nm band of bacteriochlorophyll shifts further into the infrared to 800, 850, or 870 to 890 nm, depending on the particular molecular environment. The position of the bacteriochlorophyll absorption band of longest wavelength varies among organisms, e.g., it is near 870 nm for *Rhodopseudomonas* and 882 nm for

Chromatium. Bacteriochlorophyll *in vivo* also has a Soret band (350 to 400 nm) and a small orange band at 590 to 600 nm.

When using polarized incident light, the absorption and the subsequent fluorescence by chlorophyll *in vivo* provide information on the molecular orientations and on the interactions between individual chlorophyll molecules. The electronic transition of chlorophyll to the excited singlet state responsible for the red absorption band has its electric dipole in the plane of the porphyrin ring. Polarized light of the appropriate wavelength which has its oscillating electric vector parallel to this plane is therefore preferentially absorbed by chlorophyll. With such polarized light, it has been shown that the porphyrin rings of a few percent of the Chl *a* molecules, perhaps including P_{700}, are nearly parallel to the plane of the chloroplast lamellae. However, most of the chlorophyll molecules have their porphyrin heads oriented in a random fashion in the internal membranes of the chloroplasts. If the same chlorophyll molecules which absorbed polarized light later emit quanta when they go back to the ground state, the fluorescence would be polarized to within a few degrees of the direction of the electric vector of the incident light. However, the chlorophyll fluorescence following absorption of polarized light by chloroplasts is not appreciably polarized. This fluorescence depolarization could be explained if the excitation energy had been transferred from one chlorophyll molecule to another one so many times that the directional aspect had been randomized, i.e., if the fluorescent emitter were randomly aligned relative to the chlorophyll molecule which absorbed the polarized light. This fluorescence depolarization has important implications for the excitation transfer reactions of chlorophyll which we will discuss in a later section.

Other Photosynthetic Pigments

Other molecules in photosynthetic organisms may absorb light in the visible region and pass the excitation on to Chl *a*. These molecules are known as auxiliary or "accessory" pigments. In addition to chlorophylls *b*, *c*, and *d*, the two groups of accessory pigments important photosynthetically are the carotenoids and the phycobilins. These latter two classes of accessory pigments can absorb yellow or green light, a part of the spectrum where absorption by chlorophyll (Fig. 5–2) is not appreciable.

Fluorescence studies have provided valuable information on the sequence of energy transfer to and from the accessory pigments. For example, light absorbed by carotenoids, phycobilins, and Chl *b* leads to the fluorescence of Chl *a*. However, light absorbed by Chl *a* does not lead to fluorescence of any of the accessory pigments, indicating that excitation energy is not transferred from Chl *a* to the accessory pigments. Thus, accessory pigments may increase the efficiency of photosynthesis in white light by absorbing at wavelengths where chlorophyll absorption is low, following which the excitation is transferred to chlorophyll, the initiator of the subsequent photochemical reactions.

Carotenoids. Carotenoids are found in most green plants, algae, and photosynthetic bacteria. In fact, the dominant pigments for plant leaves are the chlorophylls, which absorb strongly in the red and the blue, and the carotenoids, which absorb mostly in the blue and some in the green region of the spectrum. Thus the predominant colors reflected or transmitted by leaves are green and yellow. The yellow, orange, and red colors of leaves in the fall are mainly due to the carotenoids, which become apparent when the chlorophyll bleaches. The chlorophylls and carotenoids are embedded in the chloroplast lamellar membranes, which were discussed in Chapter 1 (cf. Fig. 1–7). When viewed with the electron microscope, these lamellae appear to have oblate spheroids about 10 by 18 nm as part of their substructure. These were named quantasomes by R. Park and were shown to contain approximately 230 chlorophylls and 50 carotenoids, which gives an indication of the relative frequency of these two pigments in higher plants. As a sidelight, it is interesting to note that animals generally cannot synthesize carotenoids. Thus brightly colored birds like canaries and flamingoes, as well as many invertebrates, obtain their yellow or reddish colors from the carotenoids occurring in the parts of the plants which they eat.

Carotenoids are 40 carbon isoprenoids composed of 8 isoprene units, where isoprene is a five-carbon compound having two double bonds ($CH_2\!=\!CCH\!=\!CH_2$). In many carotenoids, the isoprene units on one or both

$$|$$
$$CH_3$$

ends of the molecule are part of six-membered rings. (See Fig. 5–5.) Carotenoids are about 30 Å long, and those involved in photosynthesis generally contain nine or more double bonds. The wavelength position of the λ_{max} depends on the solvent, on the substitutions on the hydrocarbon backbone, and on the number of double bonds in the conjugated system. This latter point can be illustrated for carotenoids in *n*-hexane, where the central maxima of the three observed peaks in the absorption spectra are at 285 nm for 3

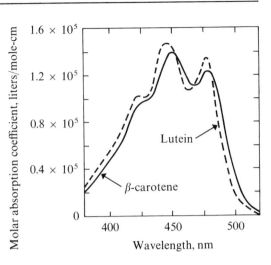

Figure 5–4. Absorption spectra for the two major carotenoids of green plants. [Data for β-carotene (in *n*-hexane) and lutein (in ethanol) are from F. P. Zscheile, J. W. White, Jr., B. W. Beadle, and J. R. Roach, *Plant Physiology* **17**, 331–46 (1942); by permission.]

conjugated double bonds, 348 nm for 5, 400 nm for 7, 440 nm for 9, and 472 nm for 11 (the only change from molecule to molecule in this series is in the number of double bonds in conjugation). Thus, the greater the conjugation, the higher is the λ_{max}, as was discussed in Chapter 4. For the 9 to 12 double bonds which occur in the conjugated systems of photosynthetically important carotenoids, the maximum absorption coefficient is greater than 10^5 liters/mole-cm.

Carotenoids serving as accessory pigments for photosynthesis absorb strongly in the blue [424 to 491 nm (Table 4–1)] and on into the green (491 to 550 nm), usually having triple-banded spectra in the region from 400 to 550 nm. For β-carotene in hexane, these three bands are centered at 425, 451, and 483 nm (Fig. 5–4) while another major carotenoid, lutein, has peaks at 420, 447, and 477 nm when dissolved in ethanol (absorption spectrum also indicated in Fig. 5–4). The three absorption bands in each spectrum differ in energy from each other by 0.17 to 0.18 ev, typical values for the spacing between adjacent vibrational sublevels. Hence, the triple-banded spectra characteristic of carotenoids most likely represent transitions to different vibrational sublevels of the same excited electronic state. It is not known with certainty which vibrational sublevels are actually involved, in part because it has proved difficult to detect any carotenoid fluorescence. The spectra of the carotenoids *in vivo* are shifted about 20 to 30 nm toward longer wavelengths compared with the absorption when the pigments are dissolved in hexane or ethanol.

Carotenoids are usually subdivided into the hydrocarbon types (carotenes) and the oxygenated ones (xanthophylls). The major carotene in green

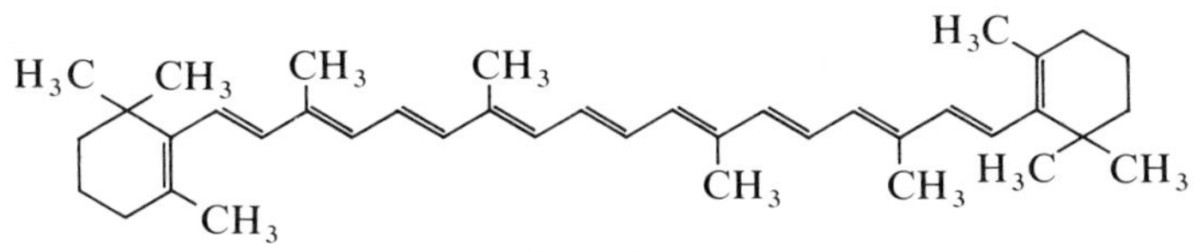

β-carotene

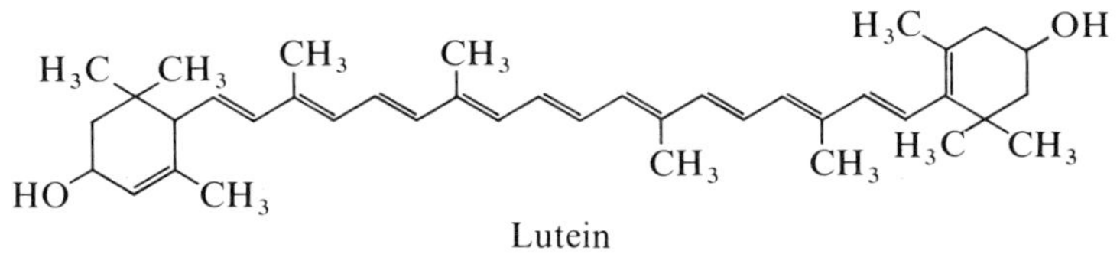

Lutein

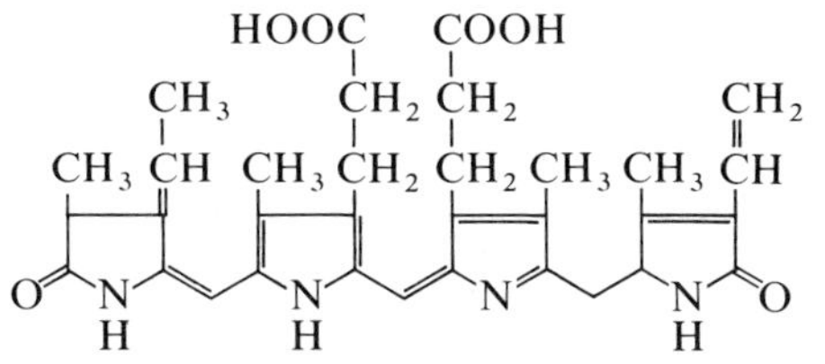

Phycoerythrobilin

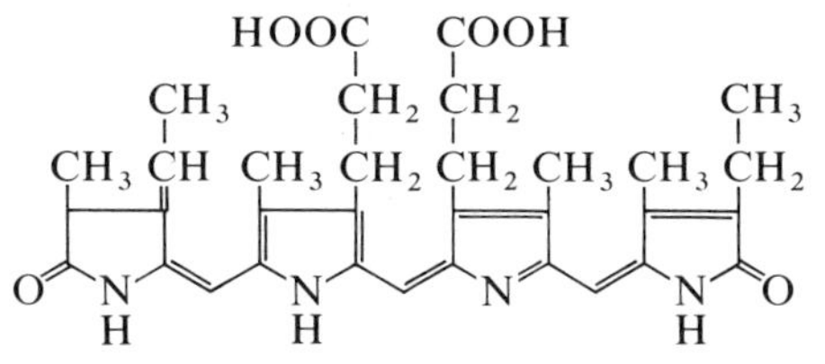

Phycocyanobilin

Figure 5–5. Structure of four important accessory pigments.

plants is β-carotene (absorption spectrum in Fig. 5–4 and structure in Fig. 5–5), α-carotene also being abundant. The xanthophylls exhibit a much greater structural diversity than do the carotenes since the added oxygen can be in hydroxyl, keto, epoxy, or methoxy groups. The three most prevalent xanthophylls in green plants are lutein (absorption spectrum in Fig. 5–4 and structure in Fig. 5–5), violaxanthin, and neoxanthin, in that order, with cryptoxanthin and zeaxanthin less frequently encountered. The major carotenoid of the photosynthetic tissue of green plants is the xanthophyll lutein. The major carotene of algae is again β-carotene while lutein is the most common xanthophyll, although great variation in the type and amount of xanthophylls is characteristic of algae. For instance, diatoms and brown algae contain considerable amounts of the special xanthophyll, fucoxanthin, which functions as the main accessory pigment in these organisms. The distribution and types of carotenoids in plants have both important evolutionary implications and also taxonomic usefulness.

In addition to functioning as accessory pigments for photosynthesis, carotenoids are also important for protecting photosynthetic organisms from destructive photooxidations. Light absorbed by chlorophyll can lead to excited states of molecular oxygen. These highly reactive states can damage chlorophyll, but their interactions with carotenoids prevent harmful effects to the organism. For instance, a mutant of *Rhodopseudomonas spheroides* lacking carotenoids performs photosynthesis in a normal manner in the absence of oxygen; when oxygen is introduced in the light, the bacteriochlorophyll becomes photooxidized and the bacteria are killed, a sensitivity not occurring in related strains containing carotenoids. In other cases, when carotenoid synthesis is inhibited, light in the presence of oxygen can be lethal to the photosynthetic organism.

Phycobilins.   The other main group of accessory pigments important in photosynthesis is the phycobilins, which are found loosely associated with the lamellar membranes in blue-green and red algae as well as in the cryptomonads. In the 1920s R. Lemberg termed these molecules *phycobilins* because they resembled bile pigments. Like the chlorophylls, phycobilins are tetrapyrroles. However, the four pyrroles in the phycobilins occur in a straight chain, not in a closed porphyrin ring as is the case for the chlorophylls. Phycobilins, which have molecular weights near 586, occur covalently bound to proteins that generally range in molecular weight from 100,000 to 300,000. Many pigment molecules are attached to the same protein since the biliproteins are about 4% phycobilins by weight. For instance, a biliprotein of 300,000 molecular weight could have (0.04)(300,000) or 12,000 grams of phycobilins per mole, which corresponds to more than 20 pigment molecules per protein in this case.

Phycobilins, which have their major absorption bands in the region from 500 to 650 nm, are higher in concentration in many algae than are the chlorophylls and thus are responsible for the color of certain species. The main phycobilins are phycocyanobilin and phycoerythrobilin (structures given in Fig. 5–5), with any other ones occurring to a much smaller extent. Phyco-

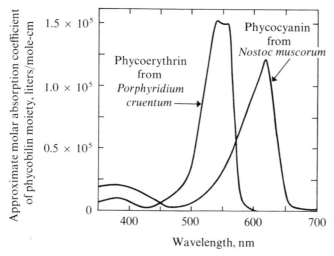

Figure 5-6. Absorption spectra of phycoerythrin and phycocyanin. [Data are replotted from C. Ó hEocha, in *Chemistry and Biochemistry of Plant Pigments*, T. W. Goodwin, ed., Academic Press, London, 1965, pp. 175–96; by permission.]

erythrobilin plus the protein to which it is attached is called phycoerythrin. Phycoerythrin is soluble in aqueous solutions, and thus absorption spectra can readily be obtained under conditions similar to those *in vivo*. Phycoerythrin is reddish since it absorbs green and has at least one main band between 530 and 570 nm. (See absorption spectrum in Fig. 5–6.) It occurs throughout the red algae, in some blue-green algae, and in the cryptomonads. Phycocyanin (phycocyanobilin plus protein) is blue, absorbing strongly from 610 to 660 nm (Fig. 5–6). Phycocyanin is the main phycobilin in the blue-green algae and is also found in the red algae and the cryptomonads. As with the carotenoids, the greater the number of double bonds in conjugation in the phycobilins, the longer are the wavelengths for λ_{max}. For example, phycoerythrobilin has 6 double bonds in the conjugated system and absorbs maximally in the green region of the spectrum while phycocyanobilin has 8 such double bonds and its λ_{max} occurs in the red (cf. the structures for these compounds given in Fig. 5–5). As is indicated in Figure 5–6, the maximum absorption coefficient of both phycobilins exceeds 10^5 liters/ mole-cm.

Interestingly enough, only two types of pigments are involved in all the known photochemical reactions in plants. These are the carotenoids and the tetrapyrroles, the latter class including the chlorophylls, the phycobilins, and phytochrome. The maximum absorption coefficients for the most intense absorption bands are slightly over 10^5 liters/mole-cm for all of these molecules. In addition, the cytochromes, which are involved in the electron transport reactions in chloroplasts and mitochondria, are also tetrapyrroles, as will be indicated later in this chapter.

Excitation Transfers Among Chlorophylls and Other Photosynthetic Pigments

Chlorophyll is at the very heart of the primary events of photosynthesis. Its intervention is necessary to convert the plentiful radiant energy from the sun into chemical bond energy that can be stored in various ways, both the conversion and storage aspects being involved in making photosynthesis such a biologically important process. In this rather extended introduction, the light absorption, excitation transfer, and photochemical steps will all be set down as chemical reactions in order to set the stage for the further consideration of the molecular details of photosynthesis.

The first step in photosynthesis is light absorption by one of the pigments. The absorption event per se (discussed in detail in Chapter 4) can be represented as follows for the various types of photosynthetic pigments described in this chapter:

$$
\begin{matrix}
\text{Accessory pigment} \\
\text{or} \\
\text{Chl } a \\
\text{or} \\
\text{Trap chl}
\end{matrix}
\quad + \ h\nu \ \longrightarrow \quad
\begin{matrix}
\text{Accessory pigment*} \\
\text{or} \\
\text{Chl } a* \\
\text{or} \\
\text{Trap chl*}
\end{matrix}
\qquad (5\text{--}3)
$$

where the asterisk refers to an excited state of the pigment molecule caused by the absorption of a light quantum, $h\nu$, and where "trap chl" indicates a special type of Chl a (e.g., P_{700}), which occurs rather infrequently and whose important excitation-trapping properties we will consider at the end of this section.

Since the photochemical reactions take place only at the trap chl molecules, the excitation resulting from light absorption by the accessory pigments or by the regular Chl a's must migrate to the trap chl before it can be used for photosynthesis. Trap chl is relatively rare compared with the other photosynthetic pigments; thus it absorbs only a small fraction of the incident light. In fact, in green plants under natural conditions over 99% of the photons are absorbed by the accessory pigments or by Chl a. The excitation migration from the initially excited species to the trap chl, the mechanism for which will be discussed below, can be represented as follows:

$$\text{Accessory pigment*} + \text{Chl } a \longrightarrow \text{accessory pigment} + \text{Chl } a* \quad (5\text{-}4)$$

$$\text{Chl } a* + \text{trap chl} \longrightarrow \text{Chl } a + \text{trap chl*} \quad (5\text{-}5)$$

In other words, the direction of excitation transfer or migration is from the accessory pigments to Chl a (Eq. 5–4) and from Chl a to the special chlorophylls (Eq. 5–5) where the actual photochemical reactions take place. Hence, the overall effect of the steps described by Equations 5–3 through 5–5 is to funnel the excitations that are caused by light to the trap chl.

A prerequisite for the storage of energy in chemical bonds is that the oxidizing (electron-accepting) and the reducing (electron-donating) species, which are produced by light absorption, must be stable and situated so as not to recombine. Once these stable oxidized and reduced species are formed, the photochemistry of photosynthesis is complete. (Oxidation and reduction will be discussed in detail in Chapter 6.) If the molecule which accepts an electron from the excited trap chl is designated as A, this electron transfer step can be represented by

$$\text{Trap chl*} + A \longrightarrow \text{trap chl}^+ + A^- \quad (5\text{-}6)$$

where A^- indicates the reduced state of the acceptor and trap chl$^+$ means that the special chlorophyll has lost an electron. This electron removed from trap chl* (Eq. 5–6) can be replaced by one coming from a donor, D, which leads to the oxidation of this latter species (D^+) and the return of the trap chl to its normal unexcited state:

$$\text{Trap chl}^+ + D \longrightarrow \text{trap chl} + D^+ \quad (5\text{-}7)$$

Equations 5–6 and 5–7 represent photochemical reactions since the absorption of a light quantum (Eq. 5–3) has led to the transfer of an electron away from a special type of chlorophyll and, consequently, has changed the number of electrons associated with various chemical species (A and D).

The generation of stable oxidized (D^+) and reduced (A^-) entities completes the conversion of light energy into chemical potential energy. To emphasize this point, Equations 5–3 through 5–7 can be added up, which gives the following relation for the overall net reaction that describes the primary events of photosynthesis:

$$A + D + h\nu \longrightarrow A^- + D^+ \quad (5\text{-}8)$$

In green plants and algae, the light-driven change in chemical potential energy represented by the conversion of $A + D$ to $A^- + D^+$ (Eq. 5-8) eventually causes chemical reactions leading to the evolution of oxygen from water, the production of a reduced compound ($NADPH_2$), and the formation of high energy phosphate bonds (ADP + phosphate → ATP). Such a conversion of light energy into chemical energy is the cornerstone of photosynthesis.

In this section, we will consider a mechanism for the transfer of excitation from an excited molecule to one in its ground state. Then the concepts that are developed will be applied to the specific case of the migration of excitation among photosynthetic pigments, i.e., reactions described by Equations 5-4 and 5-5. Finally, we will discuss the actual trapping of the excitation in special Chl a molecules, this trapping being a prelude to the separation of electrons from chlorophyll that is needed for the actual generation of chemical potential energy.

Resonance Transfer of Excitation. A number of different examples of excitation transfer between photosynthetic pigments have already been mentioned. For instance, light absorbed by the accessory pigments can lead to the fluorescence of Chl a. Also, the studies on the absorption of polarized light by chlorophyll *in vivo* have shown the phenomenon of fluorescence depolarization, which is further evidence that excitations can migrate from molecule to molecule before the energy is emitted as radiation. The simplest case to consider is the transfer of excitation between identical molecules, e.g., the excitation of the lower excited singlet state of chlorophyll can be passed on to a second chlorophyll molecule—this causes the deactivation of the originally excited molecule and the attainment of an excited singlet state in the second chlorophyll, a process described by Equation 4-6. The most widely accepted mechanism for such exchange of electronic excitation between chlorophyll molecules is by "resonance transfer," which we will consider next in a qualitative sense.

For resonance transfer of excitation to occur, the excited molecule must induce an excited state in a second molecule in close proximity. Specifically, the oscillating electric dipole representing the energetic electron in the excited state of the first molecule leads to a varying electric field which can cause an analogous oscillation of some electron in a second molecule. A transfer of electronic excitation is actually taking place when the electron oscillation in the second molecule is being induced. When excitation transfer is completed, the previously excited electron in the first molecule has ceased oscillating while some electron in the second molecule is now oscillating, leading to an excited state of that molecule. Thus resonance transfer of excitation between molecules is analogous to the process whereby light is originally absorbed, in that an oscillation of some electron in the molecule is induced by a locally varying electric field. (See Chapter 4.)

For resonance transfer of electronic excitation to occur, the energy that is available in the excited molecule must match the energy that can be accepted by a second molecule. The wavelengths for fluorescence indicate the energy which is in the excited singlet state of a molecule; thus the fluorescence spectrum usually gives the range of energies which are available for transfer to a second molecule. On the other hand, the range of wavelengths of light which can sympathetically induce an oscillation of some electron in the second molecule is given by the absorption spectrum of that molecule (Chapter 4), and therefore the absorption spectrum shows the energies which can be accepted by a molecule. As might be expected from these two considerations, the probability for resonance transfer is high when the overlap in wavelength between the fluorescent band for the excited oscillator (available energy) and the absorption band of an unexcited oscillator (acceptable energy) in a neighboring molecule is large. The absorption and the fluorescence spectra of Chl a are both given in Figure 5–2. As has already been pointed out, the overlap in the red region of the two spectra is very great, and thus excitations can be efficiently exchanged between Chl a molecules by resonance transfer.

The probability for resonance transfer of electronic excitation varies inversely with the sixth power of the separation between the two molecules. Consequently, for resonance transfer to be probable between chlorophylls, the molecules must be relatively close together. If uniformly distributed in three dimensions in the lamellar membranes of chloroplasts, the chlorophyll molecules would have a center-to-center spacing of approximately 28 Å, an intermolecular distance over which resonance transfer of excitation can readily occur. Thus, both the spectral properties of chlorophyll and its spacing in the lamellar membranes are conducive to an efficient migration of excitation from molecule to molecule by resonance transfer.

Transfers of Excitation Between Photosynthetic Pigments.   In addition to the transfer from one Chl a to another, excitations can also migrate by resonance transfer from the accessory pigments to Chl a. The transfers of excitations among Chl a's can be essentially 100% efficient while the efficiency for excitation transfer between dissimilar molecules is rather variable. In particular, the transfer of excitation from certain carotenoids such as α-carotene, β-carotene, and lutein to chlorophyll sometimes is rather inefficient. For instance, only about 40% of the excitations of these carotenoids may be transferred to Chl a. On the other hand, photons absorbed by the carotenoid fucoxanthin, which is found in the brown algae and diatoms, can approach 100% efficiency of excitation transfer to Chl a. The efficiency of excitation transfer from the phycobilins and from Chl b to Chl a can also be nearly 100%. In the red algae, 90% of the electronic excitations produced by the absorption of quanta by phycoerythrin can be passed on to phycocyanin and then to Chl a, these transfers requiring about 4×10^{-10} sec each. We will now consider the direction for excitation transfer between various photosynthetic pigments and then the times involved for internal electronic transitions and intermolecular excitation transfers of chlorophyll.

Some electronic energy is generally lost by each molecule to which the excitation is transferred, mainly by having any excess vibrational, rotational, or translational energy dissipated as heat. Therefore, the wavelength positions of the λ_{max}'s for each of the types of pigments involved in the sequential steps of excitation transfer tend to become longer in the direction in which the excitation migrates. To see why this is so, recall that the fluorescence emission spectrum of some molecule (which must appreciably overlap the absorption spectrum of the molecule to which the energy is resonantly transferred in order for transfer to take place efficiently) occurs at longer wavelengths than the absorption spectrum of that molecule (cf. Fig. 5–2 for Chl a). Therefore, for a second molecule to become excited by resonance transfer, it should have an absorption band that is shifted toward longer wavelengths compared with the absorption band for the molecule from which it receives the excitation. Thus the direction for excitation migration by resonance transfer among photosynthetic pigments is usually toward pigments having the longer λ_{max}. [Since the absorption and fluorescence emission bands of the pigments often overlap over a considerable wavelength interval, the mandatory transfer toward longer wavelengths (lower energy) does not always specify a unique pigment-to-pigment direction for an individual transfer event.]

As specific examples of the tendency for excitations to migrate toward pigments with longer λ_{max}'s, we will consider the transfer of excitations from the accessory pigments to Chl a. In red and some blue-green algae, phycoerythrin has a λ_{max} at 560 nm and passes excitation energy on to phycocyanin, which has an absorption maximum near 620 nm. This excitation can then be transferred to a type of Chl a with a λ_{max} at 680 nm (Chl a_{680}). The biliprotein, allophycocyanin, absorbs maximally at 650 nm and may intervene in the transfer of excitation between phycocyanin (λ_{max} at 620 nm) and Chl a_{680} in some blue-green and red algae. Cryptomonads contain Chl c which has a λ_{max} near 650 nm; for such organisms, excitation energy transfer may be from phycoerythrin (λ_{max} at 560 nm) to phycocyanin (620 nm) to Chl c_{650} and then to Chl a_{680}. Since some electronic excitation energy is generally dissipated as heat by each molecule, the excitation represents less energy (longer λ) after each pigment in the sequence for the individual transfers. Consequently, the overall direction for excitation migration is essentially irreversible, a point that we will return to below.

As discussed in Chapter 4, the light absorption event takes about 10^{-15} sec, consistent with the oscillations of the electric field of visible light which occur at a frequency of about 10^{15} cycles/sec (see Table 4–1). Since nuclear vibrations have a frequency of about 10^{13} cycles/sec, the nuclei essentially do not move during the absorption event, a restriction embodied in the Franck-Condon principle. However, as the nuclei vibrate back and forth after the absorption of the quantum, their collisions with other nuclei every 10^{-13} sec can lead to the dissipation in such short times of any excess electronic energy in the excited vibrational sublevels (cf. Fig. 4–4). In addition, the radiationless transition from the upper excited singlet to the lower excited singlet of Chl a [$S^b_{(\pi,\pi*)}$ to $S^a_{(\pi,\pi*)}$ in Fig. 4–3] is completed within 10^{-12} sec. The actual time for the transfer of electronic excitation energy between two Chl a molecules in $vivo$ is somewhat longer—about 1 to 2×10^{-12} sec. Thus the originally excited molecule attains the lowest vibrational sublevel of the lower excited singlet state before the excitation can be transferred to another molecule, and so the amount of energy resonantly transferred from one Chl a molecule to another generally corresponds to the electronic energy indicated by the fluorescence emission spectrum. The time for excitation transfer between Chl a's of somewhat more than 10^{-12} sec is quite rapid compared with fluorescence lifetimes, the consequences of which we will consider next.

An electronic excitation caused by light absorption is generally transferred many times among the Chl a's in $vivo$ before the assemblage of molecules becomes de-excited. As was mentioned in Chapter 4, an upper time limit in which processes involving excited singlet states must occur is provided by the kinetics of fluorescent de-excitation, the lifetime for chlorophyll fluorescence from the lower excited singlet state being about 1.5×10^{-8} sec. Thus, approximately 10,000 transfers of excitation each requiring about 10^{-12} sec could take place among the Chl a molecules before the loss of energy by fluorescence. The number of excitation transfers between Chl a molecules which actually do take place is much less than this, for reasons which will become clear shortly.

Excitation Trapping. A special type of Chl a, approximately 1 per 450 chlorophylls, was introduced previously and designated as P_{700}. This pigment absorbs at longer wavelengths than the other types of Chl a, and so the excited singlet state in P_{700} is at a lower energy. Thus, it is energetically feasible for Chl a_{680} to excite P_{700} by resonance transfer, but P_{700} does not transfer its excitation to Chl a_{680} to any appreciable extent. Therefore, the excited singlet states of other Chl a molecules can have their excitations passed on to P_{700}, but not vice versa, analogous to the irreversibility of the migration of excitations from the accessory pigments to Chl a. The excitation resulting from the absorption of radiation by the various photosynthetic pigments is thereby funneled into P_{700}, such collecting of excitations by one species being the net effect of Equations 5–3 through 5–5 given above (with the term "trap chl" replaced by P_{700}).

Since one P_{700} is present per 450 chlorophylls, only a few hundred transfers are necessary on the average to get the excitation from Chl a to P_{700}. Thus, the 10,000 possible transfers of excitation from one Chl a to another mentioned above do not occur. Since each excitation transfer takes approximately 10^{-12} sec, 100 transfers would require about 10^{-10} sec. In agreement with this, both calculations from models and ingenious experimentation have shown that over 90% of the excitations of Chl a can migrate to P_{700} in less than 10^{-9} sec.

The extent of fluorescence provides information on the lifetime of the excited singlet state of chlorophyll *in vivo* and thus on the time available for migration of excitations. Specifically, about 3% of the light absorbed by Chl a *in vivo* is lost by fluorescence (the actual amount reradiated depends on the light intensity and increases to about 7% for high light intensities). In other words, the quantum yield for fluorescence *in vivo*, Φ_{Fl}, can be considered to be 0.03. Equation 4–12 ($\Phi_i = \tau/\tau_i$) indicates that such a quantum yield is equal to τ/τ_{Fl}, where τ is the lifetime of the excited singlet state while τ_{Fl} is its fluorescent lifetime. Although τ_{Fl} is not known *in vivo*, it is reasonable to assume that it is similar to the fluorescent lifetime of Chl a *in vitro*, 1.5×10^{-8} sec. Therefore, Equation 4–12 predicts a lifetime for the excited state of Chl a *in vivo* of $(0.03)(1.5 \times 10^{-8})$ or 0.5×10^{-9} sec. This is a rough estimate of the time necessary for the excitation to migrate to the special Chl a, P_{700}.

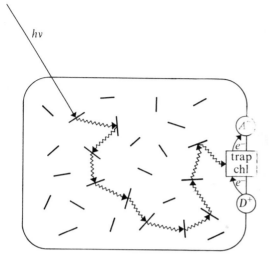

Figure 5-7. Schematic indication of a group of pigments functioning together as a photosynthetic unit which harvests the light quanta and passes the excitations on to a special trap chl. An electron (e^-) is transferred from this chlorophyll to some acceptor (A^- in the reduced form) and then replaced by another electron coming from a suitable donor (D^+ in the oxidized form).

P_{700} acts as a trap for excitations in chloroplast lamellae while in bacteria a special type of bacteriochlorophyll having a λ_{max} between 870 and 890 nm acts in an analogous manner. One of the useful features for such excitation traps is to have an excited singlet state which is lower in energy than excited states in the other pigment molecules. This ensures the directionality for migration of excitations. Another characteristic of special molecules like P_{700} is their relative rarity. Thus most of the photosynthetic pigments act as antennae or light harvesters which collect the radiation and channel the excitations toward the trap chl, as is schematically indicated in Figure 5-7. Subsequent processing of the excitation originally caused by light need take place only at the trap chl's. In fact, this participation in the subsequent, essentially irreversible, electron transfer steps is the crucial feature of an excitation trap.

When the excitation migrates to the trap chl P_{700}, this special Chl a goes to an excited singlet state as would any other Chl a. However, another unique property of P_{700} is its long lifetime, which may be conferred on it by interactions with neighboring molecules or perhaps by a transition to an excited triplet state of P_{700}. Although the relatively long lifetime of a triplet would allow time for photochemical reactions to take place, such as the reduction of A and oxidation of D in Figure 5-7, there is no direct evidence for a triplet state of P_{700} *in vivo*. On the other hand, interactions with the neighboring molecules apparently prevent the fluorescent de-excitation of P_{700}, and therefore this special trap chl can exist in the excited singlet state for a rather long time, as we will consider below.

The trap chl is so situated that when it becomes excited such as by resonance transfer from other Chl *a* molecules, it is able to donate an electron to some acceptor molecule indicated by *A* in Equation 5–6 and Figure 5–7. The donation of this electron initiates the photochemical reactions of photosynthesis and the subsequent storage of energy in stable chemical bonds. Moreover, once the trap chl has lost an electron, it can take on another one from some donor, indicated by *D* in Equation 5–7 and Figure 5–7. Thus the photochemical reactions of photosynthesis are intrinsically involved with electron flow. It can therefore be readily appreciated that an excitation trap such as P_{700} plays a key role in the conversion of radiant energy into forms of energy that are biologically useful.

Photosynthetic Units and Enhancement Effects

So far we have discussed the absorption of light by photosynthetic pigments and the ensuing transfers of excitation among these molecules, which leads to a consideration of whether there are discrete units of such pigments acting together in some concerted fashion. Such an ensemble was presented in Figure 5–7, where it was indicated that the light harvesting photosynthetic pigments greatly outnumber the special trap chl molecules, the latter possibly occurring in a one-to-one relationship with suitable electron acceptors and donors. The questions to be considered in this section are whether photosynthetic pigments are organized into functional groups, and if so, how many molecules make up one group. Also, are the various groupings of pigments identical in terms of their function in photosynthesis?

Photosynthetic Units. It has been repeatedly demonstrated that approximately eight quanta absorbed by Chl *a* or the accessory pigments are used for the photosynthetic fixation of one CO_2 molecule in green plants. Concomitantly, one molecule of O_2 is evolved. The aspect to be specifically considered here is not how many quanta are required but rather the efficiency of the use of the light quanta at low compared with high light intensities.

At low light intensities, one molecule of CO_2 can be fixed or one of O_2 evolved per approximately eight quanta absorbed by any of the photosynthetic pigments. Is one molecule of O_2 still evolved per eight quanta absorbed by photosynthetic pigments at high light intensities? This question was answered in 1932 by R. Emerson and W. Arnold who used the green alga, *Chlorella,* and exposed it to intense flashes of light. These intense flashes excited all the chlorophyll molecules and other photosynthetic pigments simultaneously. The maximum yield in such experiments was one O_2 per 2000 to 2500 quanta absorbed by chlorophyll molecules! This is roughly 250 times more quanta than are necessary to produce the same amount of oxygen at low light intensities. At low levels of illumination, there is sufficient time between the arrival of the individual quanta for the excitations of the accessory pigments and Chl a to be efficiently collected in a trap chl and used for the chemical reactions of photosynthesis. At high light intensities, on the other hand, many photosynthetic pigments become excited at the same time, and only one excited chlorophyll in as many as 250 such molecules leads to any photochemical reaction. It is as if there were a unit of 250 chlorophyll molecules acting together; when any one molecule in this *photosynthetic unit* absorbs light and becomes excited, the concomitant excitation of other chlorophyll molecules cannot be used for photosynthesis.

The above conclusion on photosynthetic units can also be considered in terms of Figure 5–7, where the trap chl is shown interacting with the electron acceptor A and donor D. Specifically, when the rate-limiting step for photosynthesis is the photochemistry leading to the dissipation of the excited state of the trap chl, then a high light intensity leads to more excitations per unit time than can be processed by the reactions yielding A^- and D^+. (The same line of reasoning can be extended to include the case where the production of A^- and D^+ is itself not rate-limiting but rather where the subsequent steps leading to O_2 evolution and CO_2 fixation are actually the relatively slow ones.) At a light intensity high enough to excite all the photosynthetic pigments in some unit simultaneously, one excitation would be used for the photochemical steps (which are relatively slow compared with the absorption and excitation transfer processes) while all the other excitations would be dissipated by the various nonphotochemical de-excitation processes that were presented in the previous chapter.

A photosynthetic unit of approximately 250 chlorophylls may well be both a functional and also a structural entity in chloroplasts. As mentioned above, chloroplast lamellae have subunits that contain 230 chlorophyll molecules. Although these might actually be photosynthetic units, the electron transfer reactions (e.g., Eqs. 5–6 and 5–7) still remain to be demonstrated for them. In some photosynthetic bacteria, 40 bacteriochlorophylls form a photosynthetic unit having 1 trap chl, which is a special form of bacteriochlorophyll absorbing maximally near 870 to 890 nm. The size of the bacterial photosynthetic unit is rather variable and often larger. Indeed, the number of chlorophylls acting together as a photosynthetic unit in the chloroplasts of higher plants has also been found to vary.

The electronic excitation originally caused by the absorption of a light quantum can be processed by the chemical reactions associated with a photosynthetic unit only about once every 10 milliseconds. This processing time has important consequences both for the efficiency of light use at different illumination levels and also for the optimal size of a photosynthetic unit. The highest light intensity normally encountered by plants is when the sun is directly overhead on a cloudless day (approximately 100,000 lux), in which case each chlorophyll molecule in an unshaded chloroplast would absorb a quantum on the average about once every 100 milliseconds. If there are 250 chlorophylls per photosynthetic unit, 25 of these molecules would be excited every 10 milliseconds. However, since the processing time per photosynthetic unit is 10 milliseconds, only one of these 25 excitations could be used photochemically, the other 24 being dissipated by nonphotochemical de-excitation reactions. Thus, although the chemical reactions will operate at their maximum rate under such conditions of high light intensity, a large fraction of the electronic excitations caused by light absorption will not be used for photosynthesis.

The high light intensity of direct sunlight on a chloroplast seldom occurs under natural conditions since chloroplasts are generally shaded by other chloroplasts in the same cell, by plastids in other cells, and perhaps by overlying leaves. Furthermore, the amount of sunlight incident on a plant is much less at sunrise or sunset and on overcast days than it is at midday. For the sake of argument, consider when the light incident on a chloroplast is twenty-five times less than it is from the direct midday sun, namely a light intensity of approximately 4000 lux. Each chlorophyll molecule in the chloroplast then absorbs a quantum once every 2.5 seconds, which is a much longer time between the arrival of quanta than the time required for processing an electronic excitation by a photosynthetic unit. However, when individual chlorophylls are excited every 2.5 seconds at this moderate light intensity of 4000 lux, some chlorophyll molecule in a photosynthetic unit of 250 chlorophylls will become excited on the average of once every 10 milliseconds. This excitation frequency per photosynthetic unit is such that the light can be efficiently used for photosynthesis. In other words, the quanta are arriving at a rate such that the excitations produced by essentially all of them can be used, and, moreover, the chemical reactions are working at their maximum capacity. Consequently, the photosynthetic unit with its associated photochemistry and enzymatic reactions will function very effectively at a moderate light intensity.

It is instructive to consider what the consequences would be if there were but one chlorophyll molecule per photosynthetic unit. If the chemical reactions still took 10 milliseconds as above, then at a light intensity of about 4000 lux, this single pigment molecule would be excited once every 2.5 seconds, and the excitation could easily be processed by the chemical reactions. However, the photochemical and subsequent enzymatic reactions would only be working at 0.4% of capacity [$(10 \times 10^{-3})/(2.5)$ or 0.004 is the fraction of the time they would be used]. In other words, although all the absorbed light quanta would be used for photosynthesis, even the slowest of the chemical steps would be idle over 99% of the time. In conclusion, the above arguments can be summarized as follows: Given the 10 millisecond processing time for the chemical reactions, the grouping of 250 chlorophylls into one photosynthetic unit connected with the appropriate enzyme machinery provides a plant with an efficient mechanism for handling the usual light intensities, both from the point of view of harvesting the light quanta and also for using the chemical reactions at a substantial fraction of their capacity.

Photosynthetic Action Spectra and Enhancement Effects.   The electronic excitations resulting from light absorption by any of the pigments in the photosynthetic unit can be transferred to the trap chl and thus lead to photochemical reactions. Therefore, it would be reasonably expected that the absorption spectrum of chloroplasts should fairly well match the action spectrum for photosynthesis. However, it is generally found that the action spectrum for photostynthesis and the overall absorption spectrum for the photosynthetic pigments in the same organism do not coincide. For instance, light absorbed by certain accessory pigments can actually be more efficient in photosynthesis than light absorbed by Chl *a* itself, although the light-induced excitations of accessory pigments must be passed on to Chl *a* before being used for photochemical reactions (cf. Eq. 5–4). L. N. M. Duysens showed this to be the case for phycocyanin in blue-green algae and for both the phycobilins in red algae. Another paradoxical phenomenon is the so-called "red drop." Wavelengths above 690 nm are relatively inefficient for photosynthesis in green plants, which means that the photosynthetic action spectrum drops off much more rapidly in the red region above 690 nm than does the absorption spectrum for the chlorophylls and other pigments, as is illustrated in Figure 5–8 for the case of a green alga.

In 1957, R. Emerson showed that the relatively low photosynthetic efficiency of *Chlorella* in far-red light (a "red drop" such as is shown in Fig. 5–8) could be increased by simultaneously using small amounts of light of a shorter wavelength in addition to the far-red light. The photosynthetic rate

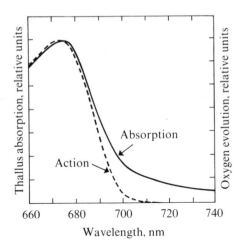

Figure 5-8. Action and absorption spectra indicating the "red drop" in photosynthesis. [Data are for *Ulva taeniata* and are taken from F. T. Haxo and L. R. Blinks, *Journal of General Physiology* **33**, 389–422 (1950); by permission.]

with the two beams was 30% to 40% greater than the sum of the rates from the far-red light and the shorter wavelength light used separately! Such synergism or enhancement suggested that photosynthesis involved the cooperation of two distinct photochemical reactions.

Specifically, light of wavelengths greater than 690 nm might mainly power only one of the reactions, and thus photosynthesis would not proceed at an appreciable rate. When shorter wavelengths are also used, the other necessary reaction could take place, resulting in a marked enhancement in the photosynthetic rate. Since photosynthesis is enhanced when a shorter wavelength is provided in addition to far-red illumination, a smaller percentage of light should then be reradiated as fluorescence. Indeed, the two wavelengths of light employed together evoke less fluorescence than the two acting individually. Finally, no matter what light intensities are used at wavelengths above 690 nm, the maximum rate of photosynthesis is not as high as the rates that can be caused by shorter wavelengths. This further supports the concept of two distinct photochemical reactions, only one of which is readily excitable by wavelengths in the far-red region above 690 nm.

Composition of the Two Photosystems.   The photosynthetic enhancement effect can be used to study the pigments in each of the two photochemical systems which are involved in photosynthesis. The system containing the pigment or pigments absorbing beyond 690 nm is referred to as Photosystem I. If the addition of shorter wavelengths in a certain region of the spectrum leads to a marked enhancement of the photosynthesis occurring in the presence of far-red light that had been acting alone, then at least some of the shorter wavelengths are being absorbed by pigments in the other system, Photosystem II. This approach has been successfully employed for assigning pigments to one or the other of the two photochemical systems. Moreover, certain of the conclusions have recently been confirmed by separation of the isolated photosystems followed by chemical identification of the components of each.

Much of the far-red absorption by Photosystem I is due to a type of Chl a having a λ_{max} from 680 to 683 nm and referred to above as Chl a_{680}. In fact, this Chl a_{680} may all be in Photosystem I as is the special Chl a, P_{700}. Therefore, light above 690 nm is absorbed mainly by Chl a_{680} and P_{700} in Photosystem I. An action spectrum for the enhancement of photosynthesis in the presence of a constant irradiation with this far-red light (i.e., wavelengths above 690 nm) should indicate the pigments in Photosystem II. For example, the action spectrum for such photosynthetic enhancement in the red alga, *Porphyra*, resembles the absorption spectrum of phycoerythrin (λ_{max} near 550 nm). In another red alga, *Porphyridium*, a marked increase in photosynthesis occurs when far-red light is supplemented by light that is absorbed by phycocyanin. Hence, in such algae it is reasonable to conclude that the phycobilins are in Photosystem II. Studies using photosynthetic enhancement also indicate that Chl b is in Photosystem II, as is fucoxanthin in the brown algae. In a related experimental approach, action spectra for the evocation of Chl a fluorescence indicate that light absorbed by the phycobilins and Chl b leads to the fluorescence of Chl a_{670}, this latter being another of the types of chlorophyll mentioned previously. Since Chl b and the phycobilins are in Photosystem II, Chl a_{670} most likely also occurs in Photosystem II. The location of certain carotenoids is less clear, and they may be associated with either or both photosystems.

Photosystems I and II of higher plants appear to be structurally distinct entities, each having 200 to 300 light-harvesting chlorophylls and a special type of chlorophyll acting as an excitation trap. In other words, each photosystem acts like one of the photosynthetic units discussed above. Photosystem I contains a few hundred Chl a_{680} molecules, very little or no Chl b, one P_{700}, and probably some carotenoids as accessory pigments. Photosystem II has most of its chlorophyll as Chl a_{670}, somewhat more than one-third as Chl b, and no P_{700} (a special chlorophyll acting as an excitation trap and having a λ_{max} near 690 nm apparently occurs). The phycobilins and most of the other accessory pigments are associated with Photosystem II. The blue-green algae also have two photosystems but do not have any Chl b. Convincing evidence has recently been presented for two separate photosystems in the photosynthetic bacteria. (Instead of oxidizing water to evolve oxygen, the photosynthetic bacteria are unique among photosynthetic organisms in oxidizing primarily organic acids or inorganic sulfur-containing compounds.)

The trap chl in any of the photosynthetic units must be accessible to the light-harvesting pigments and to the electron transfer components which become oxidized or reduced. This trap chl with the associated species which accept or donate electrons is generally referred to as a reaction center. The reaction center is the locus for the photochemistry of photosynthesis (Eqs. 5–6 and 5–7) and may be located at or near the surface of the photosynthetic unit.

Electron Flow and Photophosphorylation

As has been discussed in the preceding sections, the photochemical reactions of photosynthesis involve the removal of an excited electron from the special chlorophyll that acts as an excitation trap and the replacement of this electron by one coming from a suitable donor. The donation of the electron to some acceptor begins a series of electron transfer steps which ultimately can lead to the reduction of NADP. The oxidized trap chl, having lost an electron, can then accept another electron from a suitable donor, such as by means of the steps which lead to oxygen evolution. Coupled to the electron transfer reactions in chloroplasts is the formation of ATP, although the actual mechanism for this "photophosphorylation" is as yet unknown. In this section we will consider some of the components of chloroplasts that are involved in accepting and donating electrons and leave a discussion of the energetics of such processes until the next chapter.

The various aspects of photosynthesis specifically discussed in this text occur over a wide range of times, extending essentially from 10^{-15} second all the way up to 1 second. The absorption of light and the transfer of excitations from the accessory pigments and the Chl a molecules to the trap chl occupy a time interval from 10^{-15} to 10^{-9} sec. The photochemical events at the reaction center, which can be described by Equations 5–6 and 5–7, last from about 10^{-9} to 10^{-5} sec. The separation of the electron from the trap chl, which takes place at this time, leads to a bleaching (decrease in absorption coefficient) of this pigment. By observing the kinetics of spectral changes occurring in the far-red region where the trap chl's absorb, one is able to determine when the photochemistry takes place, an event which signals that the radiant energy has been converted to chemical potential energy. The ensuing electron flow commences approximately 10^{-5} sec after light absorption and can last into the millisecond range for the electron transfers to some of the components involved. The kinetics of the steps leading to ATP formation are not very well known but apparently extend to even longer times, such as seconds after the light absorption event.

Electron Flow.   Studies on the electron flow accompanying photosynthesis received great impetus in 1938 when R. Hill demonstrated that isolated chloroplasts could evolve oxygen and reduce certain exogenous compounds in the light. Oxygen evolution was able to proceed in the absence of carbon dioxide, suggesting that CO_2 fixation and O_2 evolution are separate processes. These pioneering investigations focused attention on the overall pathway for electron flow in photosynthesis, a topic which was not understood at that time. Using ^{18}O-labeled H_2O and ^{18}O-labeled CO_2 in separate experiments, S. Ruben and M. D. Kamen in 1941 conclusively showed that the evolved oxygen comes from water and not from CO_2. Subsequent studies have elucidated many of the steps intervening between O_2 evolution and CO_2 fixation in photosynthesis, the principal features of which we will now turn our attention to.

The point of departure for the present discussion of electron flow in photosynthesis will simply be to indicate the overall accomplishments of the process. To begin with, four molecules of water are involved in the evolution of one molecule of oxygen. Although the actual mechanism of this water oxidation is still unclear, it can be represented as follows:

$$4H_2O \longrightarrow O_2 + 4H + 2H_2O \qquad (5\text{-}9)$$

where H_2O has been included on both sides of Equation 5–9 to emphasize that each of four different molecules of water loses an electron and a proton (H in Eq. 5–9 represents $H^+ + e^-$) in the formation of one oxygen molecule. The process of CO_2 fixation into a carbohydrate involves the reduction of carbon. Specifically, four hydrogen atoms are required per carbon atom:

$$CO_2 + 4H \longrightarrow \{CH_2O\} + H_2O \qquad (5\text{-}10)$$

where $\{CH_2O\}$ represents a general carbohydrate as indicated previously (cf. Eq. 5–1). The movement of the reductant H appearing in Equations 5–9 and 5–10 can be conveniently followed by tracing the flow of the elec-

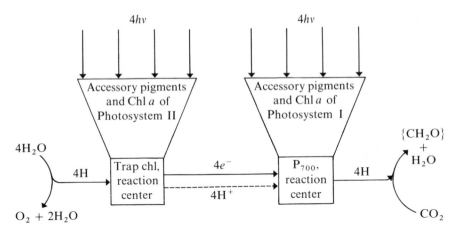

Figure 5–9. Schematic model for a series representation of the two photosystems of photosynthesis, indicating the stoichiometry of the various factors involved in the reduction of a CO_2 molecule to a carbohydrate ($\{CH_2O\}$).

trons ($H = H^+ + e^-$), which explains why the topic under consideration here is electron flow, not hydrogen flow. Moreover, reducing a compound is chemically equivalent to adding electrons while oxidation is the removal of electrons.

Some pathway for photosynthetic electron flow is needed to take the H's indicated as products in Equation 5–9 and transfer them by means of a number of electron accepting and donating components to become the H's required as reactants in Equation 5–10. This electron flow process involves both Photosystems I and II. Specifically, the oxidant involved with oxygen evolution (Eq. 5–9) is provided by Photosystem II. The primary oxidant is trap chl$^+$, which leads to the oxidation of water (cf. Eq. 5–7, trap chl$^+$ + $D \rightarrow$ trap chl + D^+). The reductant required for carbon reduction (Eq. 5–10) is produced by the excited trap chl in Photosystem I (cf. Eq. 5–6, trap chl* + $A \rightarrow$ trap chl$^+$ + A^-). These two photosystems are linked by a flow of electrons as is schematically indicated in Figure 5–9.

One electron can be removed from an excited trap chl per quantum absorbed by any of the accessory pigments or Chl a's in that photosynthetic unit. Since 4 electrons are involved per O_2 derived from water, the evolution of this 1 molecule of oxygen requires the absorption of 4 quanta by Photosystem II (cf. Eq. 5–9 and the 4 quanta indicated to be incident on Photosystem II in Fig. 5–9). An additional 4 quanta absorbed by Photosystem I are necessary for the reduction of 2 molecules of NADP and then ultimately of 1 CO_2 molecule (Eq. 5–10 and Fig. 5–9). Hence, 8 quanta are needed for the evolution of 1 molecule of oxygen and fixation of 1 molecule of carbon dioxide, consistent with the observations mentioned above when photosynthetic units were introduced. (The number of quanta necessary to provide the ATP's required for CO_2 fixation will be considered below.) Although alternatives to the series representation in Figure 5–9 do exist, the scheme that is illustrated takes into consideration the results of many investigators and has become generally accepted as an overall description of the electron flow aspects of photosynthesis.

Components of the Electron Transport Pathway.   Now let us turn to the molecules acting as electron acceptors or donors in chloroplasts. To organize some of the aspects to be mentioned here, a summary of the characteristics of the better known components is presented in Table 5–1. The discussion will begin by considering the photochemistry at the reaction center of Photosystem II and then will proceed with a consideration of the various substances in the approximate sequence in which they are involved in electron flow.

The electron lost from the excited trap chl in the reaction center of Photosystem II is replaced by one coming from water in the process leading to oxygen evolution. The molecular details of this water oxidation are unknown at the present time. Manganese may be involved, presumably while bound to some protein. Also chloride is implicated in the oxygen evolution steps. The other half of the photochemistry at Photosystem II involves the fate of the electron removed from the excited trap chl, a topic we will consider next.

The electron removed from the excited trap chl of Photosystem II is transferred through a series of molecules comprising the photosynthetic "electron transport chain," a term which is often used to describe the pathway from Photosystem II to Photosystem I. (See Fig. 5–9.) All the components involved with electron flow in this chain of molecules are not known, and also some of the molecule-to-molecule sequences for electron transfer are uncertain. One of the first molecules to accept electrons donated by the excited trap chl of Photosystem II is a plastoquinone. Chloroplast lamellae actually contain eight or more different types of quinone.

Table 5–1: Representative properties of some of the components involved with electron transport in chloroplasts. Photosystems I plus II contain about 450 chlorophyll molecules; thus the frequency of the components in the table is per 450 chlorophylls. Heme refers to an iron-containing porphyrin. Redox potentials will be discussed in Chapter 6.

Name	Molecular weight	Approximate number/450 chlorophylls	Numbers of electrons accepted or donated per molecule	Approximate midpoint redox potential in mv	Comment
Ferredoxin	12,000	1	1	−430	Nonheme protein having two iron atoms/molecule; accepts electrons excited from Photosystem I, perhaps by way of an intermediate
Ferredoxin-NADP reductase	42,000	?	...	...	An enzyme containing one flavin adenine dinucleotide/molecule; apparently bound to lamellae
NADP	743	30	2	−320	Soluble in aqueous solutions
Cytochrome b_6	?	2	1	−30	May be involved in the cyclic pathway between ferredoxin and Photosystem I
Other b cytochrome	?	2	1	(55)	Peak absorption at 559 nm; may be bound to Photosystem II
Plastoquinone A	748	65	2	113	Probably acting at the reducing end of Photosystem II; can be oxidized by Photosystem I; only some of the plastoquinone molecules may be involved in electron transport
Cytochrome f	13,000 to 60,000 per heme	1	1	360	In or bound to Photosystem I, which can oxidize it
Plastocyanin	21,000	1	2	370	Blue protein (reduced form is colorless) associated with Photosystem I; contains two copper atoms/molecule
P_{700}	893	1	1	430	A Chl a acting as the trap chl of Photosystem I

is the structure of quinone, which becomes a semiquinone,

$$\text{O}^{\bullet}$$
$$\text{OH}$$

when one hydrogen atom is added and a hydroquinone,

$$\text{OH}$$
$$\text{OH}$$

when two are added. The great variety among the quinones is due to sub-stituents attached to the ring, e.g., plastoquinone A is

these attachments often leading to polycyclic compounds such as Vitamin K. Like chlorophyll, plastoquinone A has a nonpolar terpene tail, which may serve to anchor it at the proper locations in the lamellar membranes of chloroplasts. When donating or accepting electrons, plastoquinones have characteristic absorption changes in the UV near 250 to 260 nm that can be used to study their electron transfer reactions. From the plastoquinone, electrons may be passed on to the b cytochrome having a λ_{max} at 559 nm. (Cytochrome structure will be considered shortly.) Electron flow then con-tinues energetically downhill to a blue protein termed plastocyanin or to cytochrome f. (Energetics of electron flow are discussed in the next chapter, cf. Fig. 6–1.)

Cytochromes are extremely important components of the electron trans-port pathways in both chloroplasts and mitochondria. They have three absorption bands in the visible region, referred to as the α, β, and γ bands. In 1925, D. Keilin distinguished among three different types of cytochrome based on the spectral position of their α or long wavelength band. Cyto-chromes of the a type had a λ_{max} for the α band from 600 to 605 nm, b types near 560 nm, and c types near 550 nm. All the cytochromes have β bands near 515 to 530 nm while the main short wavelength band is the γ or Soret band, which usually has a λ_{max} in the wavelength region from 415 to 430 nm.

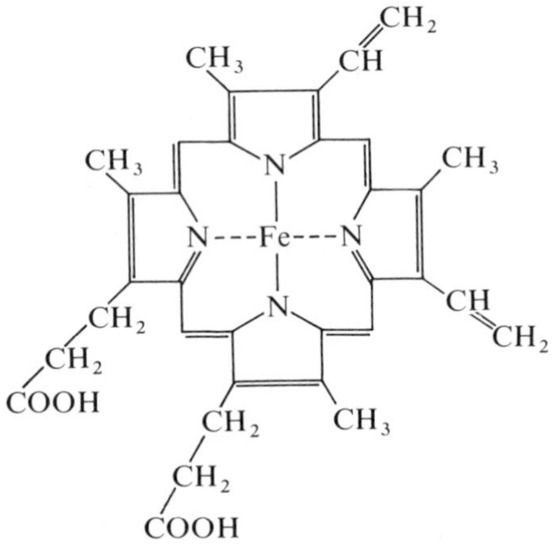

Figure 5-10. The iron-containing porphyrin known as heme, which is the chromophore for cytochrome *c*.

Cytochromes consist of an iron-containing tetrapyrrole or porphyrin known as heme (Fig. 5–10), which is bound to a protein. The various cytochromes differ in the substituents around the periphery of the porphyrin ring, in the protein to which the chromophore (light-absorbing part) is attached, and in the binding between the protein and the porphyrin. Cytochrome *f*, which occurs in chloroplasts (*f* from *frons*, the Latin for leaf), is a *c*-type cytochrome, and so contains the chromophore indicated in Figure 5–10. Many different hemoproteins of the cytochrome *b* type are found in plants, two occurring in chloroplasts (cf. Table 5–1). These various *b* cytochromes appear to have the same chromophore attached to different proteins, and thus their individual absorption properties are probably due to changes in the protein. Like the cytochromes, chlorophylls are tetrapyrroles (cf. the structure of Chl *a* given in Fig. 5–1), but they have a Mg atom in the center of the porphyrin ring while the cytochromes have an Fe. Furthermore, the acceptance or donation of an electron by a cytochrome involves a transition between the two states of its iron, Fe^{++} and Fe^{+++}, whereas the electron ejected from chlorophyll in the photochemical reactions of photosynthesis most likely is one of the π electrons in the conjugated system of the porphyrin ring.

Although absorption of light by cytochromes is presumably not involved in electron transport, spectral properties can be used for cytochrome identification, as mentioned above, and also for monitoring electron flow *in vivo*. The removal of an electron from a cytochrome (oxidation) causes its three absorption bands, which have maximum absorption coefficients of about 3×10^4 liters/mole-cm, to become less intense and more diffuse. Such changes permit a study of the kinetics of electron transport while the cyto-chrome molecules remain embedded in the internal membranes of chloro-plasts or mitochondria. For instance, monitoring the spectral changes of the chloroplast cytochromes has indicated that the electron flow in the electron transport chain between Photosystem II and Photosystem I (Figs. 5–9 and 6–1) occurs 10^{-5} to 10^{-3} sec after light absorption by some pigment molecule in the photosynthetic unit of Photosystem II.

Electrons which have traversed the electron transport chain from Photo-system II to plastocyanin or cytochrome f can then be accepted by the trap chl of Photosystem I, P_{700}, if the latter is in the oxidized form (cf. Eq. 5–7, trap chl$^+$ + D → trap chl + D^+). Photochemical changes in P_{700} can be followed spectrophotometrically since the loss of an electron causes a bleaching of both the Soret and red absorption bands while the subsequent acceptance of an electron restores the original absorption properties. For instance, it can be shown that the P_{700} bleaching takes place about 10^{-5} sec after light absorption by some photosynthetic pigment in Photosystem I. Moreover, P_{700} is bleached (oxidized) by light absorbed by Photosystem I and then restored (reduced) following the absorption of quanta by Photo-system II. Also, far-red light (above 690 nm) absorbed by Photosystem I leads to an oxidation of cytochrome f, indicating that an electron from cytochrome f can be donated to P_{700}. Thus, the electron removed from P_{700} is replaced by one coming from Photosystem II by means of the electron transport chain just discussed. (See Figs. 5–9 and 6–1.) The electron from P_{700} reduces the iron-containing protein, ferredoxin, perhaps by way of an intermediate compound. Ferredoxin contains two irons in the ferric state bound by sulfide bonds; the electron from P_{700} causes the reduction of one of these ferric atoms to the ferrous form. By means of the enzyme ferredoxin-NADP reductase, two molecules of ferredoxin reduce one molecule of NADP to yield NADPH$_2$. (NADP and NADPH$_2$ will be discussed in the next chapter.)

It has proved convenient to distinguish three different types of photo-synthetic electron flow, each one depending on the compound to which electrons are transferred from ferredoxin. In *noncyclic* electron flow, electrons coming originally from water are ultimately used to reduce NADP. The overall noncyclic electron flow is as follows: An electron from water goes to the trap chl$^+$ of Photosystem II; there, it replaces a donated electron which flows along the electron transport chain to the oxidized P_{700} in Photo-system I; the electron removed from P_{700} moves to ferredoxin, perhaps by way of an intermediate compound, and then to NADP. Such noncyclic electron flow follows essentially the same pathway as the reductant H that moves from left to right in Figure 5–9. (See also Fig. 6–1.)

For *cyclic* electron flow, the electron from the reduced form of ferredoxin moves back to the electron transport chain between Photosystems I and II and thus reduces an oxidized P_{700}. Cytochrome b_6 may act as an intermediate for this cyclic electron flow by intervening between ferredoxin and the electron transport chain. Cyclic electron flow does not involve Photosystem II at all and hence can be caused by far-red light absorbed only by Photosystem I, a fact that is often exploited in experimental studies. For instance, when far-red light alone is used, cyclic electron flow can occur, but noncyclic does not, and so no $NADPH_2$ is formed, nor is any oxygen evolved. When light absorbed by Photosystem II is added, both carbon dioxide fixation and oxygen evolution can proceed, and the photosynthetic enhancement cited above is obtained.

Electrons from ferredoxin may also reduce oxygen, which yields H_2O_2 and eventually H_2O. Since equal amounts of oxygen are evolved at Photosystem II and then consumed using reduced ferredoxin in a quite separate reaction, such electron flow is termed *pseudocyclic* (illustrated in Fig. 6–1). There is no net oxygen change accompanying pseudocyclic electron flow although it is not a cycle in the sense of having electrons cyclically traverse a certain pathway.

Many questions concerning electron flow in photosynthesis remain unanswered. For instance, what are the intermediates involved in the evolution of oxygen from water? Does the removal of an electron from each of four water molecules occur at the reaction center of a single Photosystem II, or are two or perhaps four different photosynthetic units involved? As indicated in Table 5–1, ferredoxin, the cytochromes, and P_{700} can accept or donate only one electron. These molecules must interact with NADP, plastocyanin, and the plastoquinones, all of which can transport two electrons at a time. Do the two electrons which reduce plastoquinone and plastocyanin sequentially come from the same Photosystem II, or do they come from two different ones? Similarly, do the two electrons used to reduce NADP traverse the same or different electron transport chains? Both the pyridine nucleotides and also the plastoquinones are considerably more numerous than the other molecules involved with photosynthetic electron transport (Table 5–1), which probably has important implications for the electron transfer reactions. Moreover, NADP is soluble in aqueous solutions and so could diffuse to the NADP-ferredoxin reductase where two electrons are transferred to it to yield $NADPH_2$. Although a great deal remains to be learned about photosynthetic electron flow, nevertheless much more physical and chemical information is already available describing such electron movement than is the case for the accompanying ATP formation which is somehow coupled to this electron flow.

Photophosphorylation. As was indicated in the introduction to this chapter (cf. Eq. 5–1), three ATP molecules are generally required for the reductive fixation of one CO_2 molecule into a carbohydrate. This ATP is "photophosphorylated," meaning that light absorbed by the photosynthetic pigments in the lamellar membranes leads to a flow of electrons to which is coupled the phosphorylation of ADP. The energetics of this dehydration of ADP plus phosphate to yield ATP will be considered in the next chapter.

Photophosphorylation was first demonstrated in cell-free systems in 1954. A. Frenkel, working with bacterial chromatophores, and D. Arnon and colleagues, using broken spinach chloroplasts, both observed ATP formation in the light. So far, very little is known at the molecular level about the enzymes involved in photophosphorylation or the actual mechanism for ATP formation. One difficulty is that the enzymes are localized in or on the lamellar membranes, the energy transfer steps being apparently very sensitive to disruption of the solid system. Investigation of photophosphorylation in living cells is also difficult since none of the molecular species (ADP, ATP, and phosphate) can be readily determined quantitatively *in vivo*. For instance, interconversions of these compounds in the chloroplasts cannot be monitored by measuring changes in spectral properties, a technique which is quite successful for studying the acceptance or donation of electrons by cytochromes and by trap chl's. Furthermore, all three molecules, ATP, ADP, and phosphate, take part in many different biochemical reactions, which greatly complicates the interpretation of the meager amount of kinetic data which are presently available on photophosphorylation. ATP formation coupled to electron flow in both chloroplasts and mitochondria will be further considered in the next chapter, after some of the underlying energy concepts are introduced.

Problems

5–1. Consider a spherical spongy mesophyll cell that is 40 μm in diameter and that contains 50 spherical chloroplasts that are 4 μm in diameter. Assume that such cells contain 1 mg chlorophyll/g, that the cell is 90% water by weight, and that the cellular density is 1.00 g/cm³. (a) What volume fraction of the cell is occupied by chloroplasts? (b) If the CO_2 fixation rate is 100 μmoles/mg chlorophyll-hour, how long does it take to double the dry weight of the cell? Assume that CO_2 and H_2O are the only substances entering the cell. (c) If the ratio Chl a/Chl b is 3, what is the mean molecular weight of chlorophyll? (d) Assuming that the chlorophyll is uniformly distributed throughout the cell, what is the maximum absorbance by one cell in the red and the blue regions? Use absorption coefficients given in Figure 5–2.

5–2. Suppose that some pigment has 8 double bonds in conjugation and has a single absorption band with a λ_{max} at 580 nm, which corresponds to a transition to the fourth vibrational sublevel of the excited state (cf. Fig. 4–4). A similar pigment has 10 double bonds in conjugation, which causes the lowest vibrational sublevel of the excited state to move down in energy by 0.2 ev while the lowest vibrational sublevel of the ground state moves up in energy by 0.2 ev compared with the analogous levels in the other molecule. Assume that the splitting between vibrational sublevels remains at 0.1 ev and that the most likely transition predicted by the Franck-Condon principle for this second molecule is also to the fourth vibrational sublevel. (a) What is the λ_{max} for fluorescence by each of the two molecules? (b) Can either or both molecules readily pass their excitation on to Chl a in vivo? (c) Can the absorption of blue light by Chl a lead to excitation of either of the pigments? Give your reasoning.

5–3. Suppose that chloroplasts containing 10 nanomoles of chlorophyll/ml of solution are suspended in a cuvette with a 1 cm light path. The rate of oxygen evolution is proportional to light intensity up to 6×10^{14} quanta absorbed/cm²-sec, which gives 10^{-7} M O_2 evolved/sec. For a very brief and intense flash of light, the O_2 evolution is 5×10^{-9} M. (a) Using the above data, how many quanta are required per O_2 evolved? (b) How many chlorophyll molecules are there in a photosynthetic unit? (c) How much time is required for the processing of an excitation by a photosynthetic unit? (d) An "uncoupler" is a compound which decreases the ATP formation that is coupled to photosynthetic electron flow. When such a compound is added to chloroplasts incubated at a high light intensity, the O_2 evolution rate is higher for the first few seconds and then becomes less than a control without the uncoupler. Explain.

5–4. Suppose that the absorbance of pea chloroplasts in a cuvette with a 1 cm light path is 0.1 at 710 nm and 1.0 at 550 nm. Assume that chlorophyll is the only species absorbing at 710 nm while no chlorophyll absorbs at 550 nm. For the sake of argument, suppose that no CO_2 is fixed when either 550 nm or 710 nm light is used alone, but both together do lead to CO_2 fixation. (a) Is any ATP formation caused by the 550 nm or by the 710 nm light? (b) What type of pigments are absorbing at 550 nm, and are they isoprenoids or tetrapyrroles? (c) If equal incident photon fluxes of low intensity are simultaneously used at both 550 nm and 710 nm, what is the maximum quantum yield for CO_2 fixation for each beam?

References

Boardman, N. K. 1968. The photochemical systems of photosynthesis. *Advances in Enzymology* **30**, 1–79.

Fogg, G. E. 1968. *Photosynthesis*, American Elsevier, New York.

Goodwin, T. W., ed. 1965. *Chemistry and Biochemistry of Plant Pigments*, Academic Press, London.

Hind, G., and J. M. Olson. 1968. Electron transport pathways in photosynthesis. *Annual Review of Plant Physiology* **19**, 249–82.

Kamen, M. D. 1963. *Primary Processes in Photosynthesis*, Academic Press, New York.

Thomas, J. B. 1965. *Primary Photoprocesses in Biology*, North-Holland, Amsterdam.

Vernon, L. P., and G. R. Seely, eds. 1966. *The Chlorophylls*, Academic Press, New York.

Also see references for Chapter 4.

Chapter 6

Bioenergetics

Throughout this text, we have considered various aspects of energy in biological systems. The concept of chemical potential or free energy was introduced in Chapter 2 and then applied to the specific case of water. In Chapter 3, such a thermodynamic approach was used in discussing the properties of ions in terms of their electrochemical potential energies. We also discussed the use of metabolically produced chemical energy for actively transporting some substance in an energetically uphill direction. Chapter 4 was concerned with the absorption of light, which is followed by a number of possible de-excitation reactions for the excited electronic state of the molecules. Photosynthesis (Chapter 5) involves the conversion of such electromagnetic energy trapped by the photosynthetic pigments into forms that are more useful biologically. It is this last aspect, namely the production and use of various energy currencies in biological systems, to which this chapter is devoted.

Two energy "currencies" produced in chloroplasts soon after the trapping of radiant energy are ATP and $NADPH_2$, these being representatives from the two main classes of energy storage compounds associated with the electron transport pathways of photosynthesis and respiration. We will first examine energy storage in terms of the chemical potential changes accompanying the conversion of a set of reactants into their products. This free energy consideration allows a determination of the amount of chemical or electrical energy that a given reaction can store or release. Next, the energy-carrying capacity of ATP will be evaluated in terms of the energetics of its formation and hydrolysis. $NADPH_2$ can be viewed as possessing electrical energy, the particular amount being determined relative to the oxidation-reduction potential of the system with which it interacts. After considering ATP and $NADPH_2$ as individual molecules, we will place them in their biological context, viz., as part of the bioenergetic scheme of chloroplasts and mitochondria. We will conclude with a brief comment on the overall flow of energy from the sun through the biosphere with its energy storage compounds and then back into space.

Free Energy

Energy changes accompanying biological reactions, like those for chemical reactions in general, can be calculated from thermodynamic relations. Two conditions which are usually appropriate to physiological processes greatly simplify these calculations. First, most biological reactions take place at constant temperature, i.e., they are isothermal. Second, processes in cells or tissues generally occur at constant pressure. These two special conditions make the Gibbs free energy, G, a very convenient expression for describing energetics in biology since the decrease in G for some reaction in a system at constant temperature and pressure equals the maximum amount of energy available for work by that organism. Biological work takes on a number of different forms, all the way from muscular movement to chemical synthesis and active transport. Isothermal heat exchanges, however, cannot bring about useful work and do not contribute to the change in Gibbs free energy at constant temperature and pressure. The difference in Gibbs free energy between two states can be used to predict the direction for a particular reaction as well as to indicate how much energy is required or will be released if the given reactants are converted to products. In fact, biologists are generally more interested in such changes in free energy than in its absolute amount, which must be defined relative to some arbitrary level.

The spontaneous direction for a reaction is toward a minimum of the Gibbs free energy of the reactants and products, the minimum actually being achieved at equilibrium. In principle, a spontaneous process can always be used to do a positive amount of work. To drive a reaction in the direction opposite to that in which it would proceed spontaneously requires free energy. As will be indicated below, light can be harnessed as the free energy source to cause the phosphorylation of ADP and the reduction of NADP, these two processes being prime examples of energy-requiring reactions that are at the very heart of chloroplast bioenergetics.

The concept of free energy was introduced in Chapter 2, where it was indicated that the chemical potential of an individual species could be identified as the free energy of that substance. It is often useful to consider the free energy of an entire system that will in general consist of many components. The Gibbs free energy can be used to describe the total free energy of such a system, where G is made up of contributions from each of the species present plus certain other terms. A definition of the Gibbs free energy which is appropriate for the present discussion is as follows:

$$G = \sum_j n_j \mu_j + G' \qquad (6\text{--}1)$$

where n_j is the number of moles of species j in the system being considered, μ_j is the chemical potential of species j (Eq. 2–4), the summation is over all species present, and G' includes the other terms contributing to G. At constant temperature and pressure, G' is a constant, and so Equation 6–1 is in a very useful form for the application of free energy relations to bioenergetics. It is worthwhile to point out that the chemical potential of species j, μ_j, which appears in Equation 6–1 and was extensively employed in Chapters 2 and 3, can be viewed as the increase in the Gibbs free energy of the system per mole increase of species j. More precisely, μ_j equals $(\partial G / \partial n_j)_{n_i, T, P}$, which means that the chemical potential of some species j is the partial molal Gibbs free energy obtained when the number of moles of other species, temperature, and pressure are all held constant. Next, we will turn our attention to the changes in free energy that accompany chemical reactions.

Chemical Reactions and Equilibrium Constants.   From the thermodynamic point of view, interest in bioenergetics is focused on the overall change in free energy for an individual reaction or perhaps for a sequence of reactions. To be specific, consider a general chemical reaction for which A and B are the reactants and C and D are the products:

$$aA + bB \rightleftharpoons cC + dD \qquad (6\text{--}2)$$

where a, b, c, and d appearing in Equation 6–2 are the number of moles of the various species taking part in the reaction. How much energy is stored (or released) when a certain reaction, such as that represented in Equation 6–2, proceeds in a particular direction? More specifically, what is the change in biologically useful work as expressed by the change in Gibbs free energy? Using Equation 6–1, the change in the Gibbs free energy for the reaction in Equation 6–2 proceeding in the forward direction with a moles of A and b moles of B reacting to give c moles of C and d moles of D is

$$\Delta G = -a\mu_A - b\mu_B + c\mu_C + d\mu_D \tag{6–3}$$

where the constant term, G', appearing in Equation 6–1 cancels out for the case of reactions at constant temperature and pressure. Equation 6–3 indicates that the free energy change of a chemical reaction under the conditions being considered is simply the chemical energy of the products minus that of the reactants.

To transform Equation 6–3 into a more useful form, an expression for the chemical potential of species j, μ_j, is needed. This has already been presented in Equation 2–4, where μ_j was given as a linear combination of component energies, viz., μ_j equals $\mu_j^* + RT \ln a_j + \bar{V}_j P + z_j FE$. (As mentioned previously, μ_j^* is a constant referring to a standard or reference state, a_j the activity of species j, $\bar{V}_j$ its partial molal volume, P the pressure in excess of atmospheric, z_j its charge, F the Faraday, and E the electrical potential.) Upon substituting such chemical potentials of A, B, C, and D into Equation 6–3 and collecting similar terms, one obtains:

$$\begin{aligned}
\Delta G = \ &-a\mu_A^* - b\mu_B^* + c\mu_C^* + d\mu_D^* \\
&+ RT(-a \ln a_A - b \ln a_B + c \ln a_C + d \ln a_D) \\
&+ P(-a\bar{V}_A - b\bar{V}_B + c\bar{V}_C + d\bar{V}_D) \\
&+ FE(-az_A - bz_B + cz_C + dz_D)
\end{aligned} \tag{6–4}$$

If the volume of the products $(c\bar{V}_C + d\bar{V}_D)$ is the same as that of the reactants $(a\bar{V}_A + b\bar{V}_B)$, the parenthesis multiplying P in Equation 6–4 is zero, a situation closely approached for many chemical reactions. In particular, the actual value of $P \sum_j n_j \bar{V}_j$ for biochemical reactions is usually relatively small for the pressures encountered in plant cells, and hence the term will not be retained here. The algebraic sum of the terms in the last parenthesis in Equation 6–4 equals zero because no charge is created or destroyed by the reaction given in Equation 6–2, i.e., the total charge of the products $(cz_C + dz_D)$ equals that of the reactants $(az_A + bz_B)$. The constant terms in Equation 6–4 can be collected into ΔG^*, a quantity which will be evaluated below.

Using ΔG^*, the constancy of charge, and the assumption that $P(-a\bar{V}_A - b\bar{V}_B + c\bar{V}_C + d\bar{V}_D)$ is negligible, the change in Gibbs free energy as given by Equation 6–4 for Equation 6–2 proceeding in the forward direction becomes simply

$$\Delta G = \Delta G^* + RT \ln \frac{(a_C)^c (a_D)^d}{(a_A)^a (a_B)^b} \qquad (6\text{–}5)$$

Equation 6–5 is a general expression that gives the energy stored or released by a chemical reaction.

Before continuing, let us comment on the value and meaning of ΔG^* in Equation 6–5. At equilibrium, the argument of the logarithm in Equation 6–5, $[(a_C)^c (a_D)^d]/[(a_A)^a (a_B)^b]$, is simply the equilibrium constant, K, of the reaction given by Equation 6–2. Furthermore, the free energy of a system at equilibrium is at a minimum and does not change, i.e., ΔG equals zero for such a chemical reaction proceeding a short distance in either direction. Putting these conditions into Equation 6–5 indicates that $\Delta G^* + RT \ln K$ is zero at equilibrium, and so ΔG^* equals $- RT \ln K$. In other words, ΔG^* depends in a rather simple fashion on the equilibrium constant of the particular reaction under consideration.

To see the implications of this, let us consider that the reactants (A and B) and the products (C and D) all have unit activity, i.e., $[(a_C)^c (a_D)^d]/[(a_A)^a (a_B)^b]$ is one, and hence the logarithm of the activity term is zero. Equation 6–5 indicates that for a moles of A plus b moles of B reacting to form c moles of C plus d moles of D under these conditions, the Gibbs free energy change, ΔG, is simply ΔG^*. If the equilibrium constant, K, for the reaction is greater than 1, ΔG^* is negative ($\Delta G^* = - RT \ln K$), which means that the reaction in the forward direction is spontaneous in this case. We would expect the reaction to proceed in the forward direction for an equilibrium constant greater than 1 since such a K means that at equilibrium the products are favored over the reactants {in the sense that $[(a_C)^c (a_D)^d] > [(a_A)^a (a_B)^b]$}. On the other hand, if K is less than 1, ΔG^* is positive, and so such a reaction would not proceed spontaneously in the forward direction for the given initial condition of unit activity of all reactants and products.

It is instructive to indicate numerical values that might be expected for ΔG^*. Since RT is 592 cal/mole at 25° and ln equals 2.303 log (Appendix III), an equilibrium constant of 100 corresponds to a ΔG^* of $-(592)(2.303) \log (100)$ or -2730 cal/mole while a K of 0.01 leads to a ΔG^* of $+2730$ cal/mole. In the former case, 2.73 kcal of energy/mole would be released while in the latter case the same amount of energy would be required in order to drive the reaction in the forward direction when starting with unit activity of all reactants and products.

Interconversion of Chemical and Electrical Energy.   To understand how chemical energy can be converted into electrical energy, and vice versa, we must examine a little more closely the properties of both chemical reactions and the movement of charged species. Let us first consider a chemical reaction such as the dissociation of sodium chloride: $NaCl \rightleftharpoons Na^+ + Cl^-$. Although two charged species are produced upon dissociation of NaCl, no overall change in electrical energy occurs. In other words, the electrical term, $z_j FE$, due to Na^+ ($z_{Na} = +1$) is balanced by an opposite change in the electrical energy of Cl^- ($z_{Cl} = -1$). Next consider the following type of reaction: $Ag_s \rightleftharpoons Ag^+ + e^-$, i.e., the dissociation of solid silver to an ion plus an electron. Again, no net change in electrical energy occurs for the dissociation as written. However, the production of an electron opens up various other possibilities since electrons can readily move to regions where the electrical potential may be different. Such reactions in which electrons are produced and then move to regions of different electrical potential allow for the interconversion of chemical and electrical energy. The electron producing or consuming reactions are referred to as electrode or half-cell reactions and occur not only in batteries but also in the electron transport chains located in chloroplast lamellae.

If by some external means (e.g., using the chemical energy in a battery) electrons can be moved to a lower electrical potential ($\Delta E < 0$), then the electrical energy term ($z_j FE$) of the chemical potential of the electrons is increased ($z_j = -1$ for an electron). This increase in the electrical energy of the electrons can subsequently be exploited to power a chemical reaction. For instance, the electrons can be conducted by some metal electrode into an aqueous solution containing Ag^+, which can lead to the deposition of solid silver on that particular electrode. Electrical energy is thereby converted into chemical energy. In photosynthesis, light energy is used to move electrons toward lower electrical potentials, which sets up a spontaneous flow of electrons in the other direction toward higher electrical potentials. This energetically downhill electron movement is somehow harnessed to drive the reaction $ADP + phosphate \rightleftharpoons ATP$ in the forward direction and thereby to store chemical energy, as will be discussed below.

Next, let us consider the interconversion of chemical and electrical energy in more formal terms. Suppose n moles of electrons ($z_j = -1$) are transferred from one region to another (e.g., from one half-cell to another) where the electrical potential differs by ΔE from the original region. The change in the chemical potential of the electrons is $-nF\Delta E$. (As discussed on p. 77, the charge carried by a mole of electrons is the Faraday, F, and its inclusion is necessary to obtain electrical energy per mole.) If the process is carried out slowly and close to equilibrium, then the electrical energy $(-nF\Delta E)$ can be converted to an equal amount of Gibbs free energy (ΔG):

$$\Delta G = -nF\Delta E \qquad (6\text{--}6)$$

By Equation 6–6, the amount of Gibbs free energy that can be stored or released is directly proportional to the difference in electrical potential across which the electrons move. Moreover, Equation 6–6 indicates that the flow of electrons toward more positive electrical potentials $(\Delta E > 0)$ corresponds to a decrease in free energy $(\Delta G < 0)$, and thus this movement would be expected to proceed spontaneously, as is indeed the case. We will apply these free energy considerations to the energetics of electrons moving from molecule to molecule in the electron transport chains of chloroplasts and mitochondria.

Redox Potentials.   As was indicated in Chapter 5, many organic compounds that are involved in photosynthesis can accept or donate electrons (cf. Table 5–1). These electrons spontaneously flow toward more positive electrical potentials, which are measured by so-called *redox potentials* in the case of the components involved with electron flow in chloroplast lamellae or mitochondrial membranes. Redox potentials are a measure of the relative electrical energy of electrons accepted or donated by a particular type of molecule. In fact, the oxidized and the reduced forms of each electron transport component can be viewed as an electrode or half-cell, which then interacts with the other electron accepting and donating molecules in the membrane, electrons spontaneously moving toward the components having the higher redox potentials.

Of great importance in biology is the relative tendency of various organic compounds to undergo reactions in which oxidations and reductions take place. A general reaction involving such acceptance or donation of electrons by some species can be represented as follows:

$$\text{Oxidized form} + ne^- \rightleftharpoons \text{reduced form} \qquad (6\text{--}7)$$

where n is the number of electrons transferred per molecule, and "oxidized" and "reduced" refer to different forms of the same species. Like any other chemical reaction, an oxidation-reduction reaction such as Equation 6–7 has associated with it a change in Gibbs free energy when the reactants are converted to products. Thus oxidation-reduction or "redox" reactions can be described by the relative tendency of the redox system or couple (the oxidized plus the reduced forms of the compound) to proceed in the forward direction, which means taking on electrons for Equation 6–7.

It is more useful to describe redox reactions in terms of relative electrical potentials instead of the equivalent changes in Gibbs free energy. More to the point, the electrons in Equation 6–7 come from some other redox couple, and whether or not the reaction in Equation 6–7 will proceed in the forward direction depends on the relative electrical potentials of both of these couples. Thus it is convenient to assign to a reaction which involves the acceptance or donation of electrons a particular value of an electrical potential, which is known as its redox potential. This oxidation-reduction potential can then be compared with that of another reaction in order to predict the direction for spontaneous electron flow. The redox potential of species j, E_j, is defined as follows:

$$E_j = E_j{}^* - \frac{RT}{nF} \ln \frac{(\text{reduced}_j)}{(\text{oxidized}_j)} \tag{6–8}$$

where $E_j{}^*$ is an additive constant (to be considered below), n is the number of electrons transferred (cf. n in Eq. 6–7), and (reduced_j) and (oxidized_j) refer to the activities of the two different redox states of species j. Equation 6–8 indicates that the oxidation-reduction potential of a particular redox couple is determined by the ratio of the reduced to the oxidized form plus an all-important additive constant, a quantity that we will consider next.

Equation 6–8 gives the electrical potential for a reaction going on at some electrode, whether this is a dissociation of solid silver or involves a redox couple of an organic molecule. Electrical potentials can be measured only when two electrodes or half-cells are connected and pathways for electron flow are provided. Since the sum of the electrical potentials or voltage changes going completely around such a circuit is zero, the half-cell potential for a particular electrode can be determined if that of some standard or reference electrode is known. By international agreement, the $E_j{}^*$ of a hydrogen half-cell ($\frac{1}{2}H_{2\text{gas}} \rightleftharpoons H^+ + e^-$) is arbitrarily set equal to zero for an activity of hydrogen ions of 1 N equilibrated with hydrogen gas at a pressure of 760 mm Hg. By thus fixing the zero level of the electrical potential, this definition removes the arbitrary nature of redox potentials. Consequently, $E_j{}^*$ in Equation 6–8 will henceforth be replaced by $E_j{}^{*,\text{H}}$ to emphasize the convention of referring electrode potentials to that of the standard hydrogen electrode.

When (reduced$_j$) equals (oxidized$_j$), E_j equals $E_j^{*,\mathrm{H}}$ by Equation 6–8. This $E_j^{*,\mathrm{H}}$ is commonly referred to as the midpoint redox potential (see Table 5–1) for some of the components involved with electron transport in chloroplasts. The larger is (reduced$_j$)/(oxidized$_j$), the more negative the redox potential becomes. Since electrons are negatively charged, algebraically lower E_j's correspond to higher energies for the electrons. Thus, more energy is required to increase (reduced$_j$)/(oxidized$_j$), the further Equation 6–7 is driven in the forward direction. Equivalently, the larger is (reduced$_j$)/(oxidized$_j$), the higher is the electrical energy of the electrons which the reduced form of that couple can donate. For many purposes, knowledge of $E_j^{*,\mathrm{H}}$ alone is extremely important, as we will illustrate in this chapter.

Biological Energy Currencies

In photosynthesis, light quanta are captured and an electron flow ensues leading to NADPH$_2$ production and a coupled process whereby ATP is formed. Light energy is thereby converted into chemical energy by forming an anhydride (ATP) in an aqueous environment and into electrical energy by providing a reduced compound (NADPH$_2$) under oxidizing conditions. ATP and NADPH$_2$ are the two energy storage compounds or "currencies" that will be considered in this section. Both are ions, both can readily diffuse around in the cell or subcellular organelle, and both can carry appreciable amounts of energy under biological conditions. The chemical energy stored in ATP can be used in many anabolic reactions involving the formation of anhydrous links or bonds in the aqueous milieu of the cell. Atmospheric oxygen insures that appreciable amounts of oxygen, which is a strong oxidizing agent, will be present in most biological systems, with the consequence that a reduced compound like NADPH$_2$ is also an important currency for energy storage. After briefly considering the difference between ATP and NADPH$_2$ as energy currencies, we will discuss these two compounds individually.

Redox couples or half-cells can be assigned a relative electrical energy while chemical reactions have an intrinsic chemical energy. In a chemical reaction, certain reactants are transformed into products, and the accompanying change in Gibbs free energy can be calculated. This change in chemical energy does not depend on any other system per se. In other words, if the concentrations (strictly speaking, the chemical activities) of ADP, phosphate, and ATP are the same in different parts of the plant, then the amount of chemical free energy released upon ATP hydrolysis is the same in each location. However, an oxidation-reduction couple must donate electrons to or accept electrons from another redox system, and so the change in electrical energy depends on the difference in the redox potential between the two couples. For instance, the amount of electrical energy which can be released when $NADPH_2$ is oxidized to NADP specifically depends on the redox potential of the particular couple with which it interacts.

ATP. For an understanding of chloroplast and mitochondrial bioenergetics, one needs to know how much energy is stored in ATP, which means the difference in its chemical potential compared with the chemical potentials of the reactants used in its formation, ADP plus phosphate. Armed with this information, the next step in the analysis is to look for reactions which have a large enough free energy decrease in order to drive the ATP production reaction in the energetically uphill direction. This leads to a consideration of the energetics of electron flow in the appropriate organelles, topics to be discussed in the following two sections. Of immediate concern here is: (1) the chemical reaction describing ATP formation, (2) the associated change in Gibbs free energy for that reaction, and (3) the implications of the substantial amount of energy storage in ATP.

ADP, ATP, and phosphate exist in various states of dissociation in aqueous solutions, and, moreover, all three compounds can interact with other species present, notably magnesium and calcium ions. Thus, many different chemical reactions can be used for describing ATP formation, a predominant one occurring near neutral pH in the absence of divalent cations being as follows:

$$
\begin{array}{c}
\text{Adenosine—O—P—O—P—O}^- + {}^-\text{O—P—O}^- + \text{H}^+ \\
\text{ADP} \qquad\qquad \text{phosphate}
\end{array}
$$

$$
\rightleftharpoons \text{Adenosine—O—P—O—P—O—P—O}^- + \text{H}_2\text{O} \qquad (6\text{-}9)
$$

$$\text{ATP}$$

Equation 6–9 indicates a number of features of ATP production in general. For instance, the formation of ATP from ADP plus phosphate is a dehydration while the reversal of Equation 6–9 in which the anhydride is split with the incorporation of water is known as ATP hydrolysis. Since Equation 6–9 contains H$^+$, the equilibrium constant depends on pH [$-\log (a_{H^+})$]. Furthermore, ADP, phosphate, and ATP will all exist in a number of different states of ionization, the fraction in the various forms depending on the pH. Near pH 7, about half of the ADP molecules are doubly charged and half are triply charged, the latter form being indicated in Equation 6–9. Likewise, ATP at pH 7 is about equally distributed between the forms having charges of -3 and -4. Due to their net negative charge in aqueous solutions, both ADP and ATP readily bind positive ions, in particular divalent cations like magnesium or calcium. A chelate is formed, Mg^{++} or Ca^{++} being electrostatically held between two negatively charged oxygen atoms on the same molecule (cf. the many —O$^-$'s occurring on the chemical structures indicated in Eq. 6–9). Also, inorganic phosphate can strongly interact with magnesium and other divalent cations, further increasing the number of complexed forms of ADP, ATP, and phosphate that are possible.

The activities or concentrations of a species in all its various ionization states and complexed forms are generally summed to obtain the total activity or concentration of that species. The number of relations and equilibrium constants needed to describe a reaction like ATP formation is then reduced to one, i.e., a separate equilibrium constant is not needed for every possible combination of ionization states and complexed forms of all the reactants and products. Using this convention, we can replace Equation 6–9 and many others like it that also describe ATP formation by the following general reaction for the phosphorylation of ADP:

$$\text{ADP} + \text{phosphate} \rightleftharpoons \text{ATP} + H_2O \qquad (6\text{--}10)$$

ATP formation as given by Equation 6–10 will be returned to shortly, but first two important conventions used in biochemistry need to be commented upon briefly. First, most equilibrium constants for biochemical reactions are defined at a specific pH, usually pH 7 ($a_{H^+} = 10^{-7}$ M). When the pH is maintained constant, the activity of H$^+$ does not change, and so H$^+$ need not be included as a reactant or product in the free energy expression (Eq. 6–5). In other words, the effect of H$^+$ in equations like 6–9 is actually incorporated into the equilibrium constant, which itself can depend on pH. Second, biological reactions such as photophosphorylation usually take place in aqueous solutions where the concentration of water does not change appreciably. (The concentrations of the other possible reactants and products are generally much, much less than that of water.) Hence, the (a_{H_2O}) term coming from equations like 6–10 is also generally incorporated into the equilibrium constant.

Next, we will specifically consider the equilibrium constant for ATP formation under biological conditions. Using the above conventions for H^+ and H_2O, the observed equilibrium constant for Equation 6–10 at pH 7, $K_{pH\ 7}$, is given by

$$K_{pH\ 7} = \frac{[ATP]}{[ADP][phosphate]} \cong 4.2 \times 10^{-7}\ M^{-1}\ \text{at } 25° \qquad (6\text{--}11)$$

where the total concentration of each of the three species involved is indicated in brackets in Equation 6–11, i.e., it was experimentally more convenient to measure $K_{pH\ 7}$ using concentrations, indicated in this text by brackets, instead of activities, which are designated by parentheses. The magnitude of the equilibrium constant for ATP formation depends on the concentration of magnesium ions, the actual value of $K_{pH\ 7}$ indicated in Equation 6–11 being appropriate for 1 to 10 mM Mg^{++}, a concentration range that occurs in the aqueous phases of many plant cells.

To discuss the energetics of ATP formation, the associated change in Gibbs free energy, ΔG, is needed. For a general chemical reaction, Equation 6–5 indicates that ΔG equals $\Delta G^* + RT \ln [(a_C)^c\ (a_D)^d]/[(a_A)^a\ (a_B)^b]$, where ΔG^* was shown above to be simply $-RT \ln K$. For the present case, the reactant A is ADP, B is phosphate, the product C is ATP, and the equilibrium constant is given by Equation 6–11. Therefore, the sought-after free energy relationship describing ATP formation is as follows:

$$\Delta G = -RT \ln (K_{pH\ 7}) + RT \ln \frac{[ATP]}{[ADP][phosphate]} \qquad (6\text{--}12)$$

$$\cong 8.7 + 1.36 \log \frac{[ATP]}{[ADP][phosphate]}\ \text{kcal/mole at pH 7 and } 25°$$

where ln equals 2.303 log, 2.303 RT is 1.364 kcal/mole at 25° (Appendix III), and $-(1.364) \log (4.2 \times 10^{-7})$ is 8.7. It is apparent from Equation 6–12 that ATP usually does not tend to form spontaneously because the free energy change for such a process is generally quite positive. In fact, the actual amount of energy required for the phosphorylation of ADP is rather large compared with most biochemical reactions taking place in plants.

Stated another way, much energy can be stored by converting ADP plus phosphate to ATP.

It is instructive to estimate the free energy changes that might be expected for photophosphorylation under biological conditions. For purposes of calculation, we will assume that in chloroplasts in the dark, the concentrations of ADP and phosphate are initially 10 mM while ATP is 1 mM. Thus $[ATP]/\{[ADP][phosphate]\}$ is $(10^{-3})/[(10^{-2})(10^{-2})]$ or 10 M^{-1} before illumination begins. From Equation 6–12, the free energy change required to form ATP (Eq. 6–10) is then $8.7 + 1.36 \log (10)$ or 10.1 kcal/mole. The change in Gibbs free energy required is positive, indicating that energy must be supplied to power photophosphorylation. Moreover, the amount of energy that is necessary depends in a predictable way on the concentrations of the reactants and the product. After a while in the light, ATP may increase to 10 mM with a concomitant decrease in ADP and phosphate to 1 mM. The ratio $[ATP]/\{[ADP][phosphate]\}$ then becomes $(10^{-2})/[(10^{-3})(10^{-3})]$ or 10^4 M^{-1}. The free energy required for photophosphorylation in such a case is $8.7 + 1.36 \log (10^4)$ or 14.1 kcal/mole. Consequently, the further photophosphorylation goes to completion, the greater is the energy required to form more ATP.

The high energy of ATP is not the property of a single bond but rather of the local atomic configuration in the molecule, a point that can best be appreciated by considering the phosphorus atoms in ADP, ATP, and phosphate. Phosphorus is in group V of the third period of the periodic table and has 5 electrons in its outermost shell. It can enter into a total of 5 bonds with 4 oxygen atoms, the bonding to one of the O's being a double bond (cf. structures in Eq. 6–9). In inorganic phosphate, all 4 bonds are equivalent, and so 4 different structures for phosphate exist in resonance with each other. The terminal P of ADP has but 3 resonating forms, as one of the oxygens is connected to a second phosphorus atom and does not assume a double bond configuration. (See Eq. 6–9.) When inorganic phosphate is attached to this terminal P of ADP to form ATP, a resonating form is lost both from the ADP and from the phosphate. Since configurations that have more resonating structures are in general more stable (lower in energy), energy must be supplied to form ATP from ADP plus phosphate with the consequent loss of 2 resonating forms.

NADPH$_2$. Another class of energy storage compounds consists of redox couples such as NADP-NADPH$_2$, the reduced form being produced by photosynthetic electron flow in chloroplasts. Photosynthesis in bacteria makes use of a different redox system, NAD-NADH$_2$. Moreover, the reduced member of this latter couple causes an electron flow in mitochondria and an associated formation of ATP (as will be discussed below under Mitochondrial Bioenergetics). NAD is nicotinamide adenine dinucleotide and differs from NADP by not having an extra phosphate esterified to the ribose in the adenosine part of the molecule. The present discussion will focus on the NADP-NADPH$_2$ couple, but the same arguments and also the same midpoint redox potential (to within 0.004 v) apply to the NAD-NADH$_2$ system.

As mentioned in the previous chapter, the reduction of a molecule of NADP involves the acceptance of two electrons. The actual half-cell reaction describing this reduction is as follows:

$$+ 2e^- + 2H^+ \rightleftharpoons \qquad\qquad + H^+$$

NADP   NADPH$_2$

$$(6-13)$$

where R in Equation 6–13 represents a phosphorylated ribose attached by a pyrophosphate bridge to adenosine. The reduction of NADP involves the transfer of two electrons to the nicotinamide ring, plus the attachment of one H$^+$ to the *para* position (top of the ring for the NADPH$_2$ indicated in Eq. 6–13). The convention of designating the reduced form as NADPH$_2$ has been adopted in this book simply to emphasize that two electrons are accepted by the molecule during its reduction, although one of the accompanying hydrogen ions is not attached to the reduced form as Equation 6–13 indicates. (NADP$^+$ is often used for the oxidized form and NADPH for the reduced one; to indicate that two electrons are involved, one could use NADPH + H$^+$ for the reduced species in this representation.)

A particular half-cell reaction such as Equation 6–13 has associated with it a relative tendency to accept or donate electrons. This tendency is quantified by the oxidation-reduction or redox potential for that reaction, as expressed in Equation 6–8 $\{E_j = E_j^{*,H} - (RT/nF) \ln [(\text{reduced}_j)/(\text{oxidized}_j)]\}$. The oxidized species for the NADP-NADPH$_2$ couple represents all the various ionization states and complexed forms of the oxidized nicotinamide adenine dinucleotide phosphate, with an analogous meaning for the reduced species. For redox reactions of biological interest, the standard or midpoint redox potential is generally determined at pH 7. Thus, the oxidation-reduction reaction for the NADP-NADPH$_2$ couple (Eq. 6–13) can be expressed as follows by using Equation 6–8 in which the number (n) of electrons transferred per molecule reduced is 2:

$$E = E_{pH\ 7}^{*,H} - \frac{RT}{2F} \ln \frac{(NADPH_2)}{(NADP)} \tag{6–14}$$

$$= -320 - 29.6 \log \frac{(NADPH_2)}{(NADP)} \text{ mv at } 25° \text{ and pH } 7$$

where ln has been replaced by 2.303 log and the numerical value for 2.303 RT/F of 59.2 mv at 25° (Appendix III) has been used in Equation 6–14. The standard or midpoint redox potential, $E_{pH\ 7}^{*,H}$, for the NADP-NADPH$_2$ couple is -320 mv (Table 5–1), a value achieved when (NADPH$_2$) equals (NADP).

To determine whether electrons flow toward or away from it, the redox potential of the NADP-NADPH$_2$ couple must be compared with that of some other redox system capable of accepting and donating electrons. As indicated above, electrons spontaneously flow toward more positive redox potentials while energy must be supplied to move electrons in the energetically uphill direction of algebraically decreasing redox potential. We will next consider the redox potentials of the various redox couples involved in electron flow in chloroplasts, followed by a similar section on mitochondria.

Chloroplast Bioenergetics

Various molecules involved with electron transport in chloroplasts were discussed in Chapter 5, together with a consideration of the sequence of electron flow from one component to the next. Such a discussion will be resumed now that the concept of redox potential has been introduced. Specifically, we will compare the midpoint redox potentials of the various redox systems, not only to help understand the direction for spontaneous electron flow but also to see whether enough electrical energy is available between certain pairs of redox couples to drive the ATP formation reaction in the forward direction.

Redox Couples.   Although the ratio of the reduced to the oxidized forms of species j affects its redox potential $\{E_j = E_j^{*,\mathrm{H}} - (RT/nF)\ \ln\ [(\mathrm{reduced}_j)/(\mathrm{oxidized}_j)]$ (Eq. 6–8)$\}$, the activities of the two forms are usually not known for biological studies *in vivo*. Moreover, the value of the local pH, which can affect $E_j^{*,\mathrm{H}}$, is also generally unknown. Consequently, standard or mid-point redox potentials determined at pH 7 are usually compared in order to predict the direction for electron flow in lamellar membranes of chloroplasts, and this approach will be followed here. In general, energy is necessary to transfer electrons to a compound with a more negative standard redox potential while the reverse process can go on spontaneously.

Another aspect that is particularly relevant to photosynthesis concerns the effect that absorbing a light quantum has on the redox properties of the pigment molecule. An excited molecule has an electron in an antibonding orbital, as has been discussed in Chapter 4. The removal of such an electron from the molecule takes less energy than when the electron is in the ground state, and thus the electronically excited molecule is a better reducing agent in the sense of having a considerably more negative redox potential. Once the electron is removed, the oxidized molecule (e.g., trap chl$^+$) is a very good electron acceptor, which means that it has a rather positive redox potential. First, we will estimate the redox potential spans at each of the two photosystems in chloroplasts and then diagram the overall pattern of photosynthetic electron flow.

Following light absorption by Chl *a* or an accessory pigment in Photosystem II, the excitation migrates to the trap chl, where an electron transfer reaction takes place, as discussed in Chapter 5. The electron that is removed from trap chl* of Photosystem II is replaced by one coming from water in the oxygen evolution step, which was described by Equation 5–9. (For energetic considerations, Eq. 5–9 becomes $H_2O \rightleftharpoons \frac{1}{2}O_2 + 2H$.) The water-oxygen system is a half-cell reaction and has a standard or midpoint redox potential of 0.82 v at 25°, pH 7, and an oxygen pressure of 760 mm Hg. It has been found that the water oxidation and accompanying oxygen evolution (Eq. 5–9) follow spontaneously from the photochemistry at the reaction center of Photosystem II. Thus the required oxidant for water (e.g., trap chl$^+$) must have a redox potential more positive than 0.82 v.

The electron removed from trap chl* of Photosystem II goes to plastoquinone A, presumably by one or more intermediates. The electron transfer step to plastoquinone A from the proposed intermediate is spontaneous; thus the redox potential of this precursor must be more negative than the midpoint redox potential of plastoquinone A, 0.11 v (Table 5–1). The electrical potential span in Photosystem II is thus from greater than 0.82 v for the removal of electrons from water to less than 0.11 v for the precursor which reduces plastoquinone A, or more than 0.71 v overall. Thus an energy input of more than 0.71 ev is necessary to move an electron in this energetically uphill direction, such energy being supplied by light. Photosystem II can be excited by light of wavelength 670 nm (as well as by other wavelengths, this value being near the λ_{max} for the red band of its Chl a_{670}). From Equation 4–2 ($E = hc/\lambda_{vacuum}$) and the numerical value of hc [1240 ev-nm (Appendix III)], the energy of 670 nm light is $(1240)/(670)$ or 1.85 ev/quantum. This appears to be more than sufficient energy to move the electron across the redox potential span that occurs in Photosystem II.

A similar analysis of the energetics can be made for Photosystem I, where the trap chl is P_{700}. The known redox potential span across which electrons are moved is from the midpoint redox potential of 0.43 v for P_{700} to the -0.43 v of ferredoxin, the latter being a quite negative standard redox potential. Since an intermediate with a midpoint redox potential even more negative than -0.43 v may intervene before ferredoxin and spontaneously reduce it, 0.86 v is an estimate of the minimum redox potential span for Photosystem I. Red quanta at the Chl a_{680} λ_{max}, 680 nm, which can lead to such electron transfer in Photosystem I, have an energy of 1.82 ev (Table 4–1). This is ample energy to move the electron from P_{700} to ferredoxin and also to allow extra energy for a possible intermediate with a redox potential more negative than that of ferredoxin. From ferredoxin to the next component in the noncyclic electron flow sequence, NADP, electrons go from -0.43 v to -0.32 v (midpoint redox potentials) or a ΔE of $+0.11$ v. Moving toward higher redox potentials is energetically downhill for electrons, and so this step leading to the reduction of the pyridine nucleotide follows spontaneously from the reduced ferredoxin.

In noncyclic electron flow, a pair of electrons that come originally from the water-oxygen couple with a midpoint redox potential of 0.82 v is moved to the redox level of -0.32 v for the NADP-NADPH$_2$ couple. Since a midpoint redox potential of -0.32 v is more negative than most encountered in biology, NADPH$_2$ can spontaneously reduce most other redox systems; therefore, reduced pyridine nucleotides are an important energy currency, as mentioned above. Moving electrons from 0.82 v to -0.32 v requires a considerable expenditure of free energy, which helps explain why light with its relatively large amount of energy (cf. Table 4–1) is needed. The actual free energy change for the overall process can be calculated from Equation 6–6 ($\Delta G = -nF\Delta E$), where ΔE is $-0.32 - 0.82$ or -1.14 v, n is 2, and F is 23.06 kcal/mole-v (Appendix II). Hence, ΔG equals $-(2)(23.06)(-1.14)$ or 52.6 kcal/mole for the overall movement of a pair of electrons along the pathway for noncyclic electron flow.

The energetics of the electron transfer reactions of photosynthesis can be conveniently diagrammed in terms of their midpoint redox potentials. Figure 6–1 incorporates the standard redox potentials of the various components involved with electron transport that are included in Table 5–1 and discussed in Chapter 5 as well as in this one. The direction for spontaneous electron flow to higher midpoint redox potentials is downward toward the bottom of Figure 6–1 while the absorption of light quanta with their relatively large energies corresponds to moving electrons vertically upward to higher energy. The key role played by ferredoxin as the crossroads for cyclic, noncyclic, or pseudocyclic electron flow is also illustrated in Figure 6–1.

Coupling of ATP Formation to Electron Flow. It was argued above that electrical and chemical energies are interconvertible. With this in mind, what difference in electrical potential would be sufficient to supply the energy to cause ADP plus phosphate to react to form ATP? The minimum change in redox potential necessary to power such formation of ATP can be calculated from Equation 6–6 [$\Delta G = -nF\Delta E$, F being 23.06 kcal/mole-v (Appendix II)]. The amount of Gibbs free energy, ΔG, required to phosphorylate ADP (Eq. 6–10) is generally from 10 to 14 kcal/mole. If one electron is transferred ($n = 1$ in Eq. 6–6), this would correspond to an electrical potential change of (10 to 14)/(23.06) or 0.43 to 0.61 v. If two electrons are transported per ATP that is formed, then an electrical potential span of half this amount, namely 0.22 to 0.30 v, would be necessary.

We will next focus attention on the site for coupling photosynthetic electron flow to ATP formation, using the midpoint redox potentials in Figure 6–1 to indicate the electrical energy available. Consider the difference in standard redox potentials between plastoquinone A (0.11 v) and cytochrome f (0.36 v). The redox potential drop of 0.25 v does not represent enough energy to cause ATP formation, if the free energy change of a single electron is used, since the above calculation indicates that 0.43 to 0.61 v would be necessary in such a case. However, the 10 to 14 kcal/mole needed for the phosphorylation of ADP can be supplied by two electrons moving across a span of 0.22 to 0.30 v. Thus the span of 0.25 v between the midpoint redox

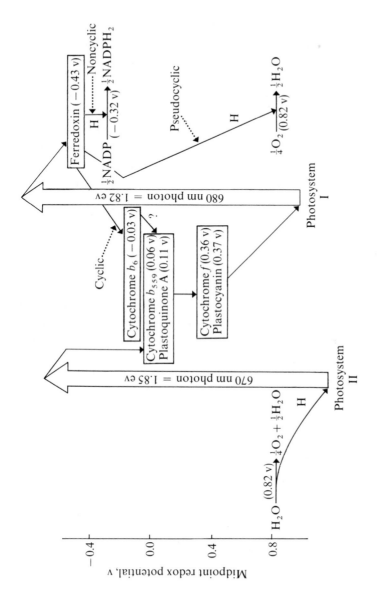

Figure 6–1. Photosynthetic electron flow showing the various midpoint redox potentials of the couples involved, the relative energy of red light at the λ_{max} of the main Chl a's in the two photosystems, and the three types of electron flow that are mediated by ferredoxin.

potentials of plastoquinone A and cytochrome f is apparently sufficient for ATP formation, if a pair of electrons traversing the electron transport pathway between Photosystems II and I is used. Such a site for photophosphorylation is thermodynamically possible, but the actual coupling site or sites for ATP formation in chloroplasts remain uncertain.

A matter related to coupling sites is the relative amounts of ATP produced and NADP reduced in chloroplasts. Three ATP molecules and 2 of $NADPH_2$ are needed per CO_2 molecule that is photosynthetically fixed, as was indicated by Equation 5–1. (Four ATP's are required per CO_2 fixed in chloroplasts from some types of plants, an added complication that we will not consider here.) If but one coupling site for ATP formation exists between Photosystems II and I, then 8 light quanta, 4 absorbed by each system, will give 2 $NADPH_2$'s and 2 ATP's (cf. Fig. 5–9). How is the third ATP produced? There may actually be two coupling sites for electrons moving in the noncyclic pathway from water to NADP although a possible location in terms of differences in midpoint redox potentials of the components is apparent for only one such coupling site. Another hypothesis is that cyclic or perhaps pseudocyclic electron flow leads to the other ATP. (As indicated in Chapter 5, no reduction of NADP accompanies either one of these types of electron flow.) This second possibility actually requires more than 8 light quanta to produce the 3 ATP's plus 2 $NADPH_2$'s which are used per CO_2 molecule fixed, a point that remains experimentally unclarified.

Another unresolved question in chloroplast bioenergetics is the mechanism for coupling electron flow to ATP formation, two hypotheses for which are currently being considered. In one, a so-called chemical hypothesis, the intermediates intervening between electron flow in the chloroplast lamellae and the joining of ADP and phosphate which is coupled to this are believed to be specific components, presumably proteins, whose actual chemical nature and properties are under investigation. The high energy electrons could conceivably cause changes or strains in the electronic configuration of the coupling molecules that are involved, a condition ultimately leading to the formation of the high energy bonding in ATP. In the other hypothesis, a so-called chemi-osmotic one proposed by P. Mitchell, the photosynthetic electron flow is envisioned as actively transporting protons across the lamellar membranes. This creates a difference in chemical potential of the hydrogen ions across the membranes, the magnitude of which can be estimated from Equation 3–23 $[\mu_{H^+}{}^i - \mu_{H^+}{}^o = F(E_M - E_{N_H^+})]$. This difference in free energy is then proposed to spontaneously drive the ATP formation reaction in the forward direction although the molecular details of the coupling of the energetically downhill H^+ flow to the formation of ATP are not known. As

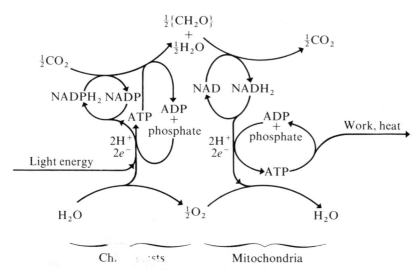

Figure 6–2. Schematic indication of the interrelationship between components involved in chloroplast and mitochondrial bioenergetics.

yet, a decision on the actual mechanism of coupling between electron flow and ATP production has not been reached, nor is it understood in molecular terms how two electrons moving in the electron transport pathway can lead to the formation of but one ATP molecule.

Mitochondrial Bioenergetics

The activities of chloroplasts and mitochondria are related in a number of ways, as is indicated in diagrammatic form in Figure 6–2. For instance, the O_2 evolved by photosynthesis is consumed during respiration while the fate of CO_2 is just the opposite for the two processes. Moreover, ATP formation is coupled to electron flow in both organelles although in mitochondria the electron flow is from a reduced pyridine nucleotide to oxygen while in chloroplasts it is in the opposite direction, as is summarized in Figure 6–2. From a few to many thousands of mitochondria occur in a given plant cell, their frequency tending to be somewhat less in cells where chloroplasts are abundant. In photosynthetic tissue at night and at all times in the nongreen parts of the plant, oxidative phosphorylation taking place in the mitochondria is the predominant supplier of ATP for the cells.

Electron Flow Components—Redox Potentials.   As is the case with chloroplasts, many compounds in mitochondria can accept or donate electrons, the direction for spontaneous electron flow being toward higher redox potentials. The reduced compounds which introduce electrons into the mitochondrial electron transport chain are $NADH_2$ and $FADH_2$. FAD is flavin adenine dinucleotide, which upon accepting two electrons becomes $FADH_2$. FAD is usually bound to a protein, the combination being referred to as a flavoprotein. Electrons from $NADH_2$ or $FADH_2$ move by an electron transport chain to O_2, which is thus reduced to H_2O. Important members of the mitochondrial electron transport chain, in order of increasing midpoint redox potential indicated in parentheses, are: $NAD-NADH_2$ (-0.32 v); $FAD-FADH_2$ (-0.22 to -0.03 v); cytochrome b (-0.04 v); cytochrome c (0.26 v); cytochrome a (0.29 v); cytochrome a_3, which is in the cytochrome oxidase complex ($\sim$0.5 v); and O_2-H_2O (0.82 v).

A given class of electron transport components in mitochondria may contain different molecular types. For instance, the various mitochondrial flavoproteins have different midpoint redox potentials in the range from -0.22 to -0.03 v, presumably reflecting different proteins binding FAD. One of the flavoproteins accepts electrons from the $NAD-NADH_2$ couple and passes them on to cytochrome b while another type apparently does not interact with $NADH_2$ at all. A number of b-type cytochromes occur in plant mitochondria, one of them being involved in an electron transport pathway that bypasses cytochrome oxidase on the way to oxygen. Mitochondria contain ubiquinone, which may also be involved with electron transport. Cytochromes a, b, and c are in roughly equal amounts in mitochondria (the ratios vary somewhat with plant species) while flavoproteins are about four times and pyridine nucleotides twenty to twenty-five times as abundant as the individual cytochromes. Likewise in chloroplasts, the pyridine nucleotides are much more abundant than are the cytochromes (see Table 5–1).

Oxidative Phosphorylation.   ATP formation coupled to electron flow in mitochondria is termed oxidative phosphorylation. Similar to the case with photophosphorylation, the mechanism is not yet understood in molecular terms. Processes like phosphorylation accompanying electron flow appear to be intimately connected with membrane integrity, and thus they are much more difficult to study than the biochemical reactions taking place in solutions. However, certain proteinaceous "coupling factors" which appear to be involved with the terminal steps of the coupling process for oxidative phosphorylation have been isolated from animal mitochondria. Due to lack of information on the local pH and the activities of the species involved, the existing redox potentials of the various mitochondrial oxidation-reduction systems are not known under physiological conditions. Nevertheless, the electrical energy available between the various redox couples can be estimated from the midpoint redox potentials in order to indicate which electron transitions might be associated with ATP formation, a topic we will turn to next.

Experiments with isolated mitochondria have shown that the number of ATP's produced per pair of electrons that are used to reduce oxygen depends on the particular compound which introduces the electrons into the electron transport pathway. For instance, when a pair of electrons moves from $NADH_2$ to oxygen, 3 ATP molecules can be produced. Certain substrates like succinate lead directly to a reduction of FAD without first reducing NAD. The oxidation of such $FADH_2$ leads to the phosphorylation of but 2 ADP's per pair of electrons moving in the mitochondrial electron transport chain. This suggests that a coupling site for ATP formation may exist between $NADH_2$ and $FADH_2$. (The flavoproteins involved with $NADH_2$ oxidation and with succinate oxidation appear to be different, and so alternative explanations are possible.) From the $NAD-NADH_2$ couple to the $FAD-FADH_2$ one, the difference in midpoint redox potentials is 0.10 to 0.29 v, depending on the particular flavoprotein being considered. Assuming a free energy requirement of 10 to 14 kcal/mole to form ATP as was done previously, an 0.22 to 0.30 v change in electrical potential would be necessary to produce ATP by a pair of electrons moving toward higher redox potentials. Thus enough energy for such oxidative phosphorylation may be available for electrons moving from $NADH_2$ to FAD, but the matter remains uncertain since the existing redox potentials are not precisely known nor is the actual ΔG for ATP formation known in mitochondria. Electrons from $FADH_2$ go to cytochrome b and then to the subsequent members of the electron transport chain. Energetically speaking, another coupling site for ATP formation may be between cytochrome b (midpoint redox potential of -0.04 v) and cytochrome c (0.26 v), where about 0.30 v is available. The third site for oxidative phosphorylation is associated with cytochrome oxidase (cytochromes a and a_3 apparently occur together in this complex), about which relatively little is presently certain.

Energy Flow

One of the characteristics of life is the formation of rather complex molecules which possess a considerably greater amount of Gibbs free energy than the constituent molecules and atoms into which they can be degraded. This extra free energy was originally obtained as radiant energy from the sun, which was trapped in the form of chemical (ATP) and electrical (NADPH$_2$) energy by photosynthesis, as indicated schematically in both Figures 5–9 and 6–1. Energy in currencies such as ATP or NADPH$_2$ can be used by cells to actively transport ions, to synthesize proteins, and to provide for growth and development. Such energy must constantly be supplied, or otherwise plants and animals would drift toward equilibrium and consequently die. In this brief section, we will consider the amount of radiant energy annually reaching the earth from the sun, estimate the relative fraction of this used in photosynthesis, and finally mention the consequent enrichment in chemical energy per atom for the nonaqueous components of cells.

The amount of energy radiated by any object depends markedly on its temperature. For instance, the maximum rate of energy radiation per unit area is given by the Stefan-Boltzmann law:

$$\text{Energy radiated} = \sigma T^4 \qquad (6\text{–}15)$$

where σ is the Stefan-Boltzmann constant and equals 8.130×10^{-11} cal cm^{-2} min^{-1} °K^{-4}. For the sun's surface (T about 5800°K), the energy radiated is $(8.130 \times 10^{-11})(5800)^4$ or 0.92×10^5 cal/cm^2-min calculated by using Equation 6–15. This extremely large amount of solar radiation leads to about 2.00 cal/cm^2-min incident on the earth's atmosphere, as was mentioned in Chapter 4. A year contains 525,600 min, and the projected area of the earth is 1.276×10^{18} cm^2. Hence, the energy input into the earth from the sun is $(2.00)(1.276 \times 10^{18})(5.256 \times 10^5)$ or 1.34×10^{24} cal/year. This energy input must be balanced by an equal energy output, or the earth would tend to heat up and life would eventually disappear. The maximum amount of energy reradiated from the earth can also be calculated from Equation 6–15. The average temperature of the earth's surface is about 287°K, and so the upper limit on the amount of heat energy reradiated into outer space is $(8.130 \times 10^{-11})(287)^4$ or 0.552 cal/cm^2-min. This thermal radiation goes out from the earth's total surface area ($4\pi r^2$) in distinction to the solar input which comes in for the projected area of the earth (πr^2). Using the figure of 0.552 cal/cm^2-min, the amount of energy lost from the earth by radiation would be $(0.552)(4)(1.276 \times 10^{18})(5.256 \times 10^5)$ or 1.48×10^{24} cal/year. Somewhat less is lost since the earth's surface does not radiate at the maximum rate. In fact, the amount of energy reradiated must be rather close to the solar input, 1.34×10^{24} cal/year.

Only a rather small fraction of the energy from the sun incident on the earth each year is actually stored as chemical energy by photosynthesis. As indicated in Chapter 5, approximately 5.0×10^{16} grams of carbon are annually fixed by photosynthesis. For each mole of CO_2 (12 g carbon) incorporated into carbohydrate, approximately 114 kcal of energy are stored. The total amount of energy stored by photosynthesis is thus $[(5.0 \times 10^{16})/(12)]$ (114,000) or 0.48×10^{21} cal/year. But 1.34×10^{24} cal/year are available as solar radiation, about half of it corresponding to light in the visible region. Thus the average annual photosynthetic efficiency for all radiation that is received over the entire surface of the earth is $[(0.48 \times 10^{21})/(1.34 \times 10^{24})](100)$ or only 0.036% (cf. the calculation in Chapter 5, where a maximum possible efficiency for photosynthesis of 34% was indicated). Nevertheless, even with this apparently very low energy conversion fraction under natural conditions, the trapping of solar energy by photosynthesis is essentially the only source of free energy that is used to sustain life.

As suggested in the beginning of this section, solar radiation incident on the earth can greatly increase the energy possessed by molecules. This can be appreciated by considering the energy enrichment in the molecules of living organisms compared with the free energy of an equilibrium system containing the same relative amounts of the various atoms. For instance, the nonaqueous components of cells have 0.27 ev per atom more Gibbs free energy than the same mixture of atoms would have at equilibrium. (As mentioned previously, equilibrium corresponds to a minimum in free energy.) The Boltzmann energy distribution used in Chapters 3 and 4 predicts that at equilibrium, the number of molecules with energy in excess of ΔE is proportional to $e^{-\Delta E/kT}$ [k is 8.617×10^{-5} ev/°K (Appendix II)]. For 25° and ΔE of 0.27 ev, $e^{-\Delta E/kT}$ is $e^{-(0.27)/[(8.617 \times 10^{-5})(298)]}$ or $e^{-10.5}$, which equals 0.000027. Thus at equilibrium only 0.000027 of the atoms would have an extra energy of 0.27 ev or more at 25°, although this is the average enrichment in Gibbs free energy per atom of the nonaqueous components in cells. It is the flux of energy from the sun through plants and animals (cf. Fig. 6–2) which leads to such an energy enrichment in the molecules and furthermore ensures that biological systems will be maintained in a state far from equilibrium, an essential feature of life.

Problems

6–1. Let us consider the reaction $A + B \rightleftharpoons C$, which has a ΔG^* of -4.09 kcal/mole at 25°. Assume that activity coefficients are unity. In which direction will the reaction proceed under the following conditions? (a) The concentrations of A, B, and C are all 1 molal. (b) The concentrations of A, B, and C are all 1 millimolal. (c) The concentrations of A, B, and C are all 1 micromolal. (d) What is the equilibrium constant for the reaction?

6–2. Consider the following two half-cell reactions at 25°:

$$A \rightleftharpoons A^+ + e^- \qquad \Delta G^* = 2.00 \text{ kcal/mole}$$

$$B \rightleftharpoons B^+ + e^- \qquad \Delta G^* = 0.70 \text{ kcal/mole}$$

Assume that the midpoint redox potential of the second reaction is $+0.118$ v and that all activity coefficients are unity. (a) If the redox potential of the B-B^+ couple is 0.000 v, what is the ratio of B^+ to B? (b) Suppose that all reactants and products are initially 1 molal but that the couples are in separate solutions of equal volume. If the half-cells are electrically connected with a metal wire, what is the initial electrical potential difference between them, and in which direction do electrons flow? (c) If all reactants and products are initially 1 molal, what is the concentration of each at equilibrium in a single solution (1.30 kcal/mole $= 2.303 \ RT \log 9$ at 25°)? (d) Qualitatively, how would the answer to (c) change if the initial conditions are as in (b), but as the electrons flow through the wire, they do electrical work?

6–3. Suppose that in the dark 2 mM ADP and 5 mM phosphate occur inside chloroplasts, which are initially devoid of ATP. Assume that the temperature is 25° and that the pH is 7. (a) What is the ATP concentration at equilibrium? (b) When the chloroplasts are illuminated, the ADP concentration decreases to 1 mM. What is the new concentration of ATP, and what is the change in Gibbs free energy for continued photophosphorylation? (c) If ferredoxin has a redox potential of -0.580 v and the activity of $NADPH_2$ is 3% of that of NADP, what is the difference in redox potential between the two couples? (d) How much Gibbs free energy is available between the two couples mentioned in (c)? Is this enough for the continued formation of ATP under the conditions of (b)?

References

Alberty, R. A. 1968. Effect of pH and metal ion concentration on the equilibrium hydrolysis of adenosine triphosphate to adenosine diphosphate. *Journal of Biological Chemistry* **243**, 1337–43.

Morowitz, H. J. 1968. *Energy Flow in Biology*, Academic Press, New York.

Spanner, D. C. 1964. *Introduction to Thermodynamics*, Academic Press, New York.

Weyer, E. M., ed. 1968. Bioelectrodes. *Annals of the New York Academy of Sciences* **148**, Art. 1, 1–287.

White, A., P. Handler, and E. L. Smith. 1968. *Principles of Biochemistry*, 4th ed., McGraw-Hill, New York.

Appendices

Frequently Used Variables and Their Units

Symbol	Description	Typical units
a	activity	same as concentration[a]
b	nonosmotic volume	μm^3
b	optical path length	cm
c	concentration	moles/liter
$\bar{c}_s$	a mean concentration of solute s	moles/cm^3
h	height	cm
k	first-order rate constant	sec^{-1}
n	amount of a substance	moles
r	radius	cm
s	amount of a substance	moles
t	time	sec
u	mobility	velocity/force
v	velocity	m/sec
x	distance	cm
z	charge of ion	dimensionless
A	area	cm^2
A	absorbance (also called "optical density")	dimensionless
C	capacitance	farads

Symbol	Description	Typical units
C'	capacitance/unit area	$\mu f/cm^2$
D	diffusion coefficient	cm^2/sec
D	dielectric constant	dimensionless
E	light energy	ev
E	electrical potential	mv
E_j	redox potential of species j	mv
$E_j^{*,H}$	midpoint redox potential of species j referred to standard hydrogen electrode	mv
E_M	electrical potential difference across a membrane	mv
E_{N_j}	Nernst potential of species j	mv
G	Gibbs free energy	kcal/mole
I	intensity of electromagnetic radiation	quanta/cm^2-sec
J	flux of moles	moles/cm^2-sec
J	flux of volume	cm/sec (i.e., cm^3/cm^2-sec)
J_j^{in}	influx of species j	moles/cm^2-sec
J_j^{out}	efflux of species j	moles/cm^2-sec
J_v	total volume flux	cm/sec
K	partition coefficient	dimensionless
K	equilibrium constant	molarity raised to some power
$K_{pH\,7}$	equilibrium constant at pH 7	molarity raised to some power
L	length	cm
L_{jk}	Onsager or phenomenological coefficient	flux/force
L_P	hydraulic conductivity coefficient (in irreversible thermodynamics)	cm/sec-bar
L_w	water conductivity coefficient	cm/sec-bar
N	mole fraction	dimensionless
P	permeability coefficient	cm/sec
P	hydrostatic pressure	bars
Q	charge	coulombs
Q_{10}	temperature coefficient	dimensionless
S	magnitude of net spin	dimensionless
T	temperature	°Kelvin
U	kinetic energy	ev
U_B	minimum kinetic energy to cross barrier	ev
V	volume	cm^3
$\bar{V}_j$	partial molal volume of species j	$cm^3/mole$

Symbol	Description	Typical units
α	contact angle	°
γ	activity coefficient	dimensionless[a]
ϵ	absorption coefficient	liters/mole-cm
η	viscosity	poise (dyne-sec/cm^2)
λ	wavelength	nm
μ_j	chemical potential of species j	cal/mole
ν	frequency of electromagnetic radiation	cycles/sec (Hertz)
π	osmotic pressure	bars
π_s	osmotic pressure due to solutes	bars
ρ	density	g/cm^3
σ	surface tension	dynes/cm
σ	reflection coefficient	dimensionless
σ_L	longitudinal stress	bars
σ_T	tangential stress	bars
τ	matric pressure or potential	bars
τ	lifetime	sec
φ_j	osmotic coefficient of species j	dimensionless
Φ	quantum yield or efficiency	dimensionless
Ψ	water potential	bars

[a]The activity, a, is often considered to be dimensionless, in which case the activity coefficient, γ, has the units of reciprocal concentration ($a = \gamma c$).

Frequently Used Constants
and Their Numerical Values

Symbol	Description	Magnitude
c	speed of light in vacuum	2.998×10^8 m/sec
e	base for natural logarithm	2.71828 $(1/e = 0.368)$
g	gravitational acceleration	980.6 cm/sec^2 (sea level[a], $45°$ latitude)
		978.0 cm/sec^2 (sea level[a], $0°$ latitude)
		983.2 cm/sec^2 (sea level[a], $90°$ latitude)
h	Planck's constant	6.6256×10^{-27} erg-sec
		0.4136×10^{-14} ev-sec
		1.584×10^{-37} kcal-sec
k	Boltzmann's constant	1.381×10^{-16} erg/$°$K
		8.617×10^{-5} ev/$°$K
F	Faraday	$96,487$ coulombs/mole
		$96,487$ joules/mole-v
		$23,060$ cal/mole-v
		23.06 kcal/mole-v
		0.02306 kcal/mole-mv
N	Avogadro's number	6.02252×10^{23}
R	gas constant	8.3143 joules/mole-$°$K
		1.987 cal/mole-$°$K
		0.082054 liter-atmosphere/mole-$°$K
		0.083141 liter-bar/mole-$°$K
ϵ_o	permittivity of a vacuum[b]	8.85415×10^{-12} coulomb^2/newton-m^2
		8.85415×10^{-12} coulomb/v-m

Symbol	Description	Magnitude
σ	Stefan-Boltzmann constant	8.130×10^{-11} cal cm^{-2} min^{-1} °K^{-4}
$\bar{V}_w$	partial molal volume of water	17.984 cm^3/mole at 20°
ρ_w	density of water	0.9982 g/cm^3 at 20°
σ_w	surface tension of water	72.8 dynes/cm at 20°
		7.18×10^{-5} atmosphere-cm at 20°
		7.28×10^{-5} bar-cm at 20°
η_w	viscosity of water	0.01002 poise (dyne-sec/cm^2) at 20°

[a]The correction for height above sea level is -0.000309 cm/sec^2 per meter of altitude.

[b]The so-called rationalized meter-kilogram-second (mks) system has been adopted for expressing electrical phenomena in this text (cf. Eq. 2–3). "Rationalized" means that the factors 2π or 4π appear in equations where they might reasonably be expected based on the geometry, e.g., in cases involving cylindrical or spherical symmetry, respectively. (In a nonrationalized system, π occurs in equations describing situations without cylindrical or spherical symmetry.) The numerical value of certain constants such as the permittivity ϵ_o depends on whether a rationalized or nonrationalized system of equations is used. In the mks system, charges are expressed in coulombs, which becomes a fundamental "dimension" like meter or kilogram. Since an ampere is a coulomb/sec, the mks system is often called an mksa system (a for ampere) to emphasize this convention of treating electrical units. In the frequently used nonrationalized centimeter-gram-second (cgs) system, no special unit is picked for charge, which must then be expressed in so-called electrostatic units, while cgs potentials are in units 299.80 times larger than ordinary volts. Amperes and ohms, which are electrical units commonly used in the laboratory, refer to the mks (mksa) system.

Conversion Factors

Quantity	Equals
Ångstrom	0.1 nm
	10^{-8} cm
	10^{-10} m
atmosphere	1.013×10^6 dynes/cm^2
	0.1013 joule/cm^3
	1.013 bars
	0.0242 cal/cm^3
	1.033 kg/cm^2 (at sea level)[a]
	76.0 cm or 760 mm Hg (at sea level)
bar	10^6 dynes/cm^2
	0.1 joule/cm^3
	0.987 atmosphere
	0.0239 cal/cm^3
	1.020 kg/cm^2 (at sea level)[a]
	75.0 cm or 750 mm Hg (at sea level)
calorie	4.184 joules
calorie/cm^3	41.84 bars
coulomb	1 joule/v
coulomb-volt	1 joule
dyne	1 erg/cm
	1 g-cm/sec^2

Quantity	Equals
dyne/cm²	10^{-6} bar
electron volt	1.602×10^{-12} erg
electron volt/molecule	23.06 kcal/mole
erg	1 dyne-cm
	6.242×10^{11} ev
	2.390×10^{-11} kcal
farad	1 coulomb/v
footcandle	10.76 lux
gram	1 dyne-sec²/cm
hc	1240 ev-nm
Hertz	1 cycle/sec
joule	1 newton-m
	1 coulomb-v
	10^7 ergs
	0.239 cal
kilocalorie/mole	0.0434 ev/molecule
kT	0.0257 ev at 25°
liter-atmosphere	24.2 cal
liter-bar	23.9 cal
ln	2.303 log
ln 2	0.693
lux	1 lumen/m²
newton	10^5 dynes
Nhc	28.60 kcal/mole-μm
	28,600 kcal/mole-nm
RT	583 cal/mole at 20°
	592 cal/mole at 25°
	22.41 liter-atmospheres/mole at 0°
	24.06 liter-atmospheres/mole at 20°
	24.47 liter-atmospheres/mole at 25°
	22.71 liter-bars/mole at 0°
	24.37 liter-bars/mole at 20°
	24.79 liter-bars/mole at 25°
2.303 RT	1.342 kcal/mole at 20°
	1.364 kcal/mole at 25°
RT/F	25.3 mv at 20°
2.303 RT/F	58.2 mv at 20°
	59.2 mv at 25°
	60.2 mv at 30°
$RT/\bar{V}_w$	32.4 cal/cm³ at 20°
	135.5 joules/cm³ at 20°
	1340 atmospheres at 20°
	1355 bars at 20°

Quantity	Equals
$\rho_w g$	0.0966 atmosphere/m (20° centigrade, sea level, 45° latitude)
	0.0979 bar/m (20° centigrade, sea level, 45° latitude)
	979 dynes/cm³ (20° centigrade, sea level, 45° latitude)
watt	1 joule/sec
	10^7 ergs/sec

[a]Often it proves convenient to express forces in units which really refer to mass. For instance, the "force"/unit area used with Young's modulus (Eq. 1–12) is often given in kg/cm². Moreover, a bar, which is 10^6 dynes of force per cm², is often referred to as 1.020 kg/cm² at sea level, where kilogram is obviously a mass unit. To see why this is possible, consider the force F exerted by gravity on a body of mass m. This force is equal to mg, g being the gravitational acceleration. (See Appendix II.) Thus F/g can be used to represent a force, but the units are those of mass. Referring to the above example, a bar is 10^6 dynes/cm², which is equivalent to $(10^6$ dynes/cm²$)/(980$ cm/sec²$)$ when a gravitational acceleration of 980 cm/sec² is used. Since (dynes)/(cm/sec²) are simply grams, a bar is equivalent at sea level to $(10^6)/(980)$ g/cm² which is $(10^3)/(980)$ kg/cm² or 1.020 kg/cm², as indicated in this appendix.

Abbreviations and Symbols

Abbreviation	Full word or expression
Å	Ångstrom (10^{-8} cm)
A	electron acceptor
ADP	adenosine diphosphate
ATP	adenosine triphosphate
cal	calorie
cm	centimeter (10^{-2} meter)
Chl	chlorophyll
D	electron donor
e	electron
ev	electron volt
f	farad
FAD	flavin adenine dinucleotide (oxidized form)
FADH$_2$	reduced form of flavin adenine dinucleotide
g	gram
$h\nu$	a light quantum or photon
i	superscript for inside
in	superscript for inward
IR	infrared
j	subscript for species j

Abbreviation	*Full word or expression*
k	kilo (as a prefix), 10^3
kcal	kilocalorie
km	kilometer
K	Kelvin
ln	natural or Napierian logarithm (to the base e where e is 2.71828 . . .)
log	common or Briggsian logarithm (to the base 10)
m	milli (as a prefix), 10^{-3}
m	meter
max	maximum
min	minute
mm	millimeter (10^{-3} meter)
mM	millimolar
mole	a mass equal to the molecular weight of the species in grams; contains Avogadro's number of molecules
M	molar (moles/liter)
n	nano (as a prefix), 10^{-9}
nm	nanometer (10^{-9} meter)
N	normal (gram equivalent weights/liter)
NAD	nicotinamide adenine dinucleotide (oxidized form)
$NADH_2$	reduced form of nicotinamide adenine dinucleotide
NADP	nicotinamide adenine dinucleotide phosphate (oxidized form)
$NADPH_2$	reduced form of nicotinamide adenine dinucleotide phosphate
o	superscript for outside
out	superscript for outward
p	pico (as a prefix), 10^{-12}
pH	$-\log(a_H+)$
P	pigment
s	subscript for solute
sec	second
S	singlet
$S_{(\pi,\pi)}$	singlet ground state
$S_{(\pi,\pi*)}$	singlet excited state where a π electron has been promoted to a π^* orbital
T	triplet
$T_{(\pi,\pi*)}$	excited triplet state
u_+	mobility of monovalent cation
u_-	mobility of monovalent anion
UV	ultraviolet
v	volt

Abbreviation	*Full word or expression*
v	subscript for volume
w	subscript for water
wv	subscript for water vapor
δ	delta, a small quantity of something, e.g., δ^- refers to a small fraction of an electronic charge
Δ	delta, a symbol which means the difference or change in the quantity which follows it
λ_{max}	wavelength position for the maximum absorption coefficient in an absorption band
μ	micro (as a prefix), 10^{-6}
μm	micron (10^{-6} meter)
μM	micromolar
π	Pi (ratio of circumference to diameter of a circle)
π	refers to an electron orbital in a molecule or an electron in such an orbital
π^*	refers to an excited or antibonding electron orbital in a molecule or an electron in such an orbital
°	degree Celsius or centigrade
°	angular degree
°K	degree Kelvin (absolute scale)
*	superscript referring to a standard or reference state
*	superscript indicating a molecule in an excited electronic state
∞	infinity
+	subscript for cation
—	subscript for anion

Natural and Common Logarithms

The following relations and tabulated numbers are presented to facilitate calculations that use both natural and common logarithms as well as their antilogarithms. For those readers who are completely unfamiliar with the properties of logarithms, a text or handbook should be consulted first.

Both the characteristics and the mantissas are given in order to speed up calculations. (Characteristics must be presented for natural logarithms.) Moreover, the minus signs in the table (for $x < 1$) refer to the entire logarithm, not just the characteristic, as they do in many common logarithm tables. Thus, log (0.20) is given as -0.699, not as $9.301 - 10$. With appropriate interpolations, three-place accuracy can be obtained for both logarithms and antilogarithms.

$$\ln (xy) = \ln x + \ln y \qquad\qquad \log (xy) = \log x + \log y$$
$$\ln (x/y) = \ln x - \ln y \qquad\qquad \log (x/y) = \log x - \log y$$
$$\ln (1/x) = -\ln x \qquad\qquad\quad \log (1/x) = -\log x$$
$$\ln x^a = a \ln x \qquad\qquad\qquad \log x^a = a \log x$$

$$\ln e = 1, \ln 10 = 2.303 \qquad\qquad \log 10 = 1, \log e = \frac{1}{2.303}$$

$$\ln x = 2.303 \log x$$

x	$\ln x$	$\log x$	x	$\ln x$	$\log x$	x	$\ln x$	$\log x$
0.00	$-\infty$	$-\infty$	0.40	-0.916	-0.398	0.80	-0.223	-0.097
0.01	-4.605	-2.000	0.41	-0.892	-0.387	0.81	-0.211	-0.092
0.02	-3.912	-1.699	0.42	-0.868	-0.377	0.82	-0.198	-0.086
0.03	-3.507	-1.523	0.43	-0.844	-0.367	0.83	-0.186	-0.081
0.04	-3.219	-1.398	0.44	-0.821	-0.357	0.84	-0.174	-0.076
0.05	-2.996	-1.301	0.45	-0.799	-0.347	0.85	-0.163	-0.071
0.06	-2.813	-1.222	0.46	-0.777	-0.337	0.86	-0.151	-0.066
0.07	-2.659	-1.155	0.47	-0.755	-0.328	0.87	-0.139	-0.060
0.08	-2.526	-1.097	0.48	-0.734	-0.319	0.88	-0.128	-0.056
0.09	-2.408	-1.046	0.49	-0.713	-0.310	0.89	-0.117	-0.051
0.10	-2.303	-1.000	0.50	-0.693	-0.301	0.90	-0.105	-0.046
0.11	-2.207	-0.959	0.51	-0.673	-0.292	0.91	-0.094	-0.041
0.12	-2.120	-0.921	0.52	-0.654	-0.284	0.92	-0.083	-0.036
0.13	-2.040	-0.886	0.53	-0.635	-0.276	0.93	-0.073	-0.032
0.14	-1.966	-0.854	0.54	-0.616	-0.268	0.94	-0.062	-0.027
0.15	-1.897	-0.824	0.55	-0.598	-0.260	0.95	-0.051	-0.022
0.16	-1.833	-0.796	0.56	-0.580	-0.252	0.96	-0.041	-0.018
0.17	-1.772	-0.770	0.57	-0.562	-0.244	0.97	-0.030	-0.013
0.18	-1.715	-0.745	0.58	-0.545	-0.237	0.98	-0.020	-0.009
0.19	-1.661	-0.721	0.59	-0.528	-0.231	0.99	-0.010	-0.004
0.20	-1.609	-0.699	0.60	-0.511	-0.222	1.00	0.000	0.000
0.21	-1.561	-0.678	0.61	-0.494	-0.215	1.1	0.095	0.041
0.22	-1.514	-0.658	0.62	-0.478	-0.208	1.2	0.182	0.079
0.23	-1.470	-0.638	0.63	-0.462	-0.201	1.3	0.262	0.114
0.24	-1.427	-0.620	0.64	-0.446	-0.194	1.4	0.337	0.146
0.25	-1.386	-0.602	0.65	-0.431	-0.187	1.5	0.405	0.176
0.26	-1.347	-0.585	0.66	-0.416	-0.180	1.6	0.470	0.204
0.27	-1.309	-0.569	0.67	-0.400	-0.174	1.7	0.531	0.230
0.28	-1.273	-0.553	0.68	-0.386	-0.167	1.8	0.588	0.255
0.29	-1.238	-0.538	0.69	-0.371	-0.161	1.9	0.642	0.279
0.30	-1.204	-0.523	0.70	-0.357	-0.155	2.0	0.693	0.301
0.31	-1.171	-0.509	0.71	-0.342	-0.149	2.1	0.742	0.322
0.32	-1.139	-0.495	0.72	-0.329	-0.143	2.2	0.788	0.342
0.33	-1.109	-0.481	0.73	-0.315	-0.137	2.3	0.833	0.362
0.34	-1.079	-0.469	0.74	-0.301	-0.131	2.4	0.875	0.380
0.35	-1.050	-0.456	0.75	-0.288	-0.125	2.5	0.916	0.398
0.36	-1.022	-0.444	0.76	-0.274	-0.119	2.6	0.956	0.415
0.37	-0.994	-0.432	0.77	-0.261	-0.114	2.7	0.993	0.431
0.38	-0.968	-0.420	0.78	-0.248	-0.108	2.8	1.030	0.447
0.39	-0.942	-0.409	0.79	-0.236	-0.102	2.9	1.065	0.462

x	$\ln x$	$\log x$	x	$\ln x$	$\log x$	x	$\ln x$	$\log x$
3.0	1.099	0.477	7.0	1.946	0.845	20	2.996	1.301
3.1	1.131	0.491	7.1	1.960	0.851	21	3.045	1.322
3.2	1.163	0.505	7.2	1.974	0.857	22	3.091	1.342
3.3	1.194	0.519	7.3	1.988	0.863	23	3.135	1.362
3.4	1.224	0.531	7.4	2.002	0.869	24	3.178	1.380
3.5	1.253	0.544	7.5	2.015	0.875	25	3.219	1.398
3.6	1.281	0.556	7.6	2.028	0.881	26	3.258	1.415
3.7	1.308	0.568	7.7	2.041	0.886	27	3.296	1.431
3.8	1.335	0.580	7.8	2.054	0.892	28	3.332	1.447
3.9	1.361	0.591	7.9	2.067	0.898	29	3.367	1.462
4.0	1.386	0.602	8.0	2.079	0.903	30	3.401	1.477
4.1	1.411	0.613	8.1	2.092	0.908	31	3.434	1.491
4.2	1.435	0.623	8.2	2.104	0.914	32	3.466	1.505
4.3	1.459	0.633	8.3	2.116	0.919	33	3.497	1.519
4.4	1.482	0.643	8.4	2.128	0.924	34	3.526	1.531
4.5	1.504	0.653	8.5	2.140	0.929	35	3.555	1.544
4.6	1.526	0.663	8.6	2.152	0.934	36	3.584	1.556
4.7	1.548	0.672	8.7	2.163	0.940	37	3.611	1.568
4.8	1.569	0.681	8.8	2.175	0.944	38	3.638	1.580
4.9	1.589	0.690	8.9	2.186	0.949	39	3.664	1.591
5.0	1.609	0.699	9.0	2.197	0.954	40	3.689	1.602
5.1	1.629	0.708	9.1	2.208	0.959	41	3.714	1.613
5.2	1.649	0.716	9.2	2.219	0.964	42	3.738	1.623
5.3	1.668	0.724	9.3	2.230	0.968	43	3.761	1.633
5.4	1.686	0.732	9.4	2.241	0.973	44	3.784	1.643
5.5	1.705	0.740	9.5	2.251	0.978	45	3.807	1.653
5.6	1.723	0.748	9.6	2.262	0.982	46	3.829	1.663
5.7	1.741	0.756	9.7	2.272	0.987	47	3.850	1.672
5.8	1.758	0.763	9.8	2.282	0.991	48	3.871	1.681
5.9	1.775	0.771	9.9	2.293	0.996	49	3.892	1.690
6.0	1.792	0.778	10	2.303	1.000	50	3.912	1.699
6.1	1.808	0.785	11	2.398	1.041	51	3.932	1.708
6.2	1.825	0.792	12	2.485	1.079	52	3.951	1.716
6.3	1.841	0.799	13	2.565	1.114	53	3.970	1.724
6.4	1.856	0.806	14	2.639	1.146	54	3.989	1.732
6.5	1.872	0.813	15	2.708	1.176	55	4.007	1.740
6.6	1.887	0.820	16	2.773	1.204	56	4.025	1.748
6.7	1.902	0.826	17	2.833	1.230	57	4.043	1.756
6.8	1.917	0.833	18	2.890	1.255	58	4.060	1.763
6.9	1.932	0.839	19	2.944	1.279	59	4.078	1.771

x	$\ln x$	$\log x$	x	$\ln x$	$\log x$
60	4.094	1.778	80	4.382	1.903
61	4.111	1.785	81	4.394	1.908
62	4.127	1.792	82	4.407	1.914
63	4.143	1.799	83	4.419	1.919
64	4.159	1.806	84	4.431	1.924
65	4.174	1.813	85	4.443	1.929
66	4.190	1.820	86	4.454	1.934
67	4.204	1.826	87	4.466	1.940
68	4.220	1.833	88	4.477	1.944
69	4.234	1.839	89	4.489	1.949
70	4.249	1.845	90	4.500	1.954
71	4.263	1.851	91	4.511	1.959
72	4.277	1.857	92	4.522	1.964
73	4.290	1.863	93	4.532	1.968
74	4.304	1.869	94	4.543	1.973
75	4.317	1.875	95	4.554	1.978
76	4.331	1.881	96	4.564	1.982
77	4.344	1.886	97	4.574	1.987
78	4.357	1.892	98	4.585	1.991
79	4.369	1.898	99	4.595	1.996
			100	4.605	2.000

Answers to Problems

1–1. (a) *Nitella,* 40.2 cm^{-1}; *Valonia,* 6 cm^{-1}; *Chlorella,* 1.5×10^4 cm^{-1}
  (b) *Chlorella*
  (c) *Valonia* (for a spherical cell, the cell wall stress is $rP/2\Delta r$)

1–2. (a) 0.625×10^{-5} cm^2/sec
  (b) 3.24×10^6 sec or 900 hours
  (c) 0.9 cm from plane of insertion

1–3. (a) $t^{\text{air}} = 0.25\ t^{\text{cell wall}}$
  (b) $D^{\text{plasmalemma}} = 1.6 \times 10^{-5}\ D^{\text{cell wall}}$
  (c) 2.5×10^4 times larger in the cell wall than in the plasmalemma

1–4. (a) 573 sec (9.6 min)
  (b) 1.15×10^5 sec (32 hours)
  (c) double
  (d) increase 100-fold

2–1. (a) 0.75 cm
  (b) 1.5 cm
  (c) 1.25 cm
  (d) 15 m
  (e) (b) and (c)

2–2. (a) 1400 bars higher on 0.1 molal side
  (b) 980 bars higher on 0.1 molal side
  (c) indefinite, since $\mu_j{}^*$ is arbitrary

2-3. (a) 0.74%
(b) 0.41 mole/liter
(c) -19.1 bars

2-4. (a) 32 μm^3
(b) 12 μm^3
(c) 5/8
(d) 3.3×10^{-15} mole/chloroplast or 2.0×10^9 molecules/chloroplast

2-5. (a) 4×10^{-5} cm/sec (flow is inward)
(b) none
(c) -3.7×10^{-4} cm/sec (flow is outward)

2-6. (a) 0.14 cm/sec or 5 m/hour
(b) -0.87×10^3 dynes/cm^3 or -0.87×10^{-3} bar/cm
(c) 1.1×10^{-8} cm/sec or 3.9×10^{-7} m/hour

3-1. (a) 3.3 mM
(b) -128 mv
(c) 3.7×10^{-13} joule

3-2. (a) K^+ is, but Mg^{++} is not
(b) 10 mM Na^+ inside; 0.1 μM Ca^{++} outside
(c) 13 mM
(d) -112 mv

3-3. (a) 1 mv, negative toward the cell
(b) a Donnan potential of 77 mv, negative at the surface of the membrane
(c) -53 mv, i.e., negative inside the cell
(d) -55 mv; -59 mv

3-4. (a) 0.5 picomole/cm^2-sec
(b) 0.95 kcal/mole, higher inside
(c) influx passive; efflux active and requires 2.7 kcal/mole
(d) 0.015 μmole/sec per liter of cells

3-5. (a) 0.78
(b) 0.65
(c) yes; -5×10^{-4} cm/sec (flow is outward)
(d) 3×10^{-4} cm/sec (flow is inward)

3-6. (a) 0.75
(b) 23 μm^3
(c) 0.00, since the chloroplast volume did not change upon addition of glycine

4-1. (a) 3.1×10^5 ev
(b) $16°$
(c) 3.0×10^{13} quanta/cm^2-sec
(d) units cannot be interconverted

4–2. (a) 333 nm in a vacuum, about 0.1 nm less in air, and 222 nm in the dense flint glass
(b) yes, but transition is improbable
(c) yes, it has enough energy
(d) 30,000 cm^{-1}

4–3. (a) 2.5×10^{-9} sec
(b) 0.75, when possible phosphorescence from the excited triplet is included
(c) essentially 10^{-12} sec

4–4. (a) 472 nm and 532 nm (distances in nm from main band are not equal)
(b) 67%
(c) 12 μM

5–1. (a) 0.05
(b) 33 hours
(c) 897.0
(d) maximum absorption occurs along diameter (40 μm)—A is 0.54 in the blue region and 0.40 in the red region

5–2. (a) 675 nm with 8 double bonds in conjugation and 862 nm with 10
(b) only the one with 8 double bonds can
(c) Blue light excites the Soret band of Chl a, which rapidly becomes de-excited to the lower excited singlet (cf. Fig. 4–3), and therefore the energy available is given by the red fluorescence of Chl a (cf. Fig. 5–2). The λ_{max} in the absorption spectrum of the pigment with 10 double bonds in conjugation is at 714 nm, and thus it can become excited by resonance transfer from Chl a while the one with the λ_{max} at 580 nm essentially cannot.

5–3. (a) $10h\nu/O_2$
(b) 200 chlorophylls/photosynthetic unit
(c) 50 milliseconds
(d) The uncoupling of ATP formation from electron flow is analogous to disengaging a clutch, which allows a motor to run faster; thus the O_2 evolution initially speeds up. After a while, the lack of ATP formation causes no CO_2 to be fixed; therefore the electron acceptors stay reduced and electron flow to them is curtailed. Moreover, electron flow may eventually switch over to the pseudocyclic type, which involves no net O_2 evolution.

5–4. (a) The 710 nm light absorbed by Photosystem I leads to cyclic electron flow and accompanying ATP formation; in the example given, 550 nm light by itself leads to excitation of Photosystem II only and no photophosphorylation.
(b) accessory (or auxiliary) pigments, presumably carotenoids, which are isoprenoids
(c) 1.00 at 710 nm and 0.23 at 550 nm

6-1. (a) $\Delta G = -4.09$ kcal/mole, and so the reaction proceeds in the forward direction

(b) $\Delta G = 0$ kcal/mole, which means that the reaction is at equilibrium and does not proceed in either direction

(c) $\Delta G = 4.09$ kcal/mole, and so the reaction proceeds in the backward direction

(d) 10^3 molal^{-1}

6-2. (a) 0.010

(b) 56 mv, electrons flowing toward the B-B^+ half-cell

(c) $[A^+] = [B] = 0.5$ molal

$[A] = [B^+] = 1.5$ molal

(d) answer unchanged

6-3. (a) 4.2×10^{-12} M

(b) 1 mM ATP; 12.0 kcal/mole

(c) 305 mv

(d) 14.1 kcal/mole; yes

Index

(Boldface type refers to figures or structural formulas, italic type to tables.)

Absorbance, 155–56
Absorption, light. *See* Light absorption
Absorption band, 154–55
  bandwidth, 173
  conjugation and λ_{max}, 157–58
  See also Rotational energy; Solvent effects; Translational energy; Vibrational sublevels
Absorption coefficient, 155–56
  and conjugation, 157–58
  See also Absorption spectrum; Molar absorption coefficient
Absorption spectrum, 138, 150, 155, 159
  carotenoids, 176, **176**
  chlorophyll, 169–70, **170**
  and the Franck-Condon principle, 154
  phycobilins, 178–79, **179**
  phytochrome, **161**, 161–62
Acceptor, electron, 181, 187–88
Accessory pigments, 174–75, 191
  light harvesting, 180–81, 187
  See also Carotenoids; Phycobilins
Action spectrum, 150, 159
  photosynthesis, 191–92, **192**
  phytochrome, **162**, 162–63

Active transport, 76, 99–100
  carriers, 18, 107–11
  energy required, 83, 106–7
  in *Nitella*, 104–7
  and Q_{10}, 100–102
Activity, thermodynamic, 43, 45, 80
Activity coefficient, 45, 79–81
  under biological conditions, 80–81
  Debye-Hückel equation, 80
  ideal solution, 45
  ionic, 79–81
  K^+ in *Chara*, 83
  nonelectrolytes, 81
  sucrose, 81
Adenosine diphosphate. *See* ADP
Adenosine triphosphate. *See* ATP
Adhesion, 37, 38
ADP, 203, 216–19
  See also ATP; Photophosphorylation; Photosynthesis
Algal cells, giant or internodal. *See* Chara; Nitella
Atomic orbitals, 140–41
ATP, 203, 216–19
  energy currency, 215–16

ATP (*continued*)
  high energy bond, 219
  and light energy, 133
  in photosynthesis, 166, 226
  and sodium-potassium pump in *Nitella*,
    107
  See also ATP formation
ATP formation, 216–17
  equilibrium constant, 218
  Gibbs free energy change, 218
    under biological conditions, 219
  redox potential change needed, 224
Auxiliary pigments. *See* Accessory pigments

Bacteria, photosynthesis, 169, 193–94,
    219–20
  See also Bacteriochlorophyll
Bacteriochlorophyll, 169
  absorption bands, 173–74
  trap chl role, 187, 189
Bandwidth of absorption band, 173
Beer's law (Beer-Lambert law), 155–56
  chlorophyll in leaf cells, 156
  chloroplast, 156–57
  derivation, 155
Biliprotein, 178
  See also Phycocyanin; Phycoerythrin;
    Phytochrome
Bioenergetics, 207–31
  ATP, 216–19
  chloroplast, 221–27
  Gibbs free energy, 208–13
  mitochondrial, 227–29
  NADP-NADPH$_2$, 219–21
  redox potentials, 213–15
Boltzmann energy distribution, 100–102,
    134
  and energy enrichment per atom, 231
  and light energy, 134
  and population of vibrational energy
    levels, 150, 152, 154
  and Q_{10}, 100–102
Boyle-Van't Hoff relation, 54
  chloroplast osmotic responses, **56**, 56–57,
    121
  classical thermodynamic derivation,
    54–55
  irreversible thermodynamic derivation,
    119–21

Calcium:
  and ATP formation, 216–17
  in cell walls, 25, 26, 97
  and *Nitella* diffusion potential, 96
Candle (candela), 135

Capacitance, 78
  membrane, 78
  spherical capacitor, 78
Capillary rise, **37**, 37–40
  in cell walls, 39–40
  height and radius of tube, 38–39
  in xylem vessels, 39
Carbohydrate:
  combustion energy, 167
  photosynthetic product, 166–67, 195
Carbon dioxide:
  diffusion coefficient, 13
  diffusion steps in photosynthesis, 7–8, 13
  photosynthetic fixation, 165–67, 195
  stomatal entry, 5
β-carotene, 176–78, **177**
  absorption spectrum, 176, **176**
Carotenes, 176–78
Carotenoids, 175–78, 179
  absorption spectra, 176, **176**
  carotenes, 176–78
  conjugation and λ_{max}, 175–76
  frequency relative to chlorophyll, 175
  photooxidation protection, 178
  in Photosystems I and II, 193
  transfer of excitations to chl a, 184
  xanthophylls, 176–78
Carrier, 18, 107–8, 110
Casparian strip, 64
Cells, 2–4, **3**
  electroneutrality in, 78, 79
  sizes, 3–4
  water content, 33
Cell sap, osmotic pressure, 56
Cell wall, 1, 2, **3**, 25–30
  composition:
    calcium, 25, 26, 97
    hemicellulose, 27
    lignin, 26, 64
    pectin, 25, 26, 27, 96
    suberin, 64
    water, 26
    See also Cellulose
  diffusion across, 27–28
  Donnan potential, 96–97
  elasticity, 28, 58–59
  interstices, 2, 26, 27
    capillary rise in, 39–40
    matric potential in, 67–69
    support of water in xylem vessels, 40
    tension in, 67–69
    water flow through, 67
  middle lamella, 25
  pits, 27–28
  plasmodesmata, 28
  primary, 25, 26, 27

secondary, 25, 26, 27
stresses, 29–30
water flow across, 67
water potential in, 67–69, *71*
Young's modulus, 28
Cellulose, 25–26, **26**
elementary microfibril, 26
microfibril, 26
Young's modulus, 28
Central vacuole. *See* Vacuole, central
Chara, 4
approximation by cylinder, 29, **29**, 30
cell wall stresses, 30
K^+ Nernst potential, 83–84
water influx, 62–63
Charge, electrical, 78
Chelate, 217
Chemical activity, 43, 45, 80
Chemical bonds, 140–42, **141**, 151
energy, 113, 166
in photosynthesis, 166–67
Chemical energy:
conversion into electrical energy, 212–13
See also Chemical potential
Chemical potential, 42–46, 76, 86–87
activity term, 45, 86–87
constant term, 44–45, 46
electrical term, 46, 76–77
and activity term for ions, 82, 84
and hydrostatic pressure term for ions, 76, 77
See also Electrical potential
matric pressure term, 49–50
See also Matric potential
pressure term, 45
See also Hydrostatic pressure
relation to Gibbs free energy, 209
See also Flux ratio; Gibbs free enrgy; Water; Water potential
Chemical reactions, 209
energy storage or release, 211
Gibbs free energy, 210–11
Chemi-osmotic hypothesis for phosphorylation, 226
Chl *a*, 168–69, **168**
absorption spectrum, 169–72, **170**
excitation transfer, 181–86
resonance, 182–83
time, 185
excited singlet states:
lifetime, 171, 185
transitions between, **143**, 145, 171, 185
fluorescence:
emission spectrum, **170**, 171
lifetime, 185, 186

quantum yield, 186
red band *in vitro*, 170, **170**
red band *in vivo*, 172–73
bandwidth, 173
Soret or blue band, **143**, **170**, 170–71
vibrational sublevels, 170–72, **172**
See also Chl a_{670}; Chl a_{680}; Chlorophyll; P_{700}
Chl a_{670}, 172
in Photosystem II, 193
Chl a_{680}, 173
in Photosystem I, 193
Chl *b*, 169
in Photosystem II, 193
red band *in vivo*, 173
Chl *c*, 169, 185
Chl *d*, 169
Chlorella:
photosynthetic unit, 188–89
red drop, 191
size, 4
Chloride:
active transport into *Nitella*, 104–7
and membrane diffusion potential, 93–95
Nitella, 95–96
in Photosystem II, 197
Chlorobium chlorophyll, 169
Chlorophyll, 142–49, 167–74, **168**
absorption spectrum, 169–72, **170**
Beer's law, leaf, 156
de-excitation processes, **143**, 145–47
energy level diagram, **143**
excited states, 142–43, **143**, 145
fluorescence, **143**, 171
depolarization, 174, 182
emission spectrum, **170**, 171
lifetime, 149, 186
quantum yield *in vitro*, 149
quantum yield *in vivo*, 186
orientation in membranes, 174
phosphorescence, **143**, 145
polarized light studies, 174
radiationless transition, **143**, 145
spacing in lamellar membranes, 183
and sunlight excitation, 190
See also Chl *a*; Chl *b*; P_{700}; Photosynthesis
Chloroplasts, 2, **18**, 18–19
Beer's law, 156–57
bioenergetics, 209, 221–27
See also Electron flow in chloroplasts; Photophosphorylation; Redox potential
electron flow. *See* Electron flow in chloroplasts
grana, **18**, 19

Chloroplasts (*continued*)
  in leaf cells, 3, 5, **5**
  membranes, 17, **18**, 18–19
  osmotic responses, 52, **56**, 56–57, 121
  reflection coefficient, 121
  stroma, **18**, 19
  stromal lamellae, **18**, 19
  thylakoids, **18**, 18–19
  volume, 52, 56–57
    effect of light, 57
  water content, 57
Chromatophores, 19
Chromophore, 160
Cohesion, 37, 38
Color, light, 131, *132*
Compartmentation, 3, 14, 18, 121, **227**
Conductivity coefficient, water, 62
  See also Hydraulic conductivity
    coefficient
Conductor, electrical, 78, 79
Conjugation, 157–59, 161
  absorption band shift for hydrocarbons,
    158
  carotenoids, 175–76
  chlorophyll, 169, 170
  energy levels of molecular orbitals, 157–
    158, **158**
  phycobilins, 179
  phytochrome, 161
Constant field assumption, 90
Constant field equation. *See* Goldman
  equation
Contact angle, **37**, 38
Continuity equation, 9–10
Coulomb's law, 41
Coupling, forces and fluxes. *See* Irrevers-
  ible thermodynamics
Coupling factors, mitochondrial, 228
Coupling sites. *See* Oxidative phosphoryla-
  tion; Photophosphorylation
Cross coefficients, 112
Cuticle, 4, **5**, 69
Cuvette, 164
Cyclic electron flow, *198*, 202, **225**
Cytochrome *a*, 199
  in mitochondria, 228, 229
Cytochrome *a₃*, 228, 229
Cytochrome *b*, 199
  in chloroplasts, *198*, 199, 200, **225**
  in mitochondria, 228, 229
Cytochrome *b₆*, *198*, 202, **225**
Cytochrome *c*, 199, **200**
  in mitochondria, 228, 229
Cytochrome *f*, *198*, 199, 200, 201
  redox potential, *198*, 224–25, **225**
Cytochrome oxidase, 228, 229

Cytochromes, 17, 180, 199–201, **200**
  absorption properties, 199, 200
  See also individual cytochromes
Cytoplasm, 2, **3**
  osmotic pressure, 53, 59

Davson-Danielli membrane. *See* Membranes, Davson-Danielli model
Debye-Hückel equation, 80
De-excitation, **143**, 144–49
  electron ejection or donation, 145–46, 147
  excitation transfer, 145, 147
  fluorescence, 144, 146
  phosphorescence, 145
  radiationless transitions, 144–45, 146
Delocalization, electron, 140–41, **141**, 151
Dielectric constant, 41
  water, 41–42
Differential permeability, 2, 54
  See also Permeability coefficient
Diffusion, 3, 7–13
  and cell size, 3, 4
  and chemical potential, 43
  and concentration gradients, 7, 8, 20
  concentration profiles, 11, **11**
  equations for solute entry into cells, 22–23
    times involved, 24–25
  facilitated, 110–11
  and movement in phloem, 125
  Q_{10}, 101–2
  statistical nature, 7, 12
  and thermal motion, 7, 8
  time-distance relation, 12–13, 24
  and unstirred layers, **20**, 20–21, 69–70
  See also Diffusion coefficient; Diffusion
    potential; Fick's first law; Fick's
    second law; Membrane permeability
Diffusion coefficient, 9
  and mobility, 86
  values for gases, 13
  values for small solutes, 12
Diffusion potential, 87–89
  and Donnan potential, 98–99
  across membranes, 92–95
    Goldman equation, 94
  across salt-bridge, 89
  in solution, derivation, 87–89
Diffusion pressure deficit, 51
Dilute solution, 47
Distance-time relation for diffusion, 12
Donnan phase, **97**, 97–99
Donnan potential, 96–99
  as diffusion potential, 98–99
  as Nernst potential, 98–99
Donor, electron, 181, 187–88
Double bonds and conjugation, 157–58, 161

Earth:
    energy radiated, 230
    solar energy input, 135–36, 230
Efflux, 91–92, 102
    See also Flux; Flux ratio
Electric dipole, 138, 182
Electrical charge, 78
Electrical conductor, 78, 79
Electrical double layer, **97**, 98
Electrical force, 41–42, 87
Electrical potential or energy, 43, 76–77
    conversion *into* chemical energy, 212–13
    and electron energy, 212–13, 215
    spherical capacitor, 78
    See also Chemical potential; Redox
        potential
Electrochemical potential, 46, 76
Electrodes, 212, 213–14
    See also Half-cells; Salt-bridges
Electrogenic process, 99–100
Electromagnetic radiation. *See* Infrared;
    Light; Ultraviolet
Electron:
    delocalization, 140–41, **141**, 151
    ejection, 130, 147
    energy and electrical potential, 212–13,
        215
    nonbonding or lone-pair (n), 141
    orbital (orbit), 137, 139, 140–42, **141**
    π, 141–42
    π^*, 141–42
    resonance with light, 138
    σ, 141
    spin, 138–39
    See also Light absorption; Redox
        potential
Electron flow in chloroplasts, 194–203
    components, 197–201, *198*, **225**
    coupled ATP formation, 194, 224–27
    cyclic, *198*, 202, **225**
    noncyclic, 195, **196**, 201–2, 223, **225**
    pathway, 196, **196**, **225**
    pseudocyclic, 202, **225**
    series representation, **196**, 197
    unanswered questions, 202, 226–27
    See also individual components
Electron flow in mitochondria, 227–29
    coupled ATP formation, 229
Electron transfer or transport pathway. *See*
    Electron flow in chloroplasts; Elec-
    tron flow in mitochondria; Electron
    transport chain
Electron transport chain:
    chloroplasts, 197, 201, 202
        coupling site for ATP formation,
        224–26

    See also Electron flow in chloroplasts
mitochondria, 227–28
    coupling sites for ATP formation,
        229
Electron volt, 100
Electroneutrality, 78, 79
    in cells, 79
    in solutions, 88
    steady-state membrane fluxes, 93
Elementary microfibril, cellulose, 26
Emerson enhancement effect, 191–93
Energy, light, *132*, 132–34
Energy barrier and Q_{10}, 101
Energy conversion, 2, 181, 212–13
Energy currencies, 2, 207, 215–16, 230
    See also ATP; NADP-NADPH$_2$
Energy enrichment per atom, 231
Energy flow, 229–31
Energy level diagram, **143**, 150–52, **151**
Energy radiated, Stefan-Boltzmann law, 230
    earth, 230
    sun, 230
Energy transfer:
    coupled to electron flow, 203
    between pigments. *See* Excitation transfer
Enhancement effects in photosynthesis,
    191–93
Epidermis:
    cuticle, 4, 69
    leaf, 4, 69
    root, 64
Equilibrium, 43, 52, 84–85, 208
    and chemical potential across membrane,
        52, 81–82
    and forces, 84
    and Gibbs free energy, 208, 211
    and membrane potentials, 105
Equilibrium constant, 211
    ATP formation, 218
    biochemical conventions, 217–18
    and Gibbs free energy, 211
Excitation transfer, 145, 147, 181–88
    from Chl a to Chl a, 183, 185–86
    funneling to trap chl, 181
    toward longer λ_{max}'s, 184–85
    between photosynthetic pigments, 183–85
    resonance transfer, 182–83
        absorption and fluorescence band
            overlap, 183
        distance, 183
    trapping, 186–87
        See also P$_{700}$; Trap chl
Excited electronic state, 141–42
    energy levels, **151**, **158**
    See also Light absorption; Molecular
        orbitals

Extinction coefficient, 155

Facilitated diffusion, 110–11
FAD-FADH$_2$, 228, 229
Ferredoxin, *198*, 201
    determinant of electron flow type, 201–2, **225**
    redox potential, *198*, 223, **225**
Ferredoxin-NADP reductase, *198*, 201
Fick's first law, 8–9
    diffusion across membrane, 19–22
    diffusion across unstirred air layer, 69–70
    relation to chemical potential, 43, 86–87
Fick's second law, 10
    mathematical solution, 10
        concentration profiles, 11, **11**
First-order process, 146, 147–48
Flavin adenine dinucleotide, *198*, 228, 229
Flavoproteins, 228
Fluorescence, **143**, 144, 146
    emitted vs. absorbed wavelength, 153
    lifetimes, 144, 146
        and dissipation time for vibrational energy, 153
    See also Chl *a*; Chlorophyll
Flux, 8, 91–92
    ions, 84–86
        across membranes, 89–95
    irreversible thermodynamics, 111–16
    neutral solutes, 21–22
    water. *See* Water flow
    See also Flux ratio; Ussing-Teorell equation
Flux ratio, 102–3
    relation to chemical potential difference, 103–4
Flux ratio equation. *See* Ussing-Teorell equation
Force:
    concentration gradient, 8, 20, 85
    electrical, 41–42, 87
    and fluxes, 85–86
        irreversible thermodynamics, 111–12
Franck-Condon principle, 152–54
    and absorption spectrum, 154
Free energy, 42–44, 208–9
    See also Chemical potential; Gibbs free energy
Frequency, light, 131–33, *132*
Fucoxanthin, 178, 184, 193

Giant algal cells. *See* Chara; Nitella
Gibbs free energy, 208–9
    ATP formation, 218–19
    chemical reactions, 210–11
    conversion to electrical energy, 212–13

enrichment per atom, 231
    and equilibrium constant, 211
    equilibrium value, 208, 211
    and noncyclic electron flow, 223–24
Goldman assumption, 90
Goldman equation, 94
    application to *Nitella*, 95–96
Gradient, 8
    concentration, 8, 20, 85
Gravity:
    acceleration, 39, 238, 239
    and capillary rise, 38
    and water movement in xylem, 66–67
    and water potential, 44, 51, 66, *71*
Grotthus-Draper law, 137, 159
Ground state, 139, 142, 150
    energy levels, **151**, **158**
Guard cells, 5, **5**, 69
Guttation, 72

Half-cell potential. *See* Half-cells; Redox potential
Half-cells, 212, 213–14
    hydrogen, 214
    NADP-NADPH$_2$, 220, **225**
    silver, 212
    water-oxygen, 222, **225**

Half-time, 144
Heat flow, 8, 44
Heat of fusion, water, 35
Heat of vaporization, water, 36
Heme, *198*, 200, **200**
Hemicellulose, 27
Hill reaction, 195
Hund's rule, 140
Hydraulic conductivity coefficient, 115
Hydrocarbons, conjugation and absorption coefficient, 158
Hydrogen bonds, **35**, 35–36
    energy, 35, 36, 42
    rupture during melting of ice, 35–36
    tensile strength of water, 40–41, 72
    and tension in cell wall water, 68
Hydrogen half-cell, 214
Hydroquinone, 199, **199**
Hydrostatic pressure, 28, 43, 48–49
    and cell wall stresses, 28–30, 58–59
    diurnal variations in, 72
    and incipient plasmolysis, 58–59
    Poiseuille flow, 66–67
    and water potential, 51

Ice, 35–36
Ideal solution, 45

Immobile charges in Donnan phase, 96–97, **97**

Impermeability and reflection coefficient, 117, 118, 122–23

Incipient plasmolysis, 58–59
and internal osmotic pressures, 59
irreversible thermodynamic analysis, 121–23
measurement of reflection coefficient by, 122–23

Influx, 91–92, 102
See also Flux; Flux ratio; Ussing-Teorell equation

Infrared, 131, *132*, 134

Interfaces:
Donnan potential at solid-liquid, 96–99
plant-air, 59–60, 61, 67
in solution. *See* Matric potential

Interstices. *See* Cell wall, interstices

Ionic activity coefficients, 79–81

Ionic strength, 80

Irreversible thermodynamics, 76, 111–12
Boyle-Van't Hoff relation, 119–21
incipient plasmolysis, 121–23
reflection coefficients, 115–18
volume flow, 114–16
water and solute flow, 112–14

Isoprene, 175, **175**

Lambert-Beer law. *See* Beer's law

Leaf, 4–5
cuticle, 4, **5**, 69
epidermis, 4, **5**, 69
intercellular air space, **5**, 69
mesophyll cells, 4–5
palisade, 4–5, **5**
spongy, 4–5, **5**
transverse section, **5**
unstirred air layer, 69–70, 72–73
vascular bundle, **6**
See also Stomata

Lecithin, **15**

Lifetime, 144, 147–49
fluorescence, 144
phosphorescence, 145
and quantum yield, 147–49
radiationless transition, 145
and rate constant, 146, 148

Light:
electric and magnetic fields, 130, 137–38
energy, *132*, 132–34
and chemical bond energies, 133
and kinetic energies, 134
π and π^* orbitals, 142
and redox potentials, 222, 223, **225**
frequency, 131–33, *132*

intensity, 134–36
photometric units, 134–35
radiometric units, 134–35
sun. *See* Sunlight
particle nature, 130, 132
velocity, 131
wave number, 164
wave theory, 130
wavelength, 131, *132*

Light absorption, 137–43
chlorophyll, 142–43
double bonds in conjugation, 157–59, **158**
electric dipole, 138
energies allowed, 137, 138
energy level diagram, **143**
excited states (π^*), 141–42
Franck-Condon principle, 152–54
and molecular orbitals, 140–42
orientation of electromagnetic field, 138
oscillating electric field, 137–38
π electrons, 141–42
and redox potentials, 222, 223, **225**
resonance, 138
role of electrons, 137–38
time, 144, 153, 185
vibrational sublevels, 149–54

Light harvesting pigments, 180–81, 187, **187**

Light intensity. *See* Light, intensity

Lignin, 26, 64

Lipid bilayer, membranes, **14**, 14–16

Lipid molecules, 14–15

Lutein, 176–78, **177**
absorption spectrum, 176, **176**

Magnesium
and ATP formation, 216–17, 218
in chlorophyll, **168**, 169, 200

Matric potential, 49–50
in cell wall, 67–69
interfacial interactions, 44, 49–50
surface tension, 67–68
in soil, 70, *71*
for wilting, 70–72

Mean activity coefficient, ionic, 80

Membrane fluxes, 89–92
and Goldman equation, 92–95
main contributors, 93
Nitella, 105–6
See also Flux; Flux ratio; Ussing-Teorell equation

Membrane permeability, 19–25
dependence on lipid solubility, 14, 21
differential aspects, 2, 54
impermeability, 117, 118, 122–23
nonselectivity, 117, 118
and reflection coefficients, 116–18

Membrane permeability (*continued*)
   and unstirred layers, **20**, 20–21
   to water, 42
   See also Diffusion; Partition coefficient;
      Permeability coefficient
Membrane potential:
   as diffusion potential, 87, 92–95
      Nitella, 95–96
   and Nernst potential, 82–83, 106–7
      Nitella, 104–5, 107
Membranes, 3
   capacitance, 78
   chloroplast, 17, 18–19
   Davson-Danielli model, **14**, 14–16
   globular substructure, 16–17
   lipid bilayer, **14**, 14–16
   mitochondrial, 16–18
   proteins, **14**, 15–16
   Q_{10} for diffusion across, 101–2
   surface tension, 15–16
   thickness, 16
   unit membrane concept of Robertson, 16
   See also Membrane fluxes; Membrane
      permeability; Membrane potential
Mesophyll cells, leaf, 4–5, **5**
Micelles, 42
Michaelis constant, 110
Michaelis-Menten formalism, **109**, 109–10
Microelectrodes, 4, 89
Microfibril, cellulose, 26
Midpoint redox potential, 215, 222
   See also Redox potential
Mitochondria, 2, 227
   bioenergetics, 227–29
   cristae, 17
   cytochromes, 17, 228, 229
   electron flow. *See* Electron flow
      in mitochondria
   matrix, 18
   membranes, 16–18
Mobility, 85–86
   anion-cation pair and diffusion potential,
      88–89
   and diffusion coefficient, 86
   in membranes, 92, 94
   and permeability coefficient, 93–94
   u_{Cl}/u_K, 89
   u_{Cl}/u_{Na}, 89
   and velocity, 85–86
Modulus of elasticity. *See* Young's modulus
Molar absorption coefficient, 156, 180
   carotenoids, **176**
   chlorophyll, 156, 170, **170**
   cytochromes, 200
   phycobilins, 179, **179**
   phytochrome, **161**, 162

Molar flux, 85, 114
Mole fraction, 47
Molecular orbitals, 140–42
   and conjugation, 157–58
   n, 141
   π (bonding), **141**, 141–42
   π^* (antibonding), **141**, 141–42
   σ, 141

NAD-NADH$_2$, 220, 228, 229
NADP-NADPH$_2$, *198*, 219–21
   electron flow component, *198*, 201, 202
   as energy currency, 208, 215–16, 223
   in photosynthesis, 166, 226
   redox potential, *198*, 221, 223, **225**
   redox reaction, 220, **225**
Nernst equation, 82
Nernst potential, 81–84
   derivation, 81–82
   and Donnan potential, 98
   K^+ in *Chara*, 83–84
   Na^+, K^+, and Cl^- in *Nitella*, 104, *105*, 107
   relation to E_M, 82–83
Nicotinamide adenine dinucleotide. *See*
      NAD-NADH$_2$
Nicotinamide adenine dinucleotide phos-
      phate. *See* NADP-NADPH$_2$
Nitella, 4
   active transport of ions, 104–7
   approximation by cylinder, 29, **29**, 30
   cell wall stresses, 30
   ionic permeabilities, 95–96
   membrane diffusion potential, 95–96
   Nernst potentials, 104, *105*, 107
   water influx, 62–63
   Young's modulus of cell wall, 28
Noncyclic electron flow, **196**, 201–2, 223,
   225
Nonequilibrium, 111
Nonosmotic volume, 54, 55
   chloroplasts, 57
Nonradiative transition, **143**, 144–45, 146
Nonselectivity and reflection coefficient,
      117, 118
Nuclear vibrations, 150–52
   frequency (period), 153, 185
   trajectories or ranges, **151**, 151–52
   turning points, **151**, 152

Onsager coefficients, 112
Onsager reciprocity relation, 112
Optical density, 155–56
Optical path length (*b*) ,155, 156
Osmotic coefficient, 54, 55, 120–21
Osmotic pressure, 46–48
   of cellular fluid, 48, 56, 59

concentration dependence, 48
and reflection coefficients, 123
and volume flow, 63, 116
and water potential, 51
Osmotic responses. *See* Boyle-Van't Hoff relation
Oxidation, 181, 196, 213
Oxidation-reduction potential. *See* Redox potential
Oxidative phosphorylation, 227–29
coupling sites, 229
Oxygen:
diffusion coefficient, 13
photosynthetic product, 165–67, 195, 197
Ozone and sunlight, 136, **136**

P_{660}. *See* Phytochrome
P_{700}, 173, *198*
bleaching, 194–95, 201
electron donation reaction, 147
as electron flow component, *198*, 201
excitation trapping, 186–87
lifetime of excited state, 187
in Photosystem I, 193, **196**
redox potential, *198*, 223, **225**
time for excitation migration to, 186
See also Trap chl
P_{730}. *See* Phytochrome
Palisade cells. *See* Leaf, mesophyll cells
Partial molal volume. *See* Volume, partial molal
Partial pressure, water vapor, 60
Partition coefficient, 21, 22, 90
effect of charge, 24
and reflection coefficient, 118
Pauli exclusion principle, 139
Pea:
leaf cells, 5
osmotic responses of chloroplasts, **56**, 56–57, 121
Pectin, 25, 26, 27, 96
Perforation plate. *See* Xylem perforation plate
Permeability, membrane. *See* Membrane permeability
Permeability coefficient, 22, 93–94
cell wall, 27
equation for, 23
and mobility, 93–94
P_{Na}/P_K and P_{Cl}/P_K for *Nitella*, 95
plasmalemma, 27
values for small molecules, 24
pH, 217
and ATP formation, 216–17
and equilibrium constants, 217
Phenomenological coefficients, 112

Phloem, **6**, 6–7, 123–26
aphid studies, 124
companion cells, **6**
diffusion in, 6, 125
sieve cells, 7, 124
sieve plate, **6**, 124
sieve tube members, **6**, 7, 124
sieve tubes, **6**, 124
solutes transported, 124–25
sucrose, 6, 124
velocity of solute movement, 125
Phosphate, 203, 216–19
See also ATP; Photophosphorylation; Photosynthesis
Phosphatidyl choline, **15**
Phospholipid, 15
Phosphorescence, **143**, 145
Phosphorus, bonding in ATP, 219
Photochemistry:
and electron ejection, 147
Grotthus-Draper law, 137, 159
primary processes, 144
Stark-Einstein law, 137
Photoelectric effect, 130
Photometric units, light, 134–35
Photon. *See* Light
Photophosphorylation, 194, 203
change in redox potential needed, 224
changes in Gibbs free energy, 219
coupling mechanisms, 226
coupling site, 224–26
Photosynthesis, 165–67
action spectrum, 191–92, **192**
ATP requirement, 166, 226
carbon dioxide fixation, 165–67, 195
chemical bond changes, 166
chemical reaction summary, 166, 195, **196**
efficiency, 167, 231
electron transfer reactions, 197–202, **225**
energy storage, 166–67
annual, 231
maximum, 167
enhancement effects, 191–93
light absorption event, 180
oxygen evolution from water, 165–67, 195, 197
photochemistry, 180–82, **187**, 189
primary events, 166, 180–82
quantum requirement, 167, 188, 196–97, 226
red drop, 191–92, **192**
time intervals, 194–95, 201
See also Chl *a*; Chlorophyll; Electron flow in Chloroplasts; Excitation transfer; P_{700}; Photophosphorylation; Photosynthetic units

Photosynthetic bacteria. *See* Bacteria, photosynthesis
Photosynthetic units, **187**, 188–91
  excitation processing time, 190
  reaction center, 194
  size, 189
  as structural entities, 189
  See also Photosystem I; Photosystem II
Photosystem I, 192–93, **196**
  contents, 193
  and cyclic electron flow, 202
  in electron flow reactions, **196**, *198*, 201
  and redox potential, *198*, 223, **225**
  reductant production, 196, **196**
Photosystem II, 193, **196**
  contents, 193
  in electron flow reactions, **196**, 197, *198*
  oxygen evolution from water, 196, **196**, 197
  and redox potentials, *198*, 222–23, **225**
Phycobilins, 178–79
  in Photosystem II, 193
  transfer of excitations to Chl *a*, 184–85
  See also Phycocyanobilin; Phycoerythrobilin
Phycocyanin, 179
  absorption spectrum, **179**
  excitation transfer reactions, 184–85
Phycocyanobilin, **177**, 178–79
Phycoerythrin, 179
  absorption spectrum, **179**
  excitation transfer to phycocyanin, 184–85
Phycoerythrobilin, **177**, 178–79
Phytochrome, **160**, 160–63
  absorption spectra,-**161**, 161–62
  action spectra, **162**, 162–63
  physiological consequences of interconversion, 163
Phytol, **168**, 169
π electrons or orbitals. *See* Electron; Molecular orbitals
Pits, cell wall, 27–28
Plasma membrane. *See* Plasmalemma
Plasmalemma, 2, **3**, 14
  permeability coefficients, 27
Plasmodesmata, 28
Plasmolysis, 58
  See also Incipient plasmolysis
Plastocyanin, *198*, 199, 201, **225**
Plastoquinone, 197, *198*, 199, 202
Plastoquinone A, *198*, 199, **199**
  redox potential, *198*, 223, 224–25, **225**
Poiseuille flow, 66–67, 125–26
Poiseuille's law, 66
  water flow through cell wall, 67

water flow in xylem, 66–67
Porphyrin, **168**, 168–69, 200, **200**
Potassium:
  active transport into *Nitella*, 104–7
  in *Chara*, 83
  and membrane diffusion potential, 93–95
    Nitella, 95–96
Pressure. *See* Hydrostatic pressure; Matric potential; Turgor pressure
Protoplasmic streaming, 19, 21, 125
Pseudocyclic electron flow, 202, **225**
Pump, sodium -potassium, 107, 108
Pyrrole, 160–61

Q_{10}, 100–102
Quanta. *See* Light
Quantum yield (quantum efficiency), 148–49
  chlorophyll fluorescence, 149, 186
Quinone, 197, **197**, 199

Radiationless transitions, **143**, 144–45, 146
Radiometric units, light, 134–35
Rate constant, 146–49
  and lifetime, 146, 148
  and quantum yield, 149
Reaction center, 194, **196**
Reciprocity relation, Onsager, 112
Red drop of photosynthesis, 191–92, **192**
Redox couples, 214
  chloroplast, *198*, 222–24, **225**
  mitochondria, 228
  See also Redox potential
Redox potential, 213–15
  change needed for ATP formation, 224
  chloroplast components, *198*, **225**
  and light absorption, 222
  midpoint, 215
  mitochondrial components, 228
  NADP-NADPH₂ couple, *198*, 220–21, **225**
  standard hydrogen electrode, 214
  See also individual components
Reduction, 181, 196, 213
Reference state, chemical potential, 46
Reflection coefficient, 2, 115–16
  average or mean, 120
  in Boyle-Van't Hoff relation, 120–21
  impermeability, 117, 118
  in incipient plasmolysis, 122–23
  nonselectivity, 117, 118
  and osmotic pressure, 123
  and partition coefficient, 118
  values, 116–18
Relative humidity, 60
  and water in air, 70
  and water potential in air, 60–62

Resonance:
  and bonding in ATP, 219
  and light absorption, 138
Resonance transfer. *See* Excitation transfer
Root, 64–65
  Casparian strip, 64
  cortex, 64
  endodermis, 64–65
  epidermis, 64
  pericycle, 65
  xylem, 65
Rotational energy, 154

Salt-bridges, 4, 89
  diffusion potential across tip, 89
Saturation vapor pressure, 60
Seed germination, phytochrome mediation, 160, 162–63
Semiquinone, 199, **199**
Sieve tubes. *See* Phloem
Silver half-cell, 212
Singlet, 139, 142
Sodium:
  active transport out of *Nitella*, 104–7
  and membrane diffusion potential, 93–95
    Nitella, 95–96
Sodium-potassium pump, 107, 108
Soil water potential, 70, *71*
  wilting, 70–72
Solar constant, 135, 230
Solvent effects on absorption band, 154, 173
Soret band, 170, 199
  Chl *a*, **170**, 170–71
Space-time relation for diffusion, 12
Specific activity, 103
Spherical capacitor, 78
Spin, 138–39
Spin multiplicity, 139
Spongy cells. *See* Leaf, mesophyll cells
Spontaneous change and free energy, 43, 208, 213
Standard hydrogen electrode, 214
Standard state, chemical potential, 46
Stark-Einstein law, 137
Stationary state, 118, 119
Steady state, 72, 85, 91
Stefan-Boltzmann law, 230
Stomata, 5, 69
  guard cells, 5, **5**, 69
  pores, 5, **5**, 69
Suberin, 64
Sucrose:
  activity coefficient, 81
  diffusion coefficient, 12
  in phloem, 6, 124
  reflection coefficient, 118

Suction pressure, 51
Sunlight, 135–36, **136**
  and chlorophyll excitation frequency, 190
  energy radiated, 230
  intensity, 135
  ozone screening, 136 ,**136**
  solar constant, 135, 230
Surface tension. *See* Water, surface tension
Symplasm, 28, 64

Temperature coefficient, 100–102
Tensile strength, 40
  water, 40–41
Tension:
  in cell wall interstices, 67–69
  in water, 40–41
Tetrapyrrole, 160, 168, 179, 200
  Soret band, 170
Time:
  light absorption, 144, 153, 185
  See also Lifetime
Tonoplast, 3, **3**, 52
Trajectories, nuclear vibrations, **151**, 151–52
Translational energy, 154
Transpiration, 5, 13
  cuticular, 69
  from leaf, 70
  heat loss, 36
  stomatal, 69
  and tensile strength of water, 41
  and unstirred air layers, 70, 72–73
  and water potential in the cell wall, 68
Trap chl, 180–81, 186–88
  energy of excited singlet state, 186, 187
  funneling of excitation to, 180–81, 186–87, **187**, **196**
  kinetics of bleaching, 194–95
  photochemistry, 181, **187**, 187–88
  in photosynthetic unit, **187**, 189, **196**
  in reaction center, 194
  See also P_{700}
Triplet, 139, 142
  excited state, 143, 145, 146
Turgor pressure, 29, 51
Turning point, nuclear, **151**, 152

Ultraviolet, 131, *132*, 133, 136
Uncoupler of photophosphorylation, 204
Unstirred layers:
  in air, 69–70, 72–73
  in solution near membrane, **20**, 20–21
Ussing-Teorell equation, 99, 102–3
  ionic fluxes of *Nitella*, 105–6

Vacuole, central, 3, **3**, 52–53
  osmotic pressure, 53, 59

Vacuole (*continued*)
  volume, 52
  water relations, 52–53
Valonia, size 4
Vascular bundle, longitudinal section, **6**
Vascular tissue, 6–7
  See also Phloem; Xylem
Velocity:
  light, 131
  and mobility, 85–86
  of phloem fluid, 125
  of xylem sap, 66
Vessels. *See* Xylem
Vibrational energy. *See* Vibrational sub-
    levels
Vibrational sublevels, 149–52, **151**
  dissipation time for energy, 153, 185
  energy splitting, 149, 154
    chlorophyll, 170, 172
  Franck-Condon principle, 152–54
  transition times, 153
Viscosity, 66
Volume:
  nonwater (nonosmotic), 54, 55, 57
  osmotic responses. *See* Boyle-Van't Hoff
    relation
  partial molal, 45
    of water, 49
Volume flow, 62–63, 114–16
  and hydrostatic pressure, 63, 116
  and osmotic pressure, 63, 116, 123
  total, 63, 114–16
  of water, 62
    into *Nitella* or *Chara*,   62–63

Water, 33–34
  activity, 46–48
    effect of interfaces, 49–50
    and osmotic pressure, 46–47
    standard state, 46
  cellular content, 33
  chemical potential, 47–51
    activity term, 47
    hydrostatic pressure, 49
    matric potential, 49–50
    See also Water potential
  conductivity coefficient, 62
  dielectric constant, 41–42
  electrical forces in, 41–42
  heat of fusion, 35
  heat of vaporization, 36
  hydraulic conductivity coefficient, 115
  hydrogen bonds. *See* Hydrogen bonds
  isotopic forms, 34
  partial molal volume, 49
  structure, 35, **35**

surface tension, 36
  in capillary rise, 37–39
  and cell walls, 67–68
tensile strength, 40–41
tension in cell wall, 67–69
tension in xylem vessels, 41
water potential. *See* Water potential
See also Capillary rise; Ice; Water flow;
    Water vapor
Water flow or flux, 62–63
  across cell wall, 67
  conductivity coefficient, 62
  from leaf, 70
  irreversible thermodynamics, 112–14
  in plants, 64–73
  resistance to, 42, 64, 72–73
  in xylem, 65–67
Water oxidation in photosynthesis, 165–67,
    195, 197
Water-oxygen half-cell, 222, **225**
Water potential, 50–51
  in air, 60–62, *71*
  in cell wall, 67–69, *71*
  at equilibrium, 52
  gravitational contribution, 51, 66, *71*
  in leaves, 61–62, *71*
  in *Nitella* and *Chara*, 63
  in soil, 70, *71*
  and water relations of cells, 57–63
  and water relations of organelles, 52–57
  and wilting, 70–72
  in xylem, *71*
Water vapor, 60
  activity, 60
  amount in air, 70
  diffusion coefficient, 13
  light absorption, 136
  loss from plant, 5, 59
    See also Transpiration
  partial pressure, 60
  saturation pressure, 60
Wave, light, 130–31
Wave number, 164
Wettable walls, 37
Wilting, water potential, 70–72

Xanthophylls, 176–78
Xylem, 6, **6**, 25, 65
  fiber cells, **6**, 28
  parenchyma cells, **6**, 28
  perforation plate, **6**, 28
  tracheids, 6, 28
  velocity of sap, 66
  vessel members, 6, **6**, 28
  vessels, **6**, 28
    capillary rise in, 39

support of water by cell wall inter-
    stices, 40
tension in, 41
diurnal changes, 72
water movement in, 6, 65–67, 72

Young's modulus, 28
    cell wall, 28
    cellulose, 28